Inviting the Holy Spirit to Church

A Practical Guide for Today's Spirituality

Ruth Willerth

SmatteringsBooks | Lancaster, NY

Copyright © 2024 by Ruth Willerth

All rights reserved. No portion of this book may be reproduced or transmitted in any form or by any means, electronic, mechanical, potocopy, recording, or otherwise without written permission from the publisher or author, except as permitted by U.S. copyright law.

Unless otherwise noted, Scripture quotations are from the ESV® Bible (The Holy Bible, English Standard Version®) by Crossway Bibles, A publishing Ministry of Good News Publishing. Used by permission. All rights reserved. Scripture is quoted also from The New American Standard Bible (1995).

This publication is designed to provide accurate and authoritative information in regard to the subject matter covered. It is sold with the understanding that neither the author nor the publisher is engaged in rendering legal, investment, accounting or other professional services. While the publisher and author have used their best efforts in preparing this book, they make no representations or warranties with respect to the accuracy or completeness of the contents of this book and specifically disclaim any implied warranties of merchantability or fitness for a particular purpose. No warranty may be created or extended by sales representatives or written sales materials. The advice and strategies contained herein may not be suitable for your situation. You should consult with a professional when appropriate. Neither the publisher nor the author shall be liable for any loss of profit or any other commercial damages, including but not limited to special, incidental, consequential, personal, or other damages.

Published by: SmatteringsBooks, 1377 Ransom Road, Lancaster, New York 14086

Trade paperback ISBN: 978-0-9800130-6-1

Hardcover ISBN: 978-0-9800130-7-8

To all those who hunger for

peace that surpasses

understanding.

With God nothing is

impossible.

CREDITS

THANK YOU TO JEFFREY Anderson, Ph.D., Thesis Chair, School of Divinity, for his expertise in editing and James Flynn, D. Min., Associate Dean of Instruction & Operations, School of Divinity, for his contributions to the final touches on my thesis version. Content was deleted from the thesis because some topics touched upon needed additional details that, if included, would require a completely separate book. Yet other topics in *Inviting the Holy Spirit to Church* cried out for clarification and elaboration. I had already exceeded my word count on the initial thesis. Some of Anderson's great comments should have been more fully developed. This led to further research and writing for this book. A wealth of information came from enrollment in the Center for Anglican Learning and Leadership Winter 2024

Celtic Spirituality and English Mysticism taught by Episcopal Rev. Daniel Deforest London, who I quoted while writing this book before I found out that he teaches classes.

In this edition, the Reformation was enlarged. Legends linking the English to Noah after the flood were added to balance the legend of Joseph of Arimathea church building in 67 A.D. The Aelred and Bernard of Clairvaux story is more complete. The impact of Shakespeare and the King James Version on the English language can now be compared with Luther's impact on the German language. Lutheran Pietism fueling the Moravian Revival changed from recluses and preachers experiencing God to revivals experienced by many.

The graphic for this book's cover came from my YouTube video depicting Genesis 1:1–9. It represents the Holy Spirit as our Triune God contemplated the earth's creation.

Preface

Inviting the Holy Spirit o Church

Inviting the Holy Spirit to Church is a practical guide for every Christian seeking more out of their relationship with God in the wake of a suffering world. The Bible shows how the Holy Spirit labored before and shortly after Christ's resurrection. The Holy Spirit continued to work as the Anglican Church seeded the Protestant Reformation. The Anglican Church grew from England's start of nationalism as it dealt with the repercussions of King John's differences with Pope Innocent III, which ignited Wycliffe's Lollards, who roamed England preaching from the first translation of the Vulgate into Old English as England fought with France and popes argued about who was pope. Examining how the Holy Spirit acted through English mystics and revivals sheds light on guiding modern clergy and laity.

The advance of the printing industry propels this story. Italians invented Times New Roman as the standard type for their printing presses, while the English chose a Gothic font. A book on a phone or tablet allows owner-selected fonts. In an electronic book, any topic is easily searchable. Print versions use alternate fonts to represent sixteen-century printing presses in the twenty-first century to help envision the print media in the Middle Ages and Renaissance.

Multiple indexes are in the back of the versions printed on paper to meet the needs of a diverse readership. Both the paperback and hardcover editions include a topic index for seekers, a general index for history buffs, an index focused on the different religions covered in this book, and a biblical index for those who prefer to start a study with Scripture.

This book offers brief glimpses highlighting the writings of Archbishops, hermits, and Christian mystics. The English Reformation starts with the conversion of the Celts. It sprinkles nuggets of wisdom on experiencing God through the eyes of Medieval and Renaissance mysticism and efforts by clergy to reform the church. Observing many small events that led to large-scale revivals where the Holy Spirit worked with people throughout the history of the Anglican Church will help rejuvenate the Anglican Church, individual seekers, and many other denominations without committing similar mistakes made by others in the past. Scripture says that our fantastic God created everything. It encourages people to connect with the Almighty. It asks for the Lord to pardon the repentant sinner so that person may grow in faith and successfully seek God.

O Lord, how manifold are your works! In wisdom have you made them all; the earth is full of your creatures. Here is the sea, great and wide, which teems with creatures innumerable, living things both small and great.

Psalm 104:24-25

For by him all things were created, in heaven and on earth, visible and invisible, whether thrones or dominions or rulers or authorities—all things were created through him and for him.

Colossians 1:16

These three were the sons of Noah, and from these the people of the whole earth were dispersed. "

Genesis (Gen.) 9:19 (ESV)

INVITING THE HOLY SPIRIT TO CHURCH

"Seek the Lord while he may be found; call upon him while he is near; et the wicked forsake his way, and the unrighteous man his thoughts; let him return to the Lord, that he may have compassion on him, and to our God, for he will abundantly pardon. For my thoughts are not your thoughts, neither are your ways my ways, declares the Lord."

Isaiah (Isa.) 55:6-8

"And without faith it is impossible to please him, for whoever would draw near to God must believe that he exists and that he rewards those who seek him."

Hebrews (Heb.) 11:6

CONTENTS

1.	Overview	1
2.	Plowing the Soil	28
3.	The Rise of Oxford	54
4.	King John The Root of English Nationalism	65
5.	Watering the Seed	74
6.	A Change in Weather	92
7.	John Wycliffe	119
8.	Mystic Writings and the Aftermath of Wycliffe	138
9.	English Roots	161
10.	Across the English Channel	165
11.	John Huss	169

12. The Hussites	177
13. Spirituality, Sugar and Gold,	182
14. Power Wealth War and Seeds of Toleration	220
15. Pietism, Moravians, Quakers, Welch, and the Great Awakening	264
16. Fueling Revivals	307
17. The 1904-1906 Welsh Revival	321
18. Conclusion	331
Appendix	340
Bibliography	344
Websites	369
Index	373
Notes	472

1
Overview

Inviting the Holy Spirit to Church

An Examination

The mainline church's population dwindles as the number of people who resist the thought and desire to attend church increases. One of the Episcopal newsletters suggested that the solution to the problem must be to ignite our churches with the Holy Spirit. According to the "Nicene Creed," the Holy Spirit is "the Lord, giver of life, who proceeds from the Father and the Son. With the Father and the Son, he is worshiped and glorified. He has spoken through the prophets."[1] What course of action could the Episcopal Church incorporate to work with the Holy Spirit? How and what would that look like?

The church has always given the power of government, to Rome, or clergy to discern God's will. Spiritualism occurs within every devout Christian despite their denomination, and many do not realize God is working within because discernment stems from a top-down process. To answer the need for spiritualism, which people think can come from whatever source if people demand the Holy Spirit, the church had better be equipped to supply it.[2] Protestant denominations tend to discourage personal relationships with God as being based on a participant's experience and not from an intellect.[3] Realigning a mainline church to the Holy Spirit differs from other religions' "spirituality" because meditation that connects people to the Trinity revolves around Scripture. 2 Peter 1:21 explains, "For no prophecy was ever produced by the will of man, but men spoke from God as they were carried along by the Holy Spirit."

E. A. Jones reminds those seeking Christian spirituality that those responsible for a recluse's spiritual supervision cautioned that Paul in 2 Corinthians (2 Cor.) 11:14–15a that Satan "disguises himself as an angel of light. So, it is no surprise if his servants also disguise themselves as servants of righteousness." [4] For instance, Satan could lure a solitary individual to undertake an impossible spiritual trial. Their failure might plunge them into the sin of despair.

Another trick of Satan is to appear in a dream as an angel of light advising that person to be healed by the Church's resident recluse from prayers or food, so the recluse falls into the sin of pride, forgetting where the power of healing originates. The danger of practicing spirituality alone is facing and surviving all Satan's tricks.[5] Hein and Shattuck Jr. explain some mistakes that seemed like the Holy Spirit, which began during Queen Elizabeth's reign. Anglican Priest Richard Hakluyt wrote about England's God-given mission to "spread its political and religious virtues" worldwide to compete with Catholic France and Spain, who spread the "wrong kind of Christianity."[6] The English studied God's Word without connecting to the Holy Spirit.

After England shipped ten thousand English settlers through the Virginia Company chartered by

King James to Jamestown starting in 1607, eighty percent had died by 1622 due to disease, hunger, and Native American warfare. Two-thirds of Anglican clergy serving in Virginia between 1607 and 1660 died within five years of landing in Jamestown. Dutch traders shipped enslaved Africans in 1619. In 1662, the House of Burgesses decreed that "the child of a black slave woman had to be a slave as well." The tobacco industry slowly replaced missionary passion to spread God's Word to every tongue and nation,[7] while the colonial military killed or drove the Native American threat westward.[8] Rowan A. Greer adds that the Bible remained central to the Church of England from the 1588 Elizabethan Settlement through James I (1603–1625) and Charles I (1625–1649). After the English Revolution (1640–1660) and the Glorious Revolution in 1688, England united with Scotland. Bible translation rotated around the shift into a "secular society."[9]

Revivals scare people. Revivals cost. Revivals injure our souls by destroying one's pride,[10] explains Geoffrey Thomas, chairman of the Grace Churches of England and Wales and of the Association of Evangelical Churches of Wales.[11] More than one

Western New York church hierarchy rejected allowing the Holy Spirit into church leadership as that church leadership core wanted to succeed. They would continue to run their church as a business. "The Holy Spirit is too chaotic!" The Holy Spirit exceeds all human comprehension expressed in church doctrine or experience because He is our God, the one we worship on Sundays, "the God who invaded our lives with His transforming presence."[12]

"What if everyone spoke the word of God?" When two men remained in the camp, and the Holy Spirit rested on them in Numbers (Num.) 11:27–28, Moses' staff came running with the same objections: "A young man ran, told Moses, and said, "Eldad and Medad are prophesying in the camp!" Joshua the son of Nun, the servant of Moses, one of his chosen men, answered, "My Lord Moses, forbid them!"

Moses exclaimed how wonderful it would be if the Holy Spirit caused everyone to speak in Num. 11:29: "Moses said to him, 'Are you jealous for my sake? I wish that all the Lord's people were prophets, that the Lord would put his Spirit on them!'"

And the Bible seems to agree that everyone can. Luke 1:15–16, 41–42, 67, Acts 2:4, 4:31, 13:9–10 show that when filled with the Holy Spirit, each person spoke the Word of God.[13]

Running churches like a business built on finances will always fail. More than one church closed its doors forever. According to the seven letters to the Churches in Revelation 1:4–4:22, they cannot succeed without the help of the Holy Spirit.

Based on Methodist Hymn Sings and Pentecostal Church Services, evidence of the Holy Spirit at work tends to be seen as loud and emotional. In contrast, Anglican congregations exhibit a detached disposition.[14] Colonial Americans quietly listened to an intellectual homily. Despite being served a pint of wine per person during Communion, they quietly congratulated the clergy on a fine sermon as the congregation exited the sanctuary.[15] Episcopal worship remains similar. Now grape juice or wine is served in shot glasses during Communion due to COVID. Since churches differ, how does one know they have connected to the Holy Spirit?

Martin Thornton (1915–1986) was an Anglican parish priest in the Church of England, a visiting lecturer at the General Theological Seminary, and spent ten years as Canon Chancellor at Truro

Cathedral. He specialized in spiritual direction to "reinvigorate Anglicanism through how it came to exist to begin.[16] Thornton says serious Christians have a faith that proved effective over a faith that proved correct.[17]

George Marchinkowski and Pieter G. R. De Villiers define "spirituality" as continuous practices done purposely to empower and flood the ongoing existence of the believer and their community. "Spiritual discipline" is an experience and exercise designed to develop a "hunger and thirst" for God without special training. Whether one attempts prayer, solitude, submission, service, Scripture study, or fasting, like any skill, one gains proficiency and becomes habit-forming as one repeats that skill. "Justification" is a term used to study the overall progress of the effect on an individual practicing spirituality.[18]

The Episcopal Church is separate from the Church of England. Each church belongs to its unique geographic and historical point for this study. "Anglican" is a worldwide umbrella that began in the seventeenth century. Thornton defines "The Church of England" and "English Spirituality" as launching in England in the twelfth century as teachings of St. Benedict of Italy and St. Anselm, who moved to Normandy before his life began at Canterbury.[19]

Benedict wrote the "Threefold Rule of Prayer" (rule of Trinity in Unity) as a guide for monks not solid enough to be anchorites.[20] Since 529, Benedict's monks gathered eight times daily to pray and read Scripture.[21] Benedict left the Church the "Threefold Rule of Prayer," which forms the *Book of Common Prayer's* structure— providing a system of prayer expressing faith in Jesus' incarnation, atonement for sins, and one Triune God. Faithfulness to Benedict's three-fold rule protects from straying from communing with the Holy Spirit. "Private devotion can be guided but not regimented."[22] The term "office" describes three regular prayer times used by the Anglican and Episcopal Church based on the third, sixth, and ninth hours (9 a.m., 12 p.m., and 3 p.m.) patterned after private Judaic prayer.[23] "Office" is also used as a job position.

Benedict classified the terms "anchorites" and "hermits" interchangeably as monastery-tested individuals trained to war with the devil.[24] Both remained separate from established religious orders.[25]

Anchorites emerged in the eleventh century as solitary devout males who lived in a cell attached to a church.[26] Hermits were monks who wandered alone in the wilderness.[27] According to Mary Clay Roberts, some hermits were charlatans.[28] Only those hermits who influenced the Reformation or individual spirituality will be covered in this study.

In spiritualism within a church, Protestants tend to stress study, service, and diverse practices of praying and worshiping together. Catholics speak of solitude, contemplative prayer, meditation, and confession.[29] The term "revival" refers to a movement in which the Holy Spirit connects many humans to God over a large geographical area.

William G. Dever states, "Religion is all *about* pragmatism— what actually *works*. Otherwise, it would have little appeal for the masses."[30] Ancients aimed to avoid God's wrath and secure blessings. Sacrifice returned to God a portion of the bounty God gave, so the ancients fed their gods.[31] Dever employs a *phenomenological approach*: "functionalism" applying "direct observations of society." Typical case studies penetrate a society from within. A "thick description" utilizes "organic inductive models," progressing from "particular to general."[32]

Biblical miracles happened in a historical context. Most books written about the Moravian Revival start with Wycliffe and Huss. Working back through historical references that Wycliffe or Huss drew on helps to understand how the Holy Spirit continues to shape history. Additionally, besides the historical account, understanding the historical context is needed. For example, how did Wycliffe and Huss perceive the world around them? What was the norm?

From this basis, the plan is to examine both single conversions with large-scale historical revivals where the Holy Spirit worked with a significant number of people in the history of the Anglican Church to help rejuvenate the Anglican Church without making similar mistakes of our ancestors. Thornton quoted David Kucharsky, "A plant severed from its roots is more likely to attract parasites than to bear fruit. There is no substitute for direct connections with the past."[33]

No single history can cover every event, and each author chooses the events illustrating their story from many sources. This study focuses mainly on the history of the British Isles unless the account of somewhere else later affects the Anglican Church, like the Moravians in Germany.

Details such as the weather, culture that caused another piece of history, and entertainment led to both revivals. History is usually written in mini timelines for each historical person. Combining dictionary or encyclopedia sketches was enough material to understand key people who influenced another sequence of Reformations and Revivals. Chronological references were chosen for their content to visualize how God works in our history, answering questions on missing data to paint a transparent backdrop for God's revivals. Studying how the Holy Spirit worked through the many English Revivals sheds light on guiding modern clergy shepherding their flocks by the light of the Holy Spirit, which will rejuvenate the church.

Gerald Bray contended that Anselm belonged to the *respublica Christiana*, meaning the "Christian commonwealth," and should not be considered Anglican since the Italian's reputation came from his work in Normandy.[34] English kings answered to the pope since the 664 Council of Whitby voted to mode their religion and civilization on the Romans.[35]

England became a nation in the sixteenth century when Henry VIII severed the pope's authority in England forever.

Archbishop Thomas Cranmer (1489–1556) reduced the eight prayer services used exclusively by the monks into two prayer services for all members of the congregation published in the *Book of Common Prayer*. Today, Anglican spirituality centers on members participating in the Morning or Evening Prayer Service.[36] The *Book of Common Prayer* says the Holy Spirit inspired canons in the Old Testament to show God's work in nature and history and proclaim Jesus' life and teachings in the New Testament.[37]

E.A. Jones collected writings of anchorites and hermits to ascertain the number and influence of solitary religious figures.[38] Frederick H. Borsch (1935–2017) served as the fifth Bishop of Los Angeles and as dean, president, and professor of New Testament at the Church Divinity School of the Pacific in Berkeley, California.[39] He explains that for Anglican Christians, the Church discerns how the Holy Spirit works in one's community. People hear and contemplate Scripture at worship services, and that Scripture extends God's power to conform people to God's will[40] through the Bible passages in the lessons from the *Roman Catholic Lexicon* and the *Book of Common Prayer*.

God requires nothing more than "belief and faithful living." Borsch cautions that the "cast of biblical language used for his disciples does not dictate what God requires or wants of his people today." He uses the abolition of slavery as an example since the Bible tackles the issue without interest. [41]

Heb. 13:8 advises remembering that "Jesus Christ is the same yesterday, today, and forever." Suppose God involved the Holy Spirit prior to the American Civil War in the conflict of slavery. The Holy Spirit might have sent missionaries to Africa to bring the warring tribes peace so the victors would stop selling their neighbors to European and Muslim traders as prisoners of war. The Holy Spirit might empower the North by improving the lives of their lower-income workers before condemning the South. What kept the United States from uniting to improve life for people experiencing poverty throughout the country?

Borsch observed that the "audio-visual era" created Bible illiteracy. The Anglican community whose lives reflect the Bible will allow Scripture to become "the architecture of our thoughts."⁴² I agree with Borsch, as I belong to an Episcopal Community whose lives, with God's help, reflect the Bible, allowing God's Word to become "the architecture of our thoughts." Most of us are older than the "audio-visual era," but grandchildren only attend church on Christmas Eve and Easter.

Craig S. Keener quotes Isa. 40:13, 48:16, 63:10–11, and Matthew (Matt). 28:19 concluding that teaching the Holy Spirit as divine and (John 14:16–17, 16:13–15, Romans (Rom.) 8:26–27, 2 Cor. 13:14) as personal.⁴³ The Anglican Church struggled with personal piety, undermining church discernment soon after the first foreign translations became prolific. The 1875 report of the British and the Foreign Bible Society criticized the evangelical biblical emphasis on individuals' piety, ignoring authority, the one body, and the church's unity in modern times. J. H Newman, a member of the Tractarian group, accused evangelicals of "standing by and doing nothing, while the very rationalist liberalism in theology and politics was destroying the Church of England." Members of this Oxford movement (the 1820s–1850s) believed a "second reformation" needed a restoration of the

Holy Spirit's works in the Early Church that centered on one holy apostolic church divinely protected from the secular world instead of a focus on Scripture.[44] Tractarian leader John Keble (1792–1886) argued that "Christians do not gain faith by applying their reason to the Bible." Instead, people must be connected to a church to learn from others."[45]

According to Mark D. Chapman, the Latin community of Rome continued to influence the Church of England in the sixteenth century when King Henry VIII broke away from Rome, Zwingli broke away in Switzerland, and Luther in Germany. Europe debated English papers, and English clergy argued European Protestant theology during the 1530s.[46]

For many years, only two Universities existed in England: The University of Oxford and the University of Cambridge. The Thirty-Nine Articles, knowledge of the Gospels in Greek, and an *Analogy of Religion* by Bishop Butler (1736) made the core requirements for a BA in Theology from Oxford in the nineteenth century when the term "Anglican Theology" first appeared.[47] Other Anglicans highly contest all Anglican Theology.[48]

G. R. Evans and J. Robert Wright provide a collection of historical Anglican documents starting with the *Order of the Church* by Clement I, Bishop of Rome (96).[49] The study of the Early Church Father's traditions taught in the church before its schisms continued in the Anglo-Catholic Church of England[50] for over a thousand years. The Church of England answered to the pope.[51] After the Reformation of the sixteenth century, under the influence of Scholastic and Puritans, the new denominations criticized individual spirituality and observed in favor of Scripture as the sole source since it is the reliable Word of God and focused on the divine actions of God's work and the depravity of humans. The mainline Protestant's ethical reflection, work ethic, and social action dominated responding to God's gift of salvation. Critical thinking grew from the Enlightenment's emphasis on reason and rational faith.

The Anglican tradition kept and perpetuated Spiritual practices in traditional rites, songs, readings, social outreach, and vast activities where people creatively expressed, investigated, and intensified Christian spiritualities.[52] Today's Anglican converts see a continuity of "Christian living" developed from the structure inside the *Book of Common Prayer*.[53] When King Henry VIII authorized Miles Coverdale's English versions of the Bible in 1535 and Tyndale and Coverdale's Great Bible in 1538, he legalized ordinary people reading the Bible.[54] The Church of England lacked the rigid authority of Calvin, Luther, and Zwingli's orthodoxy.[55] Instead, it relied on Scripture reaffirmed by the Thirty-Nine Articles and recited by laity as they followed their clergy in worship guided by the *Book of Common Prayer*.[56] This connection with past practices remains a mere starting point to sharing their faith.[57]

Many scholars outside of the Anglican Church have studied Scripture to glean how the Holy Spirit operates in the modern-day mirror Thornton's observations on "English Spiritually." Thornton believes all English spirituality comes directly from the influence of Benedict monks.[58] He defines one's soul receiving the Holy Spirit as the "art of cooperation with grace." Teaching prayer means teaching complete spirituality controlling human life in liturgical, formal, and personal prayer, ongoing remembrance altering and stimulating every moment.[59]

Timothy Lin, member of the Translation Committee of the NASB, explained that for the Holy Spirit to operate to His completeness, it is never by self-struggle or rigorous schooling but by grace that empowers God's servants.[60] William S. Banowshky's lecture at The Holy Spirit Fifth Annual Fort Worth Christian College Lectureship March 22–26, 1964, explained that God gives the Holy Spirit and the remission of sins to all who become His children through obedience to Him (Acts 5:32).[61] Lin further clarified that Luke 11:13 says that to be filled by the Holy Spirit, one must ask for it through prayer.[62] Keener adds that in James 1:6, and 2:14–26, one must ask in faith and obey the answer.[63] C. J. Horton, who spoke at "The Holy Spirit Fifth Annual Fort Worth Christian College Lectureship March 22–26, 1964," pointed out that if the Holy Spirit never absolutely controls our lives, we will never become entirely Christian. Christians are Christians only to the degree that churchgoers allow the Holy Spirit to direct their lives (Rom. 8:9–11).[64] Thornton points out that spiritual direction advances from sermons, Bible studies, discussion groups, and anything that trains the Christian faith relates to prayer bursting into life.⁶⁵

The politics governing the apostolic church our creeds profess divided our church. Whenever church leaders chose financial gain over their people and neighbors, they challenged God's will and ended in disaster. Church hierarchy opposes individuality that arises from church piety but does poorly without it. Division of the church seems to oppose the one true apostolic church but can be argued as a catalyst for necessary reforms leading the church back to the Trinity.

Knowledge of Scripture does not automatically guarantee that a church person connects to the Holy Spirit, but Scripture is necessary to tap into the Holy Spirit. Studying how the Holy Spirit worked through the history leading up to the English Revivals shows that the people instrumental in reforming their church acted by the light of the Holy Spirit.

As a member of the Trinity, the Holy Spirit does not limit His work to time or people. While Christianity was in its infancy, the Chinese invented paper to wrap stuff in and expanded on its uses, such as kites, umbrellas, lanterns, and fans. Paper replaced bamboo, silk, and wood as a material to write on by the third century in China, but Christian clergy in Europe and the British Isles wrote on parchment.[66]

The Song of Solomon, depicting the marriage of Solomon and the Egyptian Queen in the Old Testament, is an example of how God's seeds bear fruit. Parallels in Egyptian and Mesopotamian literature to the Song of Songs implied festival entertainers performed the songs in the fourth to second century B.C. for a secular audience with a literal translation[67] found among the Dead Sea Scrolls.[68] A youth in 2 A.D.[69] transposed Songs of Solomon's erotic love songs into barroom ditties. Jewish religious experts saw the sacred message in the poetry. Rabbi Akiba Ben Joseph (b.40–50 A.D.), distinguished as a great rabbi by 95–96, systemized Jewish law,[70] responded to the barroom rendition, "Whoever sings from the Song of Songs in the wine-houses and makes it a (profane) song shall have no share in the world to come."[71] Origen (185–251) wrote the first parallel Bible comparing the Hebrew Old Testament with a Greek transliteration, a literal Greek translation by Aquilla, Symmachus, the Separatist, and the Theodotion to lay a foundation for his commentaries and to counter Jewish interpretation.⁷² In his opinion, Song of Songs could only be interpreted using mysticism since it symbolically portrayed the unseeable intercourse between the soul and God's Word.⁷³ The influence of this collection of songs would continue to grow with time.

---

1. Charles Mortimer Guilbert, *The Book of Common Prayer and Administration of the Sacraments and Other Rites and Ceremonies of the Church According to the Use of the Episcopal Church* (New York: The Church Hymnal Corporation and The Seabury Press, 1977), 853.

2. Martin Thornton, *English Spirituality: An Outline of Ascetical Theology According to the English Pastoral Tradition* (Eugene, OR: Wipf & Stock Publishers, 2012), 6. Logos.

3. George Marchinkowski and Pieter G. R. De Villiers, "The Rediscovery of Spiritual Practices within Protestantism," *Stellenbosch Theological Journal* 6 no. 1 (2020): 429–56, https://doi.org/10.17570/stj.2020.v6n1.a.

4. E. A. Jones, ed., *Hermits and Anchorites in England 1200–1550,* Manchester Medieval Sources Series (Manchester: Manchester University Press, 2019), 104, 130. Kindle.

5. Ibid., 130; cf. Pro. 18:1, "Whoever isolates himself seeks his own desire …" (ESV).

6. David Hein and Gardiner H. Shattuck Jr., *The Episcopalians, Denominations in America,* Number 11 (Westport, CT; London: Praeger Publishers, 2004), 10.

7. Hein and Shattuck, *The Episcopalians, Denominations in America,* 12.

8. Ibid., 13.

9. Rowan A. Greer, *Anglican Approaches to Scripture From the Reformation to the Present* (New York, NY: A Herder & Herder Book, The Crossroad Publishing Company, 2006), 32.

10. Geoffrey Thomas, *The Holy Spirit* (Grand Rapids, MI: Reformation Heritage Books, 2011), 216. Logos.

11. "Geoffrey Thomas Author Biography," Banner of Truth USA, https://banneroftruth.org/us/about/banner-authors/geoff-thomas/.

12. Craig S. Keener, *Gift and Giver: The Holy Spirit for Today* (Grand Rapids, MI: Baker Academic, 2001), 18. Logos.

13. Graham A. Cole, *He Who Gives Life* (Wheaton, IL: Crossway, 2007), 218.

14. See, David Hein and Gardiner H. Shattuck's account in *The Episcopalians in the American Colonies.*

15. Hein and Shattuck, *The Episcopalians, Denominations in America,* 25.

16. Matthew C. Dallman, "A Biography of Martin Thornton: Akenside Press," http://akensidepress.com/thornton/about/index.html.

17. Thornton, *English Spirituality,* 9.

18. Marchinkowski and De Villiers, "The Rediscovery of Spiritual Practices within Protestantism."

19. Thornton, *English Spirituality*, xiii.

20. Philippe Aries and Georges Duby, eds., *A History of Private Life Revelations of the Medieval World,* trans., Arthur Goldhammer (Cambridge, MA, London: The Belknap Press of Harvard University Press, 1988), 514.

21. Justo L. Gonzalez, *Church History An Essential Guide* (Nashville, TN, Abingdon Press, 1996), 43. Kindle.

22. Gonzalez, *Church History An Essential Guide,* 77.

23. "Daily Office," The Episcopal Church, accessed June 7, 2023, https://www.episcopalchurch.org/glossary/daily-office/.

24. Jones, *Hermits and Anchorites in England 1200–1550*, 17.

25. Ibid., 20.

26. Ibid., 19.

27. Ibid., 15–17, 20.

28. Mary Clay Rotha, "Hermits and Anchorites. Rotha Mary Clay Chapter Twelve," *Prophets and Councilors*, accessed June 19, 2023, http://www.historyfish.net/anchorites/clay_anchorites_twelve.html.

29. Marchinkowski and De Villiers, "The Rediscovery of Spiritual Practices within Protestantism."

30. William G. Dever, *Did God Have a Wife? Archaeology and Folk Religion in Ancient Israel* (Grand Rapids, MI; Cambridge, U.K: William B. Eerdmans Publishing Company, 2008), 205. Logos.

31. Dever, *Did God Have a Wife? Archaeology and Folk Religion in Ancient Israel*, 4.

32. Ibid., 9–10.

33. Thornton, *English Spirituality*, xix.

34. Gerald Bray, *Anglicanism: A Reformed Catholic Tradition* (Bellingham, WA: Lexham Press, 2021), 7. Logos.

35. Thomas O'Loughlin, "Hagiography," *Celtic Spirituality*, ed., Bernard McGinn, trans. Oliver Davies, The Classics of Western Spirituality (New York; Mahwah, NJ: Paulist Press, 1999), 23. Logos.

36. "Daily Office."

37. Guilbert, *The Book of Common Prayer and Administration of the Sacraments*, 852–53.

38. Jones, *Hermits and Anchorites in England 1200–1550*, 21.

39. "Frederick H. Borsch," Berkeley Divinity School, accessed May 31, 2023, https://berkeleydivinity.yale.edu/news/frederick-h-borsch.

40. Frederick H. Borsch, "All Things Necessary to Salvation," *Anglicanism and the Bible,* 203-227, ed., Fredericl H. Borsch, The Anglican Studies Series (Denver, CO: Morehouse Pub Co, 1984), 224-225.

41. Borsch, "All Things Necessary to Salvation," 224.

42. Ibid., 226.

43. Keener, *Gift and Giver*, 19.

44. John Booty, "Reformers and Missionaries: The Bible in Eighteenth and Early Nineteenth Century England," *Anglicanism and the Bible,* 117–142, ed., Frederick H. Borsch, The Anglican Studies Series (Denver, CO: Morehouse Pub Co, 1984), 138–139.

45. Ibid., 141.

46. Mark D. Chapman, *Anglican Theology* (London; New Delhi; NY: Sydney: Bloomsbury, 2012), 1. Logos.

47. Ibid., 4.

48. Ibid., 9.

49. G. R. Evans, and J. Robert Wright, *The Anglican Tradition: A Handbook of Sources* (London: SPCK, 1991), 1. Logos.

50. Chapman, *Anglican Theology,* 14.

51. Evans and Wright, *The Anglican Tradition: A Handbook of Sources,* 131.

52. Marchinkowski and De Villiers, "The Rediscovery of Spiritual Practices within Protestantism."

53. Thornton, *English Spirituality,* 4.

54. Evans and Wright, *The Anglican Tradition: A Handbook of Sources,* 131.

55. Chapman, *Anglican Theology,* 3.

56. Ibid., 4, 15.

57. Marchinkowski and De Villiers, "The Rediscovery of Spiritual Practices within Protestantism."

58. Thornton, *English Spirituality*, 205.

59. Ibid., 24.

60. Timothy Lin, "The Conditions for Being Filled with the Spirit," *How the Holy Spirit Works in Beleivers' Lives Today* (Carmel, IN: Biblical Studies Ministries International, Inc., 2002). e-Sword.

61. William S. Banowshky, "The Holy Spirit Fifth Annual Fort Worth Christian College Lectureship March 22-26, 1964," *The Gift of the Holy Spirit* (Fort Worth, TX: Fort Worth Christian College, 1964). e-Sword.

62. Lin, "The Conditions for Being Filled with the Spirit."

63. Keener, *Gift and Giver*, 19.

64. C. J. Horton, "The Holy Spirit Fifth Annual Fort Worth Christian College Lectureship March 22–26, 1964," *The Holy Spirit in Christian Growth* (Fort Worth, TX: Fort Worth Christian College, 1964). e-Sword.

65. Thornton, *English Spirituality*, 25.

66. Frances Gies and Joseph Gies. *Cathedral, Forge, and Waterwheel Technology and Invention in the Middle Ages* (New York, NY: HarperCollins Publishers, 1994), 95–96.

67. Christopher M. Jones, "Song of Songs, Book Of, Critical Issues," *The Lexham Bible Dictionary*, ed., John D. Barry, et al. (Bellingham, WA: Lexham Press, 2016). Logos.

68. "Song of Solomon," *Biblical Dead Sea Scrolls: Bible Reference Index* (Bellingham, WA: Lexham Press, 2011). Logos.

69. Frank Knight Sanders, and Charles Foster Kent, "1. Introduction to Canticles, 4. Recognition of a Literal Sense," *Volume 1: The Messages of the Earlier Prophets Arranged in the Order of Time Analyzed, and Freely Rendered in Paraphrase*, 3rd ed. (New York, NY: Charles Scribner's Sons, 1899). e-Sword.

70. Isidore Singer, ed., "Akiba Ben Joseph," *The Jewish Encyclopedia: A Descriptive Record of the History, Religion, Literature, and Customs of the Jewish People from the Earliest Times to the Present Day*, 12 vols. (New York; London: Funk & Wagnalls, 1901–1906). Logos.

71. Sanders, and Kent, "1. Introduction to Canticles, 3. Allegorical Interpretation," *Volume 1: The Messages of the Earlier Prophets Arranged in the Order of Time Analyzed, and Freely Rendered in Paraphrase*.

72. Everett Ferguson, *Church History Volume One: From Christ to the Pre-Reformation, The Rise and Growth of the Church in Its Cultural, Intellectual, and Political Context* (Grand Rapids, MI: Zondervan Academic, 2013), 279.

73. Thomas C. Oden, ed., "Song of Solomon 1:1–4 The Bride and The Lover," *Ancient Christian Commentary on Scripture* (Downers Grove, IL InterVarsity Press, 2010). e-Sword.

2
Plowing the Soil
English Roots

The earliest Irish origin legend stems from the seventh century called the *Book of Invasions,* which is not the name of a book but the legend's name with many versions. Eleventh and twelfth-century versions combining poems and history started with Noah's flood. Noah's granddaughter Cesair.[1] One British legend credits Noah's grandson Brutus for first settling Britain,[2] named after Brutus according to either an eighth or tenth-century writer, Nennius, who wrote

Historia Britonum. In the twelfth century, Geoffrey of Monmouth countered that Genesis' Gomer, a son of Japheth, named as one of the recipients of the Isles of Gentiles, first settled Britain. This history continues to be debated since the Reformation, who usually favor Biblical references.[3] Archeologists confirm that people have inhabited the British Isles for a long time—artifacts found on Mount Sandel near Coleraine, Ireland, date between 7000 and 6500 BC.[4]

A central argument for the independence of the Church of England from the Church of Rome is that the English Church began independently of Rome due to the disciple of Jesus, Joseph of Arimathea, a wealthy man who served on the Sanhedrin Council who buried Jesus in his freshly made tomb (Mark 15:42–47, Luke 23:50–56, Matt. 27:57–61).[5] English historian William of Malmesbury (1080/1095–1143) first recorded the legend that the apostle Philip sent Joseph to Great Britain, where he founded Glastonbury in 63 AD. Neither historian Bede nor Gildas recorded this report.[6]

In Celtic legends of the *Quest of the Holy Grail*, the recluse, through "deep personal holiness," prophesized like a Hebrew seer from a solitary cell, regarding themselves as followers of Elijah and John the Baptist.[7] In his introduction to Bede's *A History of the English Church and People,* Leo Sherley Price states that after the Briton King Arthur,[8] under the flag of the white dragon, defeated the Saxons fighting under the banner of the red dragon,[9] the Catholic Church brought art and peace to the warring inhabitants on the British Island. Columba and Aidan carried the Gospel to the northern Celts, "Ninan to the Picts, Patrick to the Irish, David, Dewi Sant to the Celts in Cornwall and Wales, and Augustine to the Saxons."[10] Augustine built England's first church in Kent out of mud.[11]

Pelagius, a Welsh native[12] born in Britain and from a Celtic mother, studied law in Rome in 390, where he was baptized.[13] He taught that Jesus' ministry revolved around care for the poor, sick, hungry, imprisoned, and marginalized.[14]

Between 397–398, Augustine wrote his statement of faith in a biography titled *Confessions.*[15] The first nine books told of how God called Augustine to follow Him. Augustine eventually converted to Catholicism in "book ten." he conveyed God's mercy and explained how his Christian confidence stemmed from grace and the optimism[16] of experiencing God despite his lingering temptations.[17] No one had penetrated the walls of Rome for one thousand years, yet in 410, Alaric and the Goths sacked the city.

Starting in 412,[18] Pelagius argued with Augustine about why God became human. Augustine asserted that original sin robbed humans of the benefits of being created in God's image. Hence, God became human to offer atonement for sin on the cross, which passed from mother to child inside the womb.[19] Pelagius countered that God became human in Jesus to model what "being truly human looks like" since "the image of God within is indestructible. God continues to offer grace and mercy at every moment, aiding us in growth in our capacity to reflect the gracious life of God who breathes us into" existence. This debate centered on baptism. Augustine insisted a baby needed to be baptized so their soul would enter heaven, while Pelagius retorted that, of course, God would accept the infant since God created all in His image." In Pelagius' scheme, will and action made human perfection possible and thus mandatory.[20]

Many blamed Rome's fall on the decline in faith in the ancient Roman gods. To refute these claims, Augustine started writing the *City of God* in 413 to disprove the myth of humankind's dependence on an array of gods.[21]

Pope Zosimus reluctantly excommunicated and exiled Pelagius in 418.[22] Pelagianism meant meriting God's salvation by works instead of divine grace.[23] Dispute over salvation through works reappears throughout the Church's reformations. Augustine completed *City of God* in 426. Augustine died on August 28, 430.[24] The first Bishop of Urgel in Catalogna, Spain, wrote an *Exposition on the Canticle of Canticles* while Rome debated the Augustine-Pelagius controversy.[25] The 539 Council of Orange concurred with Augustine's position against Pelagius but disagreed with Augustine on predestination.[26]

Celtic churches obeyed the prayer and practices from the Christian East, asserting that God is everywhere based on Prov. 15:3 and Heb. 4:13, including homes and workplaces where his presence is received in everyday life.[27] People's bodies and lives are God's creation and dwelling residence (1 Cor. 6:19) until we die (Psalm 90:12). In Catholic tradition, Heb. 12:1 explains that a "great cloud of witness" always keeps Christians company of Christ and the Saints, so one is never alone on a spiritual path.[28] The Holy Spirit toils within each person to originate Godlike organisms as the body, mind, and soul join in God's compassion to love one's enemies.[29]

Wandering Celtic missionaries excelled at converting people to Christ, but the disciplined, stable Benedict monks could better administer a national church. Many British historians paint the participants in the Council of Whitby as turncoats who marketed their heritage to foreign dominance.[30] The 664 Council of Whitby voted to pattern their religion and civilization on the Romans.[31] Other historians, while agreeing that the Council of Whitby's decision was disastrous to the British-Celtic church, conclude that "the English Church was Protestant before the Reformation and Catholic after it."[32] Thornton argues that without this calamity, the fruit of English Spirituality would not have blossomed in the fourteenth century.[33]

Bede, a monk from the monastery of St. Peter and St. Paul's, Canterbury 709–732,[34] described Britain as "in harmony with the five books of divine law, five languages, and four nations," each had their unique language. Through the study of Scripture, Latin united them.[35] Based on his expertise in Scripture and the Early Church Fathers, Bede's commentaries and sermons uncovered the process of prayer mixed with contemplation and gave instant insight into God's nature.[36]

Seeking credit from God, social status, and a handy spot to settle relatives, feudal lords established monasteries and convents during the ninth century and afterward. One of their children served as the highest monastery official as an abbot or abbess. As patrons donated lands and treasure, monasteries and convents grew into wealthy estates, boasting three thousand manor houses and twenty thousand people. Abbots of large monasteries influenced popes. Monasteries employed agriculture and domestic labor, storing both grain and wine.[37]

Upper-class second sons or below from large families were unlikely to receive large inheritances but might earn prestige in a church. Parents gave away their sons or daughters by escorting them to the altar, wrapping their seven-year-old hand in a cloth, kissing it, and offering it to the priest.[38] Monks and nuns never wore civilian garments nor enjoyed fancy occasions enjoyed by their wealthy siblings. After the priest made the sign of the cross on their forehead, the abbot led them into the highly disciplined, regimented life of prayer under the whip of their masters.[39] Monks and nuns vowed to reside in chastity and poverty at a monastery, while nomadic hermits vowed chastity.[40] The number of solitaries and recluses was small compared to the other church positions, but they produced most Christian writings and doctrine.[41]

Charles the Bald ruled much of Gaul and became the Holy Roman Emperor in 875.[42] Based on the mastery of Greek lasting longer in Celtic countries than the academic discipline had in Gaul,[43] Irish teacher John "the Scot" Ericgena (810–877) secured Charles the Bald's patronage to translate the eastern Christian Greek *Dionysius the Areopagite* and *Maximus the Confessor* into Latin.[44]

Most likely, a Christian Syrian monk wrote *Dionysus* sometime after 475 A.D. during the sixth century.[45] *Dionysius* described the process of returning to God's image as a statue whose hidden image lies with the marble and is slowly revealed by God the sculpture. Bathing in the light of unfathomable heavenly energies radiating from the infinite God transforms a person into whom God desires them to be as one consent to the Holy Spirit of the Trinity. As one's body, mind, and soul, limitless grace causes one to shine with God's radiant light. *Maximus the Confessor* observed humans as both a miniature universe and a person who can convey knowledge and reassurance from God, allowing one to intercede for anyone anywhere. Through Jesus and the Holy Spirit, one leads in the singing praises to God on high, transforming us into Godlike creatures. Today, neither the Eastern Orthodox Church nor the Jews believe in the doctrine of original sin.[46]

Ericgena wrote his original works as well.[47] He contends that all are one in Christ because, without Christ, no one and nothing would exist (John 1:3).[48] We "engage in war" whenever we harm someone else. We defile the actual "life of God, present and vital" within all God has articulated into existence when we disrespect people's and society's general welfare.[49] Ericgena's translations would later influence Hugh and Richard of St. Victor, St. Bernard of Clairvaux, William of St. Thierry, and Robert Grosseteste,[50] which would help shape people's understanding of God.

God works through history. Many credit the printing press as the major reason for the success of the Protestant Reformation. God plowed the soil for the Reformation with discoveries and advances that took hundreds of years. For a press to have significance, the printer needed paper. The paper industry reaching Muslim Spain during the tenth century[51] illustrates how God methodically places the necessary ingredients to spread his Word, which alone seems random.

The weather that today's scholars call the "Medieval warm period" brought prosperity from around 1000 to sometime after 1200 in Europe.[52] Although infant mortality rates were fifty-fifty, between 1000 and 1300, Europe's population nearly doubled.[53] Hermits cleared forests, filled swampland for housing and crops, and built and maintained roads and bridges— otherwise, occasional gifts, indulgences, and begging licenses supported hermits.[54] Although printing still depended on a rubbing technique,[55] around 1045, a Chinese artist, Pi Sheng, improved on the expensive woodblock printing press by embedding clay characters onto iron plates glued with pine sap, wax, and ashes.[56] The Western and Eastern Church split in 1054.[57]

Medieval authors wrote on the basis that God consisted of the only valid reality as He created everything. God authored the *Book of Nature*, demonstrating God's eternal and infinite will in time and space. The Bible revealed the Word of the incarnate Christ. Salvation only occurred by conforming to God's will.[58] Early Cathedral schools began by studying the Psalms and the letters of Paul. According to the Gospels, Jesus had made the Old Testament and its laws obsolete.[59]

Since 1036, England, a part of the Danish empire, still had not mastered fighting on horseback. When heirless Edward, the Confessor, died, the Angle-Saxon nobility elected powerful Earl Harold Godwinson as their king.[60] The Norwegians attacked and lost to Harold's Army in the north by 1066.[61] William the Bastard claimed the English throne by right of succession via his great-aunt.[62] William had shaped the most consolidated feudal state in Europe. He patronized the Church and Rome, and Rome felt the Angle-Saxon church exercised too much independence. The population increase in his Dutchy in Normandy supplied archers and infantry supporting fifteen hundred knights.

In 1066, the papacy charged that the new archbishop of Canterbury was not canonically elected and deposed him. King Harold refused to carry out the papal order. Rome supported the 1066 reformation of the Angle-Saxon Church.[63] The Angle-Saxons put up a decent fight at the Battle of Hastings. Surviving Angle-Saxon peasant's life continued without change; the nobility lost their lands; their clergy faced charges under the Italian-Norman scholar Lanfranc, Archbishop of Canterbury. The French became the ruling class.[64] William the Conqueror chose all of England's clergy and ordered his bishops not to obey citations from Rome.[65] From the eleventh century onward, England boasted of her numerous anchorites and hermits pursuing solitary contemplation.[66] Anchoresses, the female counterpart of an anchorite, outnumbered anchorites in a 3:2 ratio.[67] After the 1070s, monastic scriptoria at Worcester and Rochester continued to copy Angle-Saxon collections of charters, land ownership, and legal codices in Old English until the 1170s. Canterbury documents written in Latin and Old English within the same version included royal charters and religious works.[68]

In 1070, the Archbishop of York rejected Canterbury's bid to be the Senior Archbishop in England since St. Patrick's missionary work preceded Augustine's. This continued to be a controversial issue during the eleventh century. The fact that Canterbury sat on the location of the first church with a bishop settled the controversy in the twelfth century in favor of Canterbury.[69] The pope took over the power of bishops to canonize saints during the same century.[70]

In 1078, under Scottish king Malcom III (Canmore), and his son David I, the Vikings in the north agreed to a settlement with King William. Royal Norman patronage led to land grants for loyal barons.[71] Noble families swore loyalty to their king regardless of where they resided or originated.[72] Italian-born Anselm (1033–1109) became an abbot at Bec, Normandy, in 1078, where his writings on theology and grammar drew fame and glory. Pupils flocked from everywhere, filled with questions. Anselm's answers were treated as "oracles from heaven."[73]

According to Thornton, true English *ascetical theology* sprang from Anselm's writings.[74] The Catholic Dictionary defines *ascetical theology* as the science interpreting virtue and perfection and how to obtain them, creating ordinary Christian life.[75] Ascetical practices in the Old Testament included dietary laws, fasting, purification laws, and wearing course garments. In the New Testament, Jesus said, "And calling the crowd to him with his disciples, he said to them, 'If anyone would come after me, let him deny himself and take up his cross and follow me'" (Mark 8:34).[76] Anselm addressed penance in *Cur Deus Homo?* with praying by focusing his attention completely on the divine Father and then repeating his procedure of prayer onto the Passion of Christ, which led to "ransom-to-the-devil theories"[77] because Jesus judges all humans (Acts 10:42, 17:31, John 5:22, 27, 9:39, Matt. 16:27, 25:31–46, Rom. 2:16, 2 Cor. 5:10). Anselm taught the impossibility of a credit balance leading to heaven or hell, and instead "justification by grace alone," as Christian redemption exclusively depended on Christ's sacrificial death.[78]

In Anselm's *Monologion,* he presented a process of harmonizing, delving into the reason of faith through the meditation of prayer by working through a mystery for oneself in prayer to God. His procedure began with a hymn of praise to God, then deviated from the then-common technique of using fictional characters to express theology and philosophy by directly addressing God. In *Proslogion* and *Cur Deus Homo?* he utilized his approach[79] for sincere inquiry to understand God's love.[80] Faith grew a greater, more profound faith.[81] A rational understanding underscored the foundation for both doubting and belief. Chapter 12 of the *Proslogion* described God as life, goodness, wisdom, virtue, and truth. Christians incorporate faith differently. Some embrace God's law. Others agree with God's law. Still others attempt to live in God's law as a series of regulations. All these responses abandon Christians outside of virtue and perfection. Christians must absorb God's life, goodness, wisdom, integrity, and truth and "infuse it to the depths of their soul" fortified by prayer and doctrine.[82]

Anselm disdained the 1093 title of Archbishop of Canterbury imposed upon him.[83] He accepted the position after someone forced the archbishop's staff into his hands while others dragged him into the church.[84] King William's royal advisors rejected Anselm's tribute from Canterbury, so he disbursed the money to the poor. William retaliated by refusing to restore church estates, which prohibited a monk and clergy reform council. After many arguments, Anselm sent two clergy members to Rome to determine which pope held the best claim for the papacy. Pope Urban II eventually received Anselm in Rome[85] in 1097.[86] William's bribes prevented Urban from restoring Anselm's acquiring power of office from the pope.[87]

Urban gave Anselm (1033–1109) the challenge of resolving Greek and Latin Christians on whether the Holy Spirit[88] came solely from the Father or from the Father and the Son.[89] Retiring to Lyons,[90] Anselm defended the Trinity in *De Processione Spiritus Sancti* (1102) based on the Athanasian Creed,[91] of the Trinity being one and coequal.[92] Urban died on July 1099, and William died in 1100. William's successor, King Henry I, and Pope Paschal II compromised to support Anselm's belief in the pope's power to approve clergy by agreeing that elected clergy be approved by the pope.[93]

Cistercian monks rebelled against the comfort and security provided by Cluny[94] (among the most influential orders in the Christian world in 1049–1109, located in Paris, France)[95] and other Benedict monasteries by attempting to bring back the time when St. Benedict monks in Monte Cassino lived in poverty and reflected the apostolic church.[96] The Cistercian's third abbot was an Englishman named Steven Harding (d 1134). He wrote the governing "Charter of Love" in 1119.[97] The Cistercians vowed to return to the Original Rule of Benedict, opted for plain, unadorned buildings, monks did manual labor, included uneducated lay brothers, and shortened their liturgy to leave room for contemplation.[98] They built monasteries in Britain, France, and Ireland.[99] Their focus on spirituality revolved around understanding salvation's mystery of personal experience expressed in metaphors.[100]

A Yorkshire priest, Robert of Newminister (d. 1159), joined the Benedictine Abbey of York. Robert accompanied twelve other monks from St. Mary's in York[101] who left to sign up with the Cistercian Reform at Rievaulx.[102] There, they founded Fountains Abbey in 1132. Lay brothers did routine jobs for the monks, which allowed the monks extra freedom to spend time with God. The new workforce brought Fountains wealth through cattle rearing, horse breeding, wool, lead mining, and stone quarrying.[103] After a Cistercian monastery was built near Morpeth, Robert became their Abbot. God favored him with the gifts of prophecy and miracles. He followed the teachings of Bernard of Clairvaux (1090–1153),[104] who formed the Knights Templar around 1120 so French knights would protect pilgrims traveling to the Holy Land.[105] To become self-sufficient, Cistercian monks pioneered new techniques in agriculture and sheep that later improved the economy in Northern Europe.[106] Yorkshire landowners copied the monk's innovation. By the thirteenth century, their export of wool to Flemish weavers became crucial to English foreign trade.[107]

---

1. "Leabhar Gabhála / The Book of Invasions | Royal Irish Academy," (August 31, 2015), accessed February 1, 2024. https://www.ria.ie/leabhar-gabhala-book-invasions.

2. Barbara W. Tuchman, *Bible and Sword: England and Palestine from the Bronze Age to Balfour* (New York: Ballantine Books, 1984), 2.

3. Ibid., 4-5.

4. Seamas Mac Annaidh, *Irish History* (Bath BA1 1HE: Parragon Publishing, 1999), 14.

5. Paul Avis, "Great Britain," *The SPCK Handbook of Anglican Theologians*, Alister E. McGrath ed. (London: SPCK, 1998), 3. Logos.

6. J. W. Meiklejohn, "Joseph of Arimathea," *New Bible Dictionary*, ed., D. R. W. Wood, et al. (Leicester, England; Downers Grove, IL: InterVarsity Press, 1996), 611. Logos.

7. Meiklejohn, "Joseph of Arimathea," 146.

8. Bede, *A History of the English Church and People,* trans. Leo Sherley Price (Baltimore, MD: Penguin Books, 1955), 22.

9. Kurt W. Jefferson, *Celtic Politics: Politics in Scotland, Ireland, and Wales* (Lanham, MA; Boulder; New York; Toronto; Plymouth, UK: University Press America, Inc., 2011), 18.

10. Bede, *A History of the English Church and People*, 22; "Who is David" (Pembrokeshire, England: St. David's Cathedral, https://www.stdavidscathedral.org.uk/discover/history/St-David.

11. John Fenwick, *The Free Church of England: Introduction to an Anglican Tradition* (London; New York: T&T Clark, 2004), 9. Logos.

12. O'Loughlin, "Hagiography," 4.

13. Ferguson, *Church History Volume One: From Christ to the Pre-Reformation,* 279.

14. O'Loughlin, "Hagiography," 5.

15. St. Augustine, *Saint Augustine Confessions,* trans. R. S. Pine-Coffin (New York: Barnes & Noble Books, 1992), 20.

16. Mary T. Clark, "Introduction: The Spirituality of St. Augustine," *Augustine of Hippo: Selected Writings,* ed., John Farina, trans., Mary T. Clark, The Classics of Western Spirituality (Mahwah, NJ: Paulist Press, 1984), 57. Logos.

17. Ibid., 58.

18. Ferguson, *Church History Volume One: From Christ to the Pre-Reformation*, 276.

19. O'Loughlin, "Hagiography," *Celtic Spirituality*, 4.

20. Earle, *Celtic Christian Spirituality: Essential Writings—Annotated and Explained*, 4–5; Ferguson, *Church History Volume One: From Christ to the Pre-Reformation*, 280.

21. Pine-Coffin, "Introduction," 20.

22. O'Loughlin, "Hagiography," 5.

23. John D. Barry, et al., eds., "Pelagianism," *The Lexham Bible Dictionary* (Bellingham, WA: Lexham Press, 2016). Logos.

24. Pine-Coffin, "Introduction," 20.

25. "Justus of Urgel (St.) Bp. (May 28)," *The Book of Saints* (London: A & C Black, 1921). Logos.

26. Clark, "Introduction: The Spirituality of St. Augustine," *Augustine of Hippo: Selected Writings*, 50.

27. Mary C. Earle, ed. *Celtic Christian Spirituality: Essential Writings—Annotated and Explained*, Skylight Illuminations Series (Woodstock, VT: Skylight Paths Publishing, 2011), 12. Logos.

28. Earle, *Celtic Christian Spirituality: Essential Writings—Annotated and Explained*, 13.

29. Ibid., 8.

30. Thornton, *English Spirituality*, 149.

31. O'Loughlin, "Hagiography," 23.

32. Thornton, *English Spirituality*, 149.

33. Ibid., 150.

34. O'Loughlin, "Hagiography," 333.

35. Ibid., 38.

36. "Mystics, English | Encyclopedia.Com," accessed June 17, 2023, https://www.encyclopedia.com/religion/encyclopedias-almanacs-transcripts-and-maps/mystics-english.

37. Time-Life Books, ed., *What Life Was Like in the Age of Chivalry Medieval Europe AD 800–1500* (Time-Life Education, 1997), 19.

38. Ibid., 19.

39. Time-Life Books, *What Life Was Like in the Age of Chivalry Medieval Europe AD 800–1500*, 20– 21.

40. Jones, *Hermits and Anchorites in England 1200–1550*, 195.

41. Thornton, *English Spirituality*, 168.

42. O'Loughlin, "Hagiography," 6.

43. Ferguson, *Church History Volume One: From Christ to the Pre-Reformation*, 302.

44. O'Loughlin, "Hagiography," 6.

45. Evelyn Underhill, *Mysticism: A Study in the Nature and Development of Man's Spiritual Consciousness*, 3rd ed. (New York: E.P. Dutton and Company, 1912), 545. Logos.

46. Earle, *Celtic Christian Spirituality: Essential Writings—Annotated and Explained*, 7–8; O'Loughlin, "Hagiography," 7.

47. Carl A. Volz, *The Medieval Church: From the Dawn of the Middle Ages to the Eve of the Reformation* (Nashville, TN: Abingdon Press, 1997), 175.

48. Earle, *Celtic Christian Spirituality: Essential Writings—Annotated and Explained*, 8.

49. O'Loughlin, "Hagiography," 9.

50. Cleran Hollancid, (2015) "Unknowing, Knowing: and the Link with Scripture in Pseudo-Dionysius's Mystical Theology," Journal of the Adventist Theological Society: Vol. 26: Iss. 1, Article 6.

51. O'Loughlin, "Hagiography," 96.

52. Ariel Hessayon and Dan Taylor, "The Original Climate Crisis—How the Little Ice Age Devastated Early Modern Europe," *The Conversation*, March 7, 2022, accessed July 19, 2023. http://theconversation.com/the-original-climate-crisis-how-the-little-ice-age-devastated-early-modern-europe-178187.

53. Kate Findley, "How Europe's Population in the Middle Ages Doubled," *Wondrium Daily*, October 2, 2019, https://www.wondriumdaily.com/how-europes-population-in-the-middle-ages-doubled/.

54. Jones, *Hermits and Anchorites in England 1200–1550*, 25, 159.

55. Gies and Gies, *Cathedral, Forge, and Waterwheel Technology and Invention in the Middle Ages*, 244.

56. Ibid., 98.

57. Avis, "Great Britain," 3.

58. Robert P. Miller, ed., *Chaucer Sources and Backgrounds* (New York: Oxford University Press, 1977), 3–4.

59. Lesley Smith, "The Ten Commandments in the Medieval Schools: Conformity or Diversity, " "Desplenter, Pieters, and Melion ed., 'Introduction: Exploring the Decalogue in Late Medieval and Early Modern Culture,'" *The Ten Commandments in Medieval and Early Modern Culture Intersections,* Volume 52 (Leiden; Boston: Brill, 2017). 13–29, 14.

60. Norman F. Cantor, *The Civilization of the Middle Ages A Completely Revised and Expanded Edition of Medieval History* (New York, NY: HarperCollins Publishers, 1993), 278.

61. Ibid., 280.

62. Ibid., 278.

63. Ibid., 279.

64. Ibid., 280.

65. "England," *Darkness of the Dark Ages* (London: G. Morrish, n. d.). e-Sword.

66. "Mystics, English | Encyclopedia.Com."

67. Jones, *Hermits and Anchorites in England 1200–1550*, 24.

68. J. M Dent, *The Anglo-Saxon Chronicle*, ed. and trans., M. J. Swanton (University of Exeter, Routledge, NY: Routledge, 1996), xxvii–xxviii.

69. Evans and Wright, *The Anglican Tradition: A Handbook of Sources*, 94.

70. Ferguson, *Church History Volume One: From Christ to the Pre-Reformation*, 465.

71. Jefferson, *Celtic Politics: Politics in Scotland, Ireland, and Wales*, 21.

72. Ibid., 21–22.

73. "England," *Darkness of the Dark Ages*.

74. Thornton, *English Spirituality*, 156.

75. William E. Addis and Thomas Arnold, "Ascetical Theology," *A Catholic Dictionary* (New York: The Catholic Publication Society Co., 1887), 53. Logos.

76. Greg Peters, "Asceticism," *Dictionary of Christian Spirituality*, ed., Glen G. Scorgie (Grand Rapids, MI: Zondervan, 2011). Logos.

77. Thornton, *English Spirituality*, 161.

78. Ibid., 162.

79. Ibid., 158.

80. Ibid., 159.

81. Ibid., 161.

82. Ibid., 160.

83. "England," *Darkness of the Dark Ages*.

84. "Anselm of Canterbury," The British Library (The British Library), https://www.bl.uk/people/anselm-of-canterbury.

85. "England," *Darkness of the Dark Ages*.

86. Ferguson, *Church History Volume One: From Christ to the Pre-Reformation*, 435.

87. "England," *Darkness of the Dark Ages*.

88. Evans and Wright, *The Anglican Tradition: A Handbook of Sources*, 94.

89. Sergius Bulgakov, *The Comforter*, trans. Boris Jakim (Grand Rapids, MI; Cambridge, U.K.: William B. Eerdmans Publishing Company, 2004), 75. Logos.

90. "England," Darkness *of the Dark Ages*.

91. Thomas J. Mc Kenna, "Greek and Latin Gods: Anselm's Defense of the Filioque." *Saint Anselm Journal*, vol.14, no. 1, Fall (The Catholic University of America Press, 2018): 11–131, accessed June 12, 2023. https://muse.jhu.edu/article/737780/pdf.

92. Guilbert, *The Book of Common Prayer and Administration of the*, 864–65.

93. "England," *Darkness of the Dark Ages*.

94. Cantor, *The Civilization of the Middle Ages*, 248.

95. Youngblood, Ronald F., et al., "Cluniac Order," *Nelson's New Illustrated Bible Dictionary* (Nashville, TN: Thomas Nelson, Inc., 1995).

96. Cantor, *The Civilization of the Middle Ages*, 248.

97. Ferguson, *Church History Volume One: From Christ to the Pre-Reformation*, 447.

98. Ibid., 448.

99. Ibid., 449.

100. Daniel DeForest London, "St. Aelred and Friends," *Celtic Spirituality and English Mysticism*, accessed February 13, 2024, https://www.youtube.com/watch?v=eS9pUM9YYnI&list=PLJ0h 0xfIm2qunKpHMzTv1uh5TY-U2RrOW&index=15

101. "History of Fountains Abbey | Yorkshire," National Trust, https://www.nationaltrust.org.uk/visit/yorkshire/fountains-abbe y-and-studley-royal-water-garden/history-of-fountains-abbey-and-studley-royal.

102. "Robert of Newminister (St.)," *The Book of Saints*, (London: A & C Black, 1921). Logos.

103. "History of Fountains Abbey | Yorkshire."

104. "Robert of Newminister (St.)," *The Book of Saints*.

105. Cantor, *The Civilization of the Middle Ages*, 382.

106. Ferguson, *Church History Volume One: From Christ to the Pre-Reformation*, 448.

107. Cantor, *The Civilization of the Middle Ages*, 248.

3

THE RISE OF OXFORD

ENGLISH ROOTS

TWO NEW SCHOOLS OPENED in Paris. Abelard set up the collegiate church St. Genevieve and St. Victor, founded in 1108 by William of Champeaux.[1] In 1110, born to Anglo-Saxon hereditary priest Eilaf at the church of St. Andrew, Hexham Aelred served King David I in 1124 as the king's steward in Scotland's royal court. On a diplomatic mission to Archbishop Thurstan of York in 1132, Aelred joined the monks at the two-year-old Cistercian monastery at Rievaulx Abbey in North Yorkshire, founded by Abbot William.[2]

As David I strengthened Scotland by allowing intermarriage between Norman lords and Scottish Celts during his reign from 1124–53,[3] mystic[4] Hugh of St. Victor (c. 1096–d. 1141) became director of studies in 1133 in Paris.[5] He taught that all Scripture interpretation depended on literal interpretation and the building block of history.[6] The seven deadly sins functioned as the moral code since Gregory the Great used the list as a substitute for Jewish commands in their Torah in 604. Hugh's biblical criticism emphasized the Ten Commandments' support of morality, but the use of the Ten Commandments remained intellectual, academic trivia.[7]

Victorines (followers of Hugh of St. Victor) stressed meditation as the energetic pursuit of divine love and contemplation as the enthusiasm for the concentrated peace from the union in love with God.[8] The university also taught Bernard's mysticism arising from morality, defined as the beauty of the soul's inner state, which led to inner grace and continued monastic tradition.[9] Paris University began on Saint Genevieve's Mount in the twelfth century, and every scholar hoping to succeed in the "civilized world" attended between 1150 and 1350.[10]

Aelred was appointed abbot of a new Cistercian monastery in Lincolnshire but was reassigned to serve as Rievaulx's third abbot in 1147. For the next twenty years, Aelredof Rievaulx oversaw the building and construction of Rievaulx as it enticed recruits as the monastery's fame grew at the royal courts of England, Scotland, France, and Rome. God blessed him with the gift of prophecy and miraculous healing.[11]

His friend, Bernard of Clairvaux, encouraged Aelred to write.[12] Aelred, like Bernard of Clairvaux, measured a person's progress in growing with God by defining different stages of love. Both lists began with loving oneself. Bernard's next step was the love of God based on God's rewards, followed by when one starts to compare their life with the Old Testament's Job, one turns to love "God for God's sake." Lastly, one learns to love oneself by realizing "God's calling us as His own." Aelred concentrated on different steps in loving one's neighbor, starting with family, friends, other Christians, those outside the church, and one's enemies.[13]

Aelred wrote guides to monastic life, histories, the lives of Saints, and theology.[14] He defined friendship as an eternal "visible sign of Christ's Kingdom come to earth."[15] Like all monks, he devoted four hours a day every day of the year to reading, examining, contemplating, and praying Scripture.[16] He combined Scripture with Early Church Father's and Jewish leader's wisdom,[17] Cicero's study of Plato and Aristotle in his book *On Friendship* (44 BC),[18] and practical experiences of friendship within a Christian community.[19] Hank Voss dates *Spiritual Friendship* as being written between 1164 and 1167.[20] Aelred advised in his conclusion of *On Friendship*, "Surpassing all this is prayer for each other. In remembering a friend, the more lovingly one sends forth a prayer to God with tears welling up from affection, the more effective the prayer."[21]

Although monasteries grew, and Rievaulx drew monks from all over Europe,[22] the number of students, specialization of subjects, and added literature paved the way for universities.[23] Scholars directly paid university professors. Once paid, a professor swore to obey the rector while prohibiting voting rights in the university congregation. Students required deposits for a professor's vacation leave and fined professors absent if less than five students came to a morning class or three students attended the afternoon lecture.[24]

Early twelfth-century student migration flocked around French scholastic cathedral theologians like Peter Abelard (1079–1142), head of Notre Dame 1113–1118[25] and bishop of Paris, and Peter Lombard (1100–1160) in Notre Dame.[26] Abelard figured out "a new approach to the systematic study of science" before the Muslims translated Aristotle into Latin.[27] Lombard followed Abelard as head of Notre Dame.[28] In his fourth book, the *Sentences* established the number of sacraments to seven: baptism, confirmation, penance (canons), communion, unction, marriage, and ordination based on the seven gifts of the Holy Spirit from Isa. 11:2–3 (LXX and Vulgate). The New American Standard Bible (1995) translates the text as follows: "The Spirit of the Lord will rest on Him, The spirit of wisdom and understanding, The spirit of counsel and strength, The spirit of knowledge and the fear of the Lord. And He will delight in fear of the Lord, and He will not judge by what His eyes see, Nor make a decision by what His ears hear." Traditional allegory symbolized the seven sins people fought with the seven nations the

Israelites fought after God rescued them from Egypt. It followed that God provides seven channels of love via the sacraments to fight off seven conduits of evil.[29] The University of Paris required doctoral candidates to write a commentary on Lombard's *Sentences* after 1160.[30]

King Henry II (1154–1189) encouraged English scholars studying in Paris to return to English monastic schools in Oxford in 1167.[31] Sons of nobility began studies at a university at age fourteen.[32]

Stills for making brandy, gin, and whiskey had recently been perfected for medical reasons.[33] Universities created a new economic rank called "towns" from the working class of former serfs who now labored as shopkeepers and tavern employees.[34] An 1173 London Chamber of Commerce brochure described the significant problems in their city as "the immoderate drinking of fools and the frequency of fires.[35]

Quarrels erupting between "towns and gowns" at the University of Paris propelled King Philip II to "exempt the university from the royal provost" in 1200.[36] Provost Marshals reported directly to the Earl Martial to keep the "King's Peace" backed by a feudal army.[37] Students with knives differed in nationalities and hung out with the nationality they were familiar with, so the French fought against everyone: German, English, Italian, Picard, and visa-versa.[38] Roommates fought each other about everything from dogs to women, often cutting off fingers with their knives or swords.[39] They barhopped and played dice on the cathedral altar.[40] Students and Masters arose before dawn and froze in the winter. It took four to five years to earn a Bachelor of Arts degree and another three to four years to earn a master's so one could lecture.[41] Archbishop of Genoa, Italy, Jacobus de Voragine (1228–1298), wrote, in the "pilgrimage... of our present life... wander as pilgrims amidst a thousand obstacles."[42] Pilgrimage to shrines expressed both penance and piety. The shrine of the archbishop of Canterbury Thomas Beckett (1162–70) rivaled Rome as a popular destination[43] and became the setting for Chaucer's Canterbury Tales, written in 1387.[44]

---

1. Ferguson, *Church History Volume One: From Christ to the Pre-Reformation*, 452.

2. "Aelred of Rievaulx," English Heritage, accessed July 21, 2023, https://www.english-heritage.org.uk/visit/places/rievaulx-abbey/history-and-stories/aelred-of-rievaulx/.

3. Jefferson, *Celtic Politics: Politics in Scotland, Ireland, and Wales*, 21.

4. Volz, *The Medieval Church*, 175.

5. Ferguson, *Church History Volume One: From Christ to the Pre-Reformation*, 452–453.

6. "Hugh of Saint-Victor at Encyclopedia.Com," https://www.encyclopedia.com/religion/encyclopedias-almanacs-transcripts-and-maps/hugh-saint-victor.

7. Desplenter, Pieters, and Melion, "Introduction: Exploring the Decalogue in Late Medieval and Early Modern Culture, " *The Ten Commandments in Medieval and Early Modern Culture*, Intersections, Volume 52 (The Ten Commandments in Medieval and Early Modern Culture, Leiden; Boston: Brill, 2017), 1–12, 1.

8. Ferguson, *Church History Volume One: From Christ to the Pre-Reformation*, 452–453.

9. Ibid., 452.

10. Anne Fremantle and Bryan Holme, *Europe A Journey with Pictures* (Scranton, PA: The Studio Publications, Inc., 1954), 29.

11. "Aelred of Rievaulx."

12. Hank Voss, *Spiritual Friendship: Learning to Be Friends with God and One Another*, trans. Mark F Williams, Sacred Roots Spiritual Classics 3 (Wichita, KS: TUMI Press, The Urban Ministry Institute, 2022), accessed June 29, 2023, https://pillars.taylor.edu/cgi/viewcontent.cgi?article=1005&context=spiritualclassics, 5.

13. London, "St. Aelred and Friends."

14. "Aelred of Rievaulx."

15. Voss, *Spiritual Friendship*, 5.

16. Ibid., 6.

17. Ibid., 8.

18. Ibid., 7.

19. Ibid., 10.

20. Voss, *Spiritual Friendship*, 21.

21. Daniel DeForest London, "Spirt Friendship Practice Inspired by St. Aelred of Rievaulx," *Celtic Spirituality and English Mysticism*, https://www.youtube.com/watch?v=WCwoZYO0Uh4&list=PLJ0h0xfIm2qunKpHMzTv1uh5TY-U2RrOW&index=15.

22. "Aelred of Rievaulx."

23. Ferguson, *Church History Volume One: From Christ to the Pre-Reformation*, 487.

24. Michael Kuh et al., "The Age of Chivalry," *Questing Life of the Scholar*, ed. Merle Serverly and Fredrick G. Vosburgh, First Printing, vol. Man Library (Washington, D. C.: National Geographic Society, 1969), 282.

25. Ibid., 440.

26. Volz, *The Medieval Church*, 130.

27. Gies and Gies, *Cathedral, Forge, and Waterwheel Technology and Invention in the Middle Ages*, 160.

28. Ferguson, *Church History Volume One: From Christ to the Pre-Reformation*, 456.

29. Ibid., 457.

30. Volz, *The Medieval Church*, 132.

31. Louis B. Wright, "The Thames Mirrors Britain's Glory," *This England*, eds., Merle Serverly, Seymour L. Fishbein, and Edwards Park, World in Color Library (Washington, D. C.: National Geographic Society, 1966), 79–103, 101.

32. Volz, *The Medieval Church*, 133.

33. Gies and Gies, *Cathedral, Forge, and Waterwheel Technology and Invention in the Middle Ages*, 163.

34. Time-Life Books, ed., *What Life Was Like in the Age of Chivalry Medieval Europe AD 800–1500*, 10.

35. Cantor, *The Civilization of the Middle Ages*, 476.

36. Volz, *The Medieval Church*, 131.

37. "History of the Royal Military Police and Its Antecedents," accessed March 27, 2023, https://rhqrmp.org/rmp_history.html.

38. Kuh, "The Age of Chivalry," 295.

39. Ibid., 290–295.

40. Ibid., 290.

41. Ibid., 295–96.

42. Italy Jacobus de Voragine, *Book of the Legends of the Saints Collected by Brother Jacobus of Genoa, of the Order of Preacher*, as quoted in Miller, *Chaucer Sources and Backgrounds*, 14.

43. Ferguson, *Church History Volume One: From Christ to the Pre-Reformation*, 465.

44. Ibid., 469.

4
King John the Root of English Nationalism
English Roots

Jean Henri Merle D'Aubigne (1791–1872) strove to capture the Holy Spirit's influence on history[1] and credits the "madness of John," founding English nationalism that eventually led to the Anglican church.[2] King John's life is an example of God using unbalanced, despicable people to plant seeds, leading to reformations, revivals, and awakenings.

Crusader and King Richard the Lionhearted (reigned 1189–1199) proclaimed his youngest brother, John (reigned 1199–1216), his heir on his deathbed.[3] A cross bolt pierced his shoulder while surveying the castle's defenses eleven days earlier.[4] King Philip attacked Normandy in support of twelve-year-old Arthur of Brittany's claim to the throne. This ended in a military draw and cost England twenty thousand marks for Philip's lordship on the continent.[5] In 1200, John married twelve-year-old Isabella of Angouleme, who was betrothed to Hugh de Lusignan since his first marriage to Isabella of Gloucester was invalid because they were relatives.[6]

By 1200, Cistercian monasteries floundered in wealth gained from charging high rents to secular landlords and lending money to nobles. Their downfall led to forming the Dominican and Franciscan friar's spiritual life, coupled with vows of chastity, poverty, and obedience to labor that directly contributed to society's benefit.[7] The Fourth Lateran Council in 1201 guaranteed churches the freedom to use altered rites and ceremonies in different locations.[8]

In 1201, Philip summoned John to appear at his court for a judgment against Hugh de Lusignan. The following year, John retaliated by capturing Artur and his men.[9] Toward the end of 1203, rumors claimed that in a drunken rage, John killed Arthur in the castle Rouen in Normandy, tied a heavy stone to his neck, and threw his body into the Seine River.[10] Philip retaliated, and his army took over the northern half of John's continental territories from 1203–1205.[11]

In 1205, the monks at Christ Church chose Reginald as their new archbishop of Canterbury[12] and sent him to Rome.[13] Neither the bishop nor the king approved their selection, so on December 11, 1205, the Christ Church monks voted for the king's favorite, John de Gray. Pope Innocent III (1160–1216) acknowledged the monks' right to select an archbishop but rejected both candidates because the monks failed to follow Church canon.[14]

Students solved rent and cost of living disputes by relocating elsewhere.[15] Three thousand students abandoned Oxford in 1209, leading to Cambridge University's formation and the suspension of study at Oxford for five years.[16] In 1210, Innocent III gave

Francis of Assisi (1182–1226) Order of Little Brothers permission to exist.[17]

John disputed the Canterbury appointment with Innocent III and continued the argument until 1213 when the Pope excommunicated him.[18] Innocent III proposed that Philip take the English crown while placing England under interdict, which canceled all regular church services for six years. On May 15, 2013, John surrendered England, delivering his crown to the Pope's legate, who kept it for five days, igniting a national protest.[19] John promised to pay 700 marks a year from England and 300 marks per year from Ireland.[20]

The Lateran Council of 1214 recommended monotone murmured confessions and prayers as a "voice of the soul" to nurture an intimate relationship with God. People continued a practice that started in the fourth century as they prayed by focusing on a string of pearls, counting five hundred wounds of Christ or the one thousand bloody steps to death on the cross at Calvary.[21]

Philip II, aided by Pope Innocent III and Frederick of Hohenstaufen, won leadership over Germany by soundly defeating King John and King Otto of

Germany at the Battle of Bovines. England lost King Henry II's inheritance of western France. Philip annexed the duchy of Normandy, and Anjou County, The duchy of Brittany, became a fief under the French king.[22] The barons forced John to sign the *Magna Carta* between June 15 and 19, 1215.[23]

Throughout this period, lay Christians wanted to learn more about their faith.[24] The 1215 Fourth Lateran Council responded by making the principles of the Ten Commandments the basics for catechism and private penance.[25] The Council accepted Peter Lombard's *Four Books of Sentences* as orthodox,[26] which guaranteed the Ten Commandments inclusion in university curriculums everywhere.[27] The council confirmed the Western Latin view on the procession of the Holy Spirit as proceeding from the Father and the Son.[28] Doctrine decreed that Christians should take communion once a year.[29] It branded Jews as heretics and created the Inquisition since Pope Innocent III said, "God condemned Jews to eternal slavery for the death of Christ."[30] From 1215 onward, parish priests received income based on tithe revenue.[31] In France, the papal legate regulated academic dress, fees, and lecture length,[32] while Oxford became a University, and Robert Grosseteste (1170–1253) served as Oxford's first chancellor and continued until 1221.[33]

In 1216, the barons got Philip to order his son Louis to lead the army defending their side of England's civil war, which ended when John died of dysentery.[34] Innocent III died June 16, 1216, in Perugia while touring Italy[35] to aid the Fifth Crusade authorized at the Fourth Lateran Council.[36] French cardinal Fifth Crusade historian Jacques de Vitry (1160–1240) witnessed Innocent III's reeking, almost naked body on his tomb because looters stole the expensive clothes that the Pope would be buried in.[37] England resented the gold sent to Rome every year afterward.[38]

---

1. J. H. Merle d' Aubigne, *The Reformation in England Volume One*, trans. H. White (Edinburgh, England; Carlise, PA: The Banner of Truth Trust, 1977), 10.

2. Aubigne, *The Reformation in England Volume One*, 74–75.

3. "King John, Son of Henry II and Eleanor of Aquitaine," https://www.englishmonarchs.co.uk/plantagenet_3.htm.

4. Time-Life Books, *What Life Was Like in the Age of Chivalry Medieval Europe AD 800–1500*, 78.

5. "Your Guide to King John, the Monarch Who Issued Magna Carta," HistoryExtra, accessed March 19, 2024, https://www.historyextra.com/period/medieval/king-john-facts-life-death/.

6. "King John, Son of Henry II and Eleanor of Aquitaine."

7. Cantor, *The Civilization of the Middle,* 380–81.

8. Evans and Wright, *The Anglican Tradition: A Handbook of Sources,* 107.

9. "Your Guide to King John, the Monarch Who Issued Magna Carta."

10. "King John, Son of Henry II and Eleanor of Aquitaine."

11. "Your Guide to King John, the Monarch Who Issued Magna Carta."

12. "Innocent III, Pope," *The Catholic Encyclopedia* (The Catholic Church, 1908). e-Sword.

13. Joseph R. Strayer and Dana C. Munro, *The Middle Ages 395–1500,* 4th ed. (New York: Appleton-Century-Crofts, Inc., 1959), 291.

14. "Innocent III, Pope," *The Catholic Encyclopedia.*

15. Kuh, "The Age of Chivalry," 272–95, 279.

16. Volz, *The Medieval Church,* 130.

17. Ferguson, *Church History Volume One: From Christ to the Pre-Reformation,* 481.

18. John B. Harrison and Richard E. Sullivan, *A Short History of Western Civilization* (New York: Alfred A. Knopf, Inc., 1962), 250.

19. No author, *Lights and Shadows of the Reformation* (London, Great Briton: G. Morrish, 1915). e-Sword; Aubigne, *The Reformation in England Volume One*, 69.

20. *Lights and Shadows of the Reformation.*

21. Aries and Duby, *A History of Private Life Revelations of the Medieval World*, 621.

22. Harrison and Sullivan, *A Short History of Western Civilization*, 239–40.

23. Wright, "The Thames Mirrors Britain's Glory," 82–83.

24. Desplenter, Pieters, and Melion, "Introduction: Exploring the Decalogue in Late Medieval and Early Modern Culture," *The Ten Commandments in Medieval and Early Modern Culture*, 1.

25. Smith, "The Ten Commandments in the Medieval Schools," 10–11.

26. Ferguson, *Church History Volume One: From Christ to the Pre-Reformation*, 456.

27. Lesley Smith, "The Ten Commandments in the Medieval Schools" (Harris Manchester College, Oxford University, 2014), 132, https://bibleinterp.arizona.edu/sites/bibleinterp.arizona.edu/files/docs/Smith1.pdf., 1.

28. S. R. Holmes, "Lateran Councils," in *New Dictionary of Theology: Historical and Systematic*, eds., Martin Davie, et al. (Downers Grove, IL: InterVarsity Press, 2016). Logos.

29. Ward R. Holder, *Crisis and Renewal The Era of the Reformations (Westminster History of Christian Thought)* (Louisville, KY: Westminster John Knox Press, 2009), Kindle location, 447. Kindle.

30. George Bailey, *Germans The Biography of an Obsession* (Toronto; New York: The Free Press, Maxwell Macmillan Canada and Maxwell Macmillan International, 1991), 163.

31. Bray, *Anglicanism: A Reformed Catholic Tradition*, 6.

32. Volz, *The Medieval Church*, 131.

33. "No. 1153: Grosseteste and Bacon," accessed July 5, 2023, https://www.uh.edu/engines/epi1153.htm.

34. "Your Guide to King John, the Monarch Who Issued Magna Carta."

35. "Innocent III, Pope," *The Catholic Encyclopedia*.

36. John McManners, ed., *The Oxford Illustrated History of Christianity* (Oxford, NY: Oxford University Press, 1991), 209–210.

37. "Jacques de Vitry | French Cardinal and Bishop | Britannica," https://www.britannica.com/biography/Jacques-de-Vitry.

38. Thomas B. Costain, *The Three Edwards The Pageant of England* (Garden City, NY: Doubleday & Company, Inc., 1958), 409.

5
Watering the Seed
English Roots

People during this era often prayed the Psalms.[1] Liturgical prayers, prayers written by Church Fathers, and prayers to the Virgin Mary frequently turned into emotional pleas and thanksgiving for multiple circumstances.[2] Anchoresses outnumbered anchorites in a 3:1 ratio. Most anchorites had once been priests, monks, or friars.[3] Anchoresses grew up in towns or burrows as daughters of someone governing the town or their father belonged to the nobility. The Church of England followed guidelines outlined in *Ancrene*

Wisse by Aelred for accepting and scrutinizing anchorite candidates.[4]

Along with friends, family, spiritual advisors,[5] and a bishop's approval,[6] anchorites required an endowment. Endowments, donations, and gifts came from the laity, barons, and kings.[7] After a grave-sized cell had been attached to the church, the candidate attended their own funeral. Poll bearers carried the anchoress through the cemetery to the living tomb. The bishop sprinkled dust on the anchoress, consecrated them by sprinkling the cell with Holy Water and incense, and sealed the door. The open grave on the cold north side of the church had a slit overlooking the high altar just large enough to permit partaking in communion while kneeling. A second window attached to the servant quarters was large enough that a servant could pass in food and waste could be passed out. A third window,[8] just large enough for a guest to view the white veil hiding the anchoress' face,[9] opened into a parlor where guests could be received. A curtain or shutter covered all three windows.[10]

The anchoress' repetitions of "Our Fathers" upon each hour reflected the Benedictine monk's practice.

Alternating reading, meditation, prayer, and manual labor mimicked monastery life.[11] Both cloth work and copying manuscripts qualified as relevant jobs. Like monks, most anchoress days were spent in silence, even when communicating with their servants.[12] People looked to them for advice since they were good listeners and stopped talking after the question was answered.[13]

In Wales, royalty sought bards who composed songs praising King, Queens, and God. Irish monks and hermits continued to pen prayers and poems. Scotland's oral tradition left songs and prayers about the "intimate awareness of God's presence in every aspect and moment of life."[14]

From 1214–1294, Europe remained free from major wars. Nobles elaborately decorated and furnished their castles and chateaus, which became homes. Men enjoyed hunting. Townsfolk life depended on the cathedral or castle.[15]

Dominicans set up preaching missions at the University of Paris in 1217, followed by the Franciscans in 1219.[16] Dominicans focused on enlightening the mind, while Franciscans advocated changing one's heart.[17]

To evangelize the rise of small communities, Franciscans focused less on prayer services. They created a liturgical songbook[18] containing Psalms, hymns, lessons, and prayers called the *Breviary*, still used in the Roman Catholic Church.[19] Franciscans developed "The Stations of the Cross,"[20] a devotional from fourteen pictures or statues depicting the Passion of Christ, starting with Pilate and ending with Jesus' burial.[21]

Sir William Marshal, first Earl of Pembroke, Wales (1146–1219), served five English kings[22] and became nine-year-old Henry III (1216–1272) regent, undoing King John's wrongs.[23] The barons had Henry sign a revised version of the *Magna Carta*.[24] No royalty levied a single tax without the consent of the barons afterward.[25] Marshal granted government control to the eleven-year-old king and pledged his body to the Knights Templar before he died in 1219 of illness.[26] That same year, Francis of Assisi joined the Fifth Crusade and obtained permission to preach in Muslim lands.[27]

Inspired by the 1220 Fourth Lateran Council, the earliest chancellor of Cambridge University (1215–1232), Richard of Wetheringsett, Suffolk, published *Summa*, or *Mirror of Churchmen*, which contained his treatise *Qui bene present*. His book became the most popular pastoral manual in the British Isles in the late Middle Ages. A short or a longer revised version appears in sixty-three medieval manuscripts identifying the twelve topics preachers must master before delivering a sermon.[28] A preacher should be fluent in the creed with its twelve articles of faith, the Lord's Prayer, the gifts of the Holy Spirit, the virtue and vices, the seven sacraments, the two rules about loving God and one's neighbor, the Ten Commandments, the heaven's rewards over the pains of hell, mistakes people make, things to be avoided, and a must to-do list.[29] He gave the fourth commandment of honoring your mother and father the most attention in his treatment of the Ten Commandments. Modern twelfth-century practical solutions to social injustice, examples, commentaries, and memory aids distinguished his book over others.[30]

King John's son, Henry III, allowed the Church to tax England and heavily fill church offices with foreigners.[31] When the Paris University masters went on strike for two years in 1229, Henry wrote a letter offering to accept student transfers to any English college. Pope Gregory IX gave Paris University a charter granting the school to become self-governing under papal protection.[32] In 1232, Henry seized the synagogue in London and established the Domus Conversorum to house the converted one hundred expulsed Jews. All their property now belonged to the King.[33] While in Paris, Grosseteste wrote a French religious romance, the *Château d'Amour*. He moved to Oxford when elected bishop of Lincoln in 1235.[34] Parliament began as Henry's sixty-year experiment to placate the barons in 1236.[35]

In Oxford, hostels lodging scholars became colleges. Oxford colleges remain small and spread out.[36] As head of Oxford University, Grosseteste appointed at least four archdeaconries. He excelled at mathematics, science, perspectives, multiple languages, saints, and philosophies.[37] Since God is light, then by understanding light, one understands God. Since light follows Euclid's rules of geometry, mathematics also led to understanding God.[38] Grosseteste investigated how the sun creates heat and how the moon affects tides.[39] He deduced that refracted light created rainbows.[40] Notes from his lectures on theology, his commentaries, and sermons are among the earliest documents in the Oxford libraries as he willed all his books and notes to the Oxford Franciscans.[41] His lectures stressed moral issues and studying Scripture. Grosseteste mentored Franciscan Roger Bacon (1220–1292),[42] who taught Aristotelian natural philosophy at Oxford[43] and invented gunpowder.[44]

In France, biographer William of St. Thierry documented the life of mystic[45] Bonaventure of Bagnoregio (1217–1274), who became a Franciscan friar in 1243 and studied in Paris.[46] Thierry described theology as an "act of adoration" while mystical knowledge depended on "the ascent of one's soul under the Holy Spirit's influence.[47] Grosseteste served on a parliament committee of twelve to bring about reforms in 1244.[48] Early Church Fathers Clement of Alexandria and Origen defined *purgatory* as a state of sleep that dead Christians experienced in which Christ cleans them from all sin prior to the general resurrection. The mystic Italian Dominican philosopher and theologian Thomas Aquinas (1225–1274)[49] saw purgatory as a place like heaven and hell where fire painfully purged one's soul from sin. In his theological philosophy, he wrote that Jews were "assigned in eternal bondage to the princes as the desserts of their guilt."[50] The First Council of Lyon (1245) canonized his doctrine.[51] While magistrate Wang Chen crafted the first practical moveable type press in China,[52] while Thomas' studies in Cologne during 1248 and as a Paris lecturer from 1252–1259[53] revolved around reconciling Aristotelian philosophy with Christianity.[54] He defined "mysticism" correlating to the Church as the body of Christ shapes "with its head one single mystical person," signifying through the achievement of the Holy Spirit, "Head and body" comprise "one single and unique organism of grace." He counted on the mystical sense to interpret Scripture from the literal sense.[55] In his *Sentences Commentary*, he explained theology as a contemplative science based on Matt. 5–8, "Blessed are the pure of heart, for they shall see God."[56]

Grosseteste pushed to train clergy to preach effectual instruction to the laity in addition to sacramental duties.[57] Grosseteste often received Pope Innocent IV's support, but in his last year, Grosseteste received a letter explaining the Pope's nephew Frederick di Lavagna into a vacant Lincoln canonry.

Anyone in opposition faced excommunication. Innocent IV answered Grosseteste's protest with a November 1253 bull restoring the rights of English church authorities' full rights to election and presentation.[58] Grosseteste's last words defined heresy as "an opinion conceived by carnal motives, contrary to Scripture openly taught and obstinately defended."[59] Knights from towns like York and Lincoln were elected to sit at the first parliament in 1254.[60] Bacon attempted to convince the Papacy that math and science qualified as the appropriate limb of theology by describing the wonders that would surge from science. He predicted flying machines, better medicines leading to longer lifespans, telescopes, and eyeglasses.[61]

Bonaventure, with a Master of Theology from the University of Paris 1257, taught Christ is the "one true master;" knowledge begins with faith that spawns a mystical union with God, perfecting rational understanding based on God creating humans in His image.[62] In *Mind's Journey to God*, he stated, "All learning is directed to the love of God ... Every object speaks to us of God ... When we seek God within, we turn towards him, for there is a small spark of pure divine light within the soul. The ordinary person of goodwill, as well as the scholar, can see God clearly."[63] Jews mocked Christians for asserting they adhered to the Ten Commandments since Christians distorted the Jewish Sabbath, honoring "God's rest after creation" for Sunday, keeping the "day of Christ's resurrection."[64] Bonaventure countered that the moral law required a "quiet observance" once a week. What day of the week when this quiet observance occurred was ceremonial law that can be altered.[65]

Simon Hinton taught at Oxford from 1248–1254 as Oxford Dominican priory and served as provincial for the English Dominicans from 1254–1261. After the general chapter removed him from office for refusing to accept foreign students at the Dominican stadium, he lectured at the Dominican school in Cologne. Oxford permitted Hinton to return to England a year later. He wrote a manual for practical theology, *Summa ad instructionem,* which received a wide readership throughout the fifteenth century.[66] Where Peter Lombard in *Four Books of Sentences* had treated the Ten Commandments as a complete unit mimicking the structure of the Trinity prescribing a Christian life filled with Christ's virtues, Hinton divided the rules into individual rules, demonstrating how to avoid evil toward God or humans.[67]

Thomas continued his Greek philosophy studies in Italy while working as a theologian for the papal court from 1259–1268.[68] Aristotle-based teaching added to and replaced what the Church had incorporated into their theology from Plato.[69] In *Summa Theologiae,* he showed theology scientifically developed from the revelation of Scripture. According to Aristotle, science acquired by another science depends on the first. Optics depends on geometry. Music depends on mathematics. God's mystery of his trinitarian existence and salvation can only be partially accessed by faith, making faith a critical component of theology. A theologian must connect with and experience the living God through faith[70] for the theologian's work to have any authentic content.[71]

In Oxford, Merton became a college in 1264.[72] During the same year, Simon de Montfort led the Baron's War against Henry III. While in power, Simon organized a parliament.[73] Since many barons did not support Simon, he invited lesser landholders and townsfolk to participate, which later became the precedent for the House of Commons. From then on, explaining and justifying government policy to the lower classes became necessary. Edward, who would become King Edward I, raised an army that defeated Simon at Evesham Plain in 1265.[74]

In 1271, an Oxford merchant willed his savings to nine Oxford anchorites.[75] In 1282, The archbishop of Canterbury shut down all places of Jewish prayer. In 1290, Edward decreed that all Jews had six months to leave England.[76]

Paper was cheaper but perishable.[77] It started to take hold in Europe in the twelfth century as the price of paper decreased due to linen rags becoming more plentiful.[78] The "Dark Ages" is so named because the book publishing business ceased after the fall of the Roman Empire. Only monks and nuns could read and write. Texts on parchment often took a year to complete as monks had other duties.[79] As paper became cheaper and people wanted to read more, books were hand printed by full-time university copyists instead of the monasteries' expensive scribes.[80]

Eyeglasses from Italy were invented sometime before 1292, improving sight for the farsighted.[81] Copyists working in their writing shops found it impossible to keep up with the book demand.[82] Archaeologists confirmed the Chinese production of gun barrows in 1300.[83]

---

1. Ferguson, *Church History Volume One: From Christ to the Pre-Reformation*, 464.

2. Aries and Duby, *A History of Private Life Revelations of the Medieval World*, 625.

3. Jones, *Hermits and Anchorites in England 1200–1550*, 24.

4. Ibid., 193.

5. Ibid., 34.

6. Ibid., 26.

7. Ibid., 25.

8. Ibid., 73.

9. Ibid., 104.

10. Ibid., 73.

11. Ibid., 105.

12. Ibid., 106.

13. Ibid., 107.

14. O'Loughlin, "Hagiography," 3.

15. Cantor, *The Civilization of the Middle Ages*, 476.

16. Ferguson, *Church History Volume One: From Christ to the Pre-Reformation*, 489.

17. Ibid., 494.

18. Thornton, *English Spirituality*, 77.

19. F. L. Cross and Elizabeth A. Livingstone, eds., "Breviary," *The Oxford Dictionary of the Christian Church* (Oxford; New York: Oxford University Press, 2005), 238.

20. Thornton, *English Spirituality*, 90.

21. Cross and Livingstone, "Stations of the Cross," *The Oxford Dictionary of the Christian Church* (Oxford; New York: Oxford University Press, 2005), 1549.

22. "William Marshal, 1st Earl of Pembroke," geni_family_tree, May 12, 1146, accessed March 30, 2023, https://www.geni.com/people/William-Marshal-1st-Earl-of-Pembroke/6000000002459854209; Mark Cartwright, "Sir William Marshal," *World History Encyclopedia*, accessed March 30, 2023, https://www.worldhistory.org/Sir_William_Marshal/.

23. Time-Life Books, *What Life Was Like in the Age of Chivalry Medieval Europe AD 800–1500*, 78.

24. Harrison and Sullivan, *A Short History of Western Civilization*, 251.

25. Strayer and Munro, *The Middle Ages 395–1500*, 295.

26. Time-Life Books, *What Life Was Like in the Age of Chivalry Medieval Europe AD 800–1500*, 78.

27. Ferguson, *Church History Volume One: From Christ to the Pre-Reformation*, 481.

28. Greti Dinkova-Bruun, "The Ten Commandments in the Thirteenth-Century Pastoral Manual Qui Bene Presunt," Desplenter, Pieters, and Melion ed., "The Ten Commanaments in Medieval and Early Modern Culture," *Intersections*, Vol. 52 (Leiden: Brill, 2017), 113–132, 114–115.

29. Ibid., 115.

30. Ibid., 125–126.

31. Harrison and Sullivan, *A Short History of Western Civilization*, 251.

32. Volz, *The Medieval Church*, 131.

33. "London," https://www.jewishvirtuallibrary.org/london.

34. "Grosseteste, Robert," *The Catholic Encyclopedia*.

35. Strayer and Munro, *The Middle Ages 395–1500*, 481.

36. Wright, "The Thames Mirrors Britain's Glory," *This England*, 101.

37. "Grosseteste, Robert," *The Catholic Encyclopedia*.

38. "No. 1153: Grosseteste and Bacon."

39. Gies and Gies, *Cathedral, Forge, and Waterwheel Technology and Invention in the Middle Ages*, 227.

40. "No. 1153: Grosseteste and Bacon."

41. Cross, and Livingstone, "Grossetteste," 721.

42. Gies and Gies, *Cathedral, Forge, and Waterwheel Technology and Invention in the Middle Ages*, 227.

43. Tim Noone and R. E. Houser, "Saint Bonaventure," *The Stanford Encyclopedia of Philosophy*, Edward N. Zalta ed., Winter 2020 (Metaphysics Research Lab, Stanford University, 2020), accessed August 7, 2023, https://plato.stanford.edu/archives/win2020/entries/bonaventure/.

44. Costain, *The Three Edwards The Pageant of England*, 409.

45. Volz, *The Medieval Church*, 175.

46. Noone and Houser, "Saint Bonaventure."

47. Volz, *The Medieval Church*, 175.

48. "Grosseteste, Robert," *The Catholic Encyclopedia*.

49. Jean-Pierre Torrell, *Christ and Spirituality in St. Thomas Aquinas*, ed., Matthew Levering and Thomas Joseph White, trans. Bernhard Blankenhorn, Vol. 2. Thomistic Ressourcement Series (Washington, D.C.: The Catholic University of America Press, 2011), xii, 1–8. Logos.

50. Bailey, *Germans The Biography of an Obsession*, 163.

51. Jack Kilcrease, "Purgatory," in *Lexham Survey of Theology*, eds., Mark Ward, et al. (Bellingham, WA: Lexham Press, 2018). Logos.

52. Gies and Gies. *Cathedral, Forge, and Waterwheel Technology and Invention in the Middle Ages*, 98.

53. Brian L. Hanson, "Thomas Aquinas," *The Essential Lexham Dictionary of Church History*, ed., Michael A. G. Haykin (Bellingham, WA: Lexham Press, 2022). Logos.

54. Ferguson, *Church History Volume One: From Christ to the Pre-Reformation*, 491.

55. Torrell, *Christ and Spirituality in St. Thomas Aquinas*, 1–2.

56. Ibid., 6.

57. McManners, *The Oxford Illustrated History of Christianity*, 221.

58. "Grosseteste, Robert," *The Catholic Encyclopedia*.

59. Aubigne, *The Reformation in England Volume One*, 74.

60. "10 Facts About Simon de Montfort," History Hit, https://www.historyhit.com/facts-about-simon-de-montfort/.

61. "No. 1153: Grosseteste and Bacon."

62. Noone and Houser, "Saint Bonaventure."

63. Ferguson, *Church History Volume One: From Christ to the Pre-Reformation*, 495.

64. Smith, "The Ten Commandments in the Medieval Schools," 3.

65. Smith, *The Ten Commandments in Medieval and Early Modern Culture*, 18.

66. "Simon Hinton: Encyclopedia.Com," accessed June 15, 2023, https://www.encyclopedia.com/religion/encyclopedias-almanacs-transcripts-and-maps/simon-hinton.

67. Smith, "The Ten Commandments in the Medieval Schools: Conformity or Diversity?," 21.

68. Ferguson, *Church History Volume One: From Christ to the Pre-Reformation*, 490.

69. Ibid., 491.

70. Torrell, *Christ and Spirituality in St. Thomas Aquinas*, 4, 5.

71. Ibid., 4.

72. Wright, "The Thames Mirrors Britain's Glory," *This England*, 101.

73. Harrison and Sullivan, *A Short History of Western Civilization*, 251.

74. Strayer and Munro, *The Middle Ages 395–1500*, 379–380.

75. Jones, *Hermits and Anchorites in England 1200–1550*, 23.

76. Bailey, *Germans The Biography of an Obsession*, 163.

77. Gies and Gies, *Cathedral, Forge, and Waterwheel Technology and Invention in the Middle Ages*, 95–96.

78. Ibid., 182–83.

79. Time-Life Books, *What Life Was Like in the Age of Chivalry Medieval Europe AD 800-1500*, 130.

80. Gies and Gies, *Cathedral, Forge, and Waterwheel Technology and Invention in the Middle Ages*, 182–83.

81. Ibid., 227.

82. Time-Life Books, *What Life Was Like in the Age of Chivalry Medieval Europe AD 800–1500*, 131.

83. Gies and Gies, *Cathedral, Forge, and Waterwheel Technology and Invention in the Middle Ages*, 207.

6

A Change in Weather

English Roots

According to the Gospel's account of Jesus calming the storm in the Sea of Galilee, God controls the weather (Matt. 8:23–27, Mark 4:35–41, and Luke 8:22–25). The "Medieval warm period" brought prosperity from around 1000 to sometime after 1200 ended.[1] Wars righted a wrong or backed a noble cause against a wicked enemy. God joined the righteous, which was always your side. The devil led the opposition.[2]

In November 1292, Edward I acknowledged John Balliol as Scotland's rightful heir and loyalty to the English King.³ A year later, King Philip IV (1268–1314), "the Fair" of France, reneged on the 1279 Treaty of Amiens and promised an inheritance to King Edward I that French-occupied Gascon castles become controlled by the English.⁴ In 1294, King Balliol's magnates allied themselves with France, who now fought the English after Balliol appeared at Westminster when Edward summoned him.

Edward decimated Scotland's financial capital, Berwick, in March 1296. Balliol renounced his allegiance to England in April. Edward designed and began to rebuild Berwick before his forces took Edinburgh Castle and Balliol surrendered. Edward ordered the Stone of Destiny on which Scottish kings had been crowned at Scone, relocated to London, and then placed in the Coronation Chair in Westminster Abbey.⁵

William Wallace became Scotland's hero when he utilized guerilla tactics to beat the English Army at Stirling Bridge on Sept. 11, 1297, in the name of Scottish freedom from England. His troops plundered Northern England. Scottish nobles knighted him with the title "Guardian of Scotland." On July 22, 1298, Wallace's troops lost to the English at Falkirk and continued to France, where they fought the English.[6] During the truce in 1303, Edward married Philip's daughter.[7]

The "Little Ice Age" began about 1300— average temperatures cooled by two degrees Celsius in the British Isles.[8] Winters throughout Europe grew colder and longer.[9] Seas and rivers froze, paralyzing trade, harvests, and livestock.[10]

In 1303, Philip fought Pope Boniface VIII about the authority to appoint clergy, plotted to kill him, and eventually had him kidnapped.[11] Boniface died after his rescue. Philip's councilor Guillaume de Nogaret is still suspected of poisoning Pope Benedict XI, who died in less than a year.[12] In 1305, the English captured Wallace and executed him in London.[13] In 1306, Pope Clement V (1305–1314) excommunicated Robert the Bruce for stabbing his cousin John Comyn and letting him die in a church to seize the Scottish crown.[14]

Although Edward requested his bones be carried into Scottish campaigns and his heart carried into Crusaders, in 1307, he ended up buried in a candlelit black marble coffin at Westminster Abbey.[15] Italy lost control of the papacy when Philip IV conspired with French Pope Clement V to annihilate the Knights

Templar, charged with heresy, homosexuality, idol worship, fraud, and not donating as other orders did[16] and relocate the papacy seat from Rome to Avignon on the Rhine.[17] The Church of Scotland and many clans supported Scotland's crowned David Bruce as king at Scone in 1309 despite his excommunication from the Church of Rome.[18]

On March 22, 1312, the Council of Venice dissolved the Knights Templar by papal decree.[19] On June 23, 1314, Bruce's 12,000 men victory over Edward II's army of 20,000 at Bannockburn, Scotland, ensured Bruce's reign would last another fifteen years.[20] Germans ruled the empire, and the French owned the University of Paris.[21] (1315–1317) Two successive harvest failures caused by bad weather, murrain epidemics, and cow disease brought on famine.[22]

John Wycliffe would echo the words of Marsilius of Padua and John of Jandun in the future.[23] These French authors wrote the *Defensor Pacis* in 1324 during a dispute where the French Pope John XXII (1316–1334) refused to recognize the claim of Emperor Louis the Bavarian (1314–1347) of land with Fredrick of Austria caused by the election of the German pope.[24] They argued for the power of a lay government in church matters because the clergy and the pope lacked special privilege in speaking for the church as that right belonged to the people.[25] A papal election is unnecessary as a local council composed of the faithful holds the authority to elect a bishop. State supremacy relied on the power of the people.[26] Pope John XXII excommunicated both authors in 1327, and they found protection in Bavaria from the emperor.[27] The Black Death in 1331 began demolishing Central Asia as it traveled along the Silk Road as rodents fled famine-struck lands.[28]

From 1333 to 1341, King Philip VI hosted Scottish king David Bruce in France and then funded his reinstatement on the throne. On April 16, 1341, the Scots retook Edinburgh Castle. Under a truce, Scotland and England stared each other down across the Scottish-English border.[29] An inventory of Pope John XXII's estate after he died in 1334 revealed eighteen million gold florins in coins and seven million in jewels and plates. Pope Benedict XII used the money to renovate the Pope's Palace in Avignon.[30]

Counseling and preaching hermits roamed the countryside.[31] These laymen begged and worked construction jobs.[32] A nineteen-year-old dropped out of Oxford because religion was the only subject that interested him. During a break, he returned home, asked his sister for two of her tunics and his father's rain jacket, and made himself a hermit's habit.[33] Hermit, mystic, and poet Richard Rolle (1290–1349) Rolle translated the Psalms into his Northern dialect in Hampole, a small village in Yorkshire near Doncaster,[34] near a Cistercian nunnery.[35] Rolle's version included commentary[36] reflecting the works of Augustine, Bernard, and St. Victor.[37] Others rewrote Rolle's translation into their local dialects.[38] Rolle's writings greatly influenced the Lollards[39] and may have inspired Julian of Norwich and Walter Hilton of Thurgarton, as Rolle's fame included spiritual guidance.[40] Two titles from a list of his popular books were *Meditations on the Passion* and *The Forme of Perfect Living*.[41] He recommended this grace to Margaret Kirbey, a nun who decided to embrace the strict life of an anchorite in 1348:[42] "Be not negligent in meditating and reading the Scripture and most in those places where it teaches manners, and to eschew the deceits of the fiend, and where it speaks of God's love and contemplative life. Hard sayings may be left to disputers and to wise men used for a long time in holy doctrine."⁴³

Rolle combined belief and faithfulness with the freedom of spiritual expression. He enjoyed sitting while praying because he "loved God more" when he felt comfortable.⁴⁴ Offering a short prayer when thinking of God becomes constant as a person becomes aware that God's presence is everywhere. It is a vital link between corporate worship and private prayer. God demanded all.⁴⁵ After Rolle died, England revered him as a saint.⁴⁶ The Hampole nuns sent Rolle's anecdotes, readings, and quotes to Rome in hopes that Rolle would be canonized, which was rejected.⁴⁷

Theologian Thomas Bradwardine (1290–1349), a Fellow of Balliol College and Merton College, Oxford, was ranked highly among the top astronomers, mathematicians, and philosophers.⁴⁸ Arguing against William of Occam's position that information could be incorporated outside of Scripture, Bradwardine insisted everything taught in the church come directly from canonical Scripture.⁴⁹

England and France fought against each other in the Hundred Years War from 1337 until 1453, which started when King Edward III (1312–1377) responded to attacks on his French land holdings by claiming the French throne.[50] In 1337, Bradwardine became Chancellor of St. Paul's Cathedral and was made Confessor to Edward, whom he occasionally accompanied during the wars with France.[51]

Edward's 1342 army of 6,000 men-at-arms and 12,000 archers arrived at Brest, France, in four hundred warships on October 27. They ransacked the French countryside up to the town of Vannes, where on November 25, he united with Robert of Artois' army, which had besieged Vannes for almost a month. After the English attacked Nantes, Rennes, and Dinan, King Philip VI led a large French army to the scene but refused to fight for two weeks until Pope Clement VI's papal legates negotiated the Truce of Malestroit. The English military sailed home on February 22, 1343.[52] Edward invested in restoring King Author's round table at Windsor Castle.[53]

In 1344, English Franciscan theologian John of Reading warned that women wearing tight-fitting clothing with fox tails to hide their behinds would invoke God's wrath.[54] Unmoved, Edward announced a series of tournaments at Windsor Castle in January.

By February, carpenters and masons banged away, reproducing King Arthur's Round Table for the freshly created Knights of the Blue Garter.[55]

Bradwardine wrote *De Causa Dei Contra Pelagium* (1344) as mathematical reasoning for a preordained universe based on the writings of Augustine,[56] who maintained that good works alone only produce a moral code.[57] Bradwardine opposed the concept of good deeds leading to salvation. He complained that the British population preferred purchasing indulgences for grace rather than receiving grace freely from God.[58]

In 1346, Edward III took on a larger French army to reclaim French lands with Bradwardine as his chaplain.[59] Bradwardine served among the commissioners who attempted peace negotiations between England, France, and Scotland.[60] Pope Clement VI's truce ended. Edward sent two armies that assaulted French outposts in Brittany and Gascony.[61] Edward and his sixteen-year-old eldest son, the Black Knight, Edward King of Wales (1330–1376), accompanied[62] his army aboard 700 to 1000 ships and pillaged the French side of the English Channel from April to July.[63] From land and ships along the English

Channel, English troops invaded the town outside the castle Caen built by William the Conqueror and Henry I, which surrendered after the English forces massacred over 2,5000 villagers.[64]

Edward III marched northward toward a friendly Flemish army[65] but decided to confront the French army of one hundred thousand with fifty thousand at Crecy.[66] Crecy boasted of a church, a manor house, a miller, a smith, and a few peasants.[67] The French announced the battle with drums and horns. The English answered back with the sound of cannons.[68] After the English victory, from 1346 to 1347, Edward's forces of thirty-two thousand besieged Calais.[69] Welsh archers dressed in green and white marched under the Black Prince and the flag of the red dragon.[70] The longbow and tactics brought England triumph.[71] Although canons had yet to be made by the Chinese, twenty cannons and lots of sulfur and saltpeter bombarded the walls of Calais.[72]

Meanwhile, in northern England, the Scottish Army led by King David Bruce took Cumberland and Westmoreland with few casualties.[73] The Scots engaged a substantial army, which included archers, cavalry, and infantry, at Neville's Cross near Durham

Cathedral.[74] Upon the English victory, the troops heard the monk's cheers and prayers thanking God from the Cathedral tower.[75]

Back in Oxford, Bradwardine revived the study of Augustine, promoting predestination, a personal relationship with God and soul, and preached grace over merit.[76] He taught that everything in nature reflects the Trinity as in "mind, knowledge, and love of God" used in a "three-point meditation." God's indwelling inside the soul commands reason, which directs sensual desires. God's love caused creation, but Adam's fall caused sickness, vice, and sorrow.[77] A human being loves their self without concern for others.[78] A Christian must begin by analyzing their soul. One cannot form a meaningful relationship with God without facing the truth about oneself.[79] Humans must give up their free will and submit to God's will, which can only be obtained through God's grace and accessed by prayer.[80] At this point, a Christian loves God for their own sake. In the last phase, the person cooperates with grace through prayer, meditation, reading Scripture, and obedience according to the person's needs. The person tastes "how sweet the Lord is, mimicking Psalms 33 and

34. In the final stage, only God matters.[81] Although Christians must strive for perfection in charity and justice, this model only happens after death.[82]

Bradwardine's Augustine revival influenced Wycliffe, Huss, Luther, and Calvin.[83] Eighteenth century, Puritan Congregational pastor Jonathon Edward's (1703–1758) doctrine of free will as an illusion mimicked Bradwardine's.[84]

While England rejoiced in their victorious military conquests in 1346, the Mongol army led by Kipchak Khan Janiberg besieged Caffa, Crimea, the commercial headquarters for outposts on the Black Sea,[85] owned by Italian shipbuilders from Geneva in Northwest Italy.[86] The port city harbored one of Europe's biggest slave markets.[87] Genghis Khan's lieutenants catapulted their plague victims over the city walls.[88] As the decaying human carcasses fell from the sky, the Christian Genoese dumped them into the sea.[89] The rotting bodies continued to foul the air and poisoned the water for days.[90] Ships trying to escape spread the disease to every Mediterranean Sea port. A large earthquake shook Greece and Italy, followed by a "thick, stinking mist." A pillar of fire above the Palace of the Popes at Avignon at sunset lit the sky.

Many countries reported seeing large meteors. On one August evening, a fireball lit the Paris sky.[91]

The Black Death (1348–1350) arrived in Sicily on a ship from the east in 1347,[92] shortly after Edward III's victory after a two-year siege in Calais.[93] Edward mourned his daughter Joan's death from the plague in Bordeaux while en route to marry the Infante Pedro of Castile, Spain.[94] In Europe, Christians decided that the Jews had poisoned the water, so on the mainland, Europeans killed many Jews.[95]

Edward rededicated the royal chapel in the lower ward of Windsor Castle,[96] built by Henry III,[97] to Saint George, the third-century dragon slayer, Saint Edward the Confessor, and the Virgin Mary on August 22, 1348.[98] Edward rededicated St. George[99] from a Byzantine army saint[100] to the special patron of England.[101] He founded the College of St. George to care for St. George Chapel and to pray daily for his newly established Knights of the Garter. The King awarded twenty-five knights, each with a deputy knight mirroring the dean, canon, and vicars from the colleges. Each deputy had a Poor Knight who attended daily services for the deputies.[102] The Poor Knights were impoverished retired or disabled veterans of the Battle of Crecy.[103] At the dedication held for the "reincarnated knights of the Holy Grail," two lines of knights dressed in blue robes with badges filed into the chapel behind Edward and the Black Knight as they listened to anthems. They participated in righteousness and blessing from the clergy of St. George College.[104]

During the same year, riders warned about the approaching Black Death falling ill as they rode into town.[105] News from France said that Avignon churchyards "could not hold the dead. The Pope consecrated the Rhone so that bodies might be committed to the waters."[106] The disease terminated "tens of millions" of people across Europe[107] in one to three days after symptoms appeared.[108] Rumors in England claimed the plague started in India with a rain of frogs, lizards, and serpents on the first day. Thunder boomed. Lightning and sheets of fire lit the sky on the second day. A fowl-smelling smoke obliterated everything as it traveled across the land. The plague followed on day number four. Perhaps an earthquake had uncovered graves, and the wind bore infection from the corpses.[109]

Longbowmen who had recently returned from Crecy as heroes with ropes of flowers around their necks died painful, horrible deaths.[110] The dead and dying discarded by terrified friends and relatives littered the streets.[111] People died without properly confessing their sins,[112] thus lacking the priest's absolution, intensifying purgatory as a hope.[113] Was God punishing the boasting, riches, and fierce national pride?[114] As England lost half her population,[115] villagers saw bolting crops, cows crying to be milked, dead infants, filthy wandering orphans, and missing parish priests.[116]

Warren Holder blamed the Black Death on "plaque-infested rats" and the lack of technology to properly store grain as it should be, thus spreading the disease.[117] Schama reports that a 1347 lawyer, Gabriel de Mussis from Piacenza, Italy, blamed a form of anthrax carried by Asian rats infected the Mongol army during the siege of Caffa.[118] Cantor agrees about the parasitic rats but theorizes that the epidemic may have been a rare strain of murrain since domestic animals exhibited the same symptoms.[119]

In 1351, the English government passed the Statute of Provisors, forbidding the pope to assign priests as a benefit.[120] Differences of opinion on ruling and papal authority sprang from this law. Agreement from both the pope and local authorities meant imprisonment of the appointee.[121] In 1353, the Statute of Praemunire forbade appeals to Rome.[122]

Philip VI died during the Black Death, and John the Good succeeded him.[123] New outbreaks of the Black Death struck every ten years for the rest of the century.[124] The sudden decrease in labor started a wage war, increasing the cost of living.[125] Parliament issued a Statute of Laborers in 1351 that froze wages to what they had been before the plague, forcing less pay with a higher cost of living and restricting all to the parish where they lived.[126] Edward III replaced the status of one's lineage with one's wealth by changing the obligations of feudal knights to fight for their nobles or king without pay. Great fortunes could be made at war by plundering and ransoming.[127]

On February 10, 1355, a quarrel over the quality of wine in an Oxford tavern escalated into a longbow shootout between the "towns and gowns" as St. Mary's bells welcomed the feast of St. Scholastica. Everyone missed each other.[128] On the next day, the "towns" murdered several "gowns" involved in recreation in

Beaumont fields. A riot broke out as church bells rang, as more "towns" burned student halls and broke into chapels to mutilate and kill more students. Stout, thick walls protected Merton College, but most "gowns" vacated Oxford. The Church interdict denied Oxford residents the sacraments. The royal investigation found the university innocent. From then on, the Chancellor and the other university officials would govern the town above the mayor. They ensured clean streets, checked weights and measures, and oversaw rents and the quality of ale, wine, and bread. The town did penance on St. Scholastica day with a special service in the university church; the mayor, bailiffs, and sixty burghers left a penny on the altar until 1825.[129]

In the 1356 Battle of Poitier, the Black Prince's army annihilated the French and captured Good King John.[130] The French paid the English a substantial ransom for their king, and Edward III gained control of a third of France in the Treaty of Bretigny. Good King John died still a captive in 1364.[131]

---

1. Hessayon and Taylor, "The Original Climate Crisis–How the Little Ice Age Devastated Early Modern Europe."

2. Logan Kilsdonk, "The Thirty Years War(s)," *Lawrence University Honors Projects* (Lawrence University, 2018), accessed July 8, 2023, https://lux.lawrence.edu/luhp/120, 18.

3. "Edward I 'Longshanks' (r. 1272–1307) | The Royal Family."

4. "France - EU, Diplomacy, Trade | Britannica," accessed July 5, 2023, https://www.britannica.com/place/France/Foreign-relations.

5. "Edward I 'Longshanks' (r. 1272-1307) | The Royal Family."

6. Jefferson, *Celtic Politics: Politics in Scotland, Ireland, and Wales*, 22–3.

7. "France - EU, Diplomacy, Trade | Britannica."

8. Hessayon and Taylor, "The Original Climate Crisis – How the Little Ice Age Devastated Early Modern Europe."

9. Cantor, *The Civilization of the Middle Ages*, 482.

10. Hessayon and Taylor, "The Original Climate Crisis–How the Little Ice Age Devastated Early Modern Europe."

11. Jessica Parks, "The Decline of the Papacy in the Middle Ages," *Church History Themes*, ed., Zachariah Carter (Bellingham, WA: Faithlife, 2022). Logos.

12. "Rise and Fall of the Knights Templar," accessed July 5, 2023, https://northumberlandkt.com/?page_id=2370.

13. Jefferson, *Celtic Politics: Politics in Scotland, Ireland, and Wales*, 23.

14. Ibid., 23–4.

15. "Edward I 'Longshanks' (r. 1272–1307) | The Royal Family."

16. Helen Nicholson, "Saints or Sinners? The Knights Templar in Medieval Europe," History Today, vol. no. 44.12, 1994, https://www.academia.edu/9510024/Saints_or_Sinners_The_Knights_Templar_in_Medieval_Europe.

17. Williston Walker, *A History of the Christian Church*, 3rd ed. (New York, NY: Charles Scribner's Sons, 1970), 262.

18. Jefferson, *Celtic Politics: Politics in Scotland, Ireland, and Wales*, 24.

19. "Rise and Fall of the Knights Templar."

20. Jefferson, *Celtic Politics: Politics in Scotland, Ireland, and Wales*, 24.

21. Kuh, "The Age of Chivalry," 283.

22. Gies and Gies, *Cathedral, Forge, and Waterwheel Technology and Invention in the Middle Ages*, 173.

23. Addis and Arnold, "Wycliffites," 886.

24. Walker, *A History of the Christian Church*, 263–64.

25. Colin Morris, "Christian Civilization," *The Oxford Illustrated History of Christianity*, ed., John McManners (Oxford, NY: Oxford University Press, 1991), 229.

26. Robert G. Clouse, *The Church from Age to Age A History from Galilee to Global Christianity*, eds., A. Edward, et al. (Saint Louis, MO: Concordia Publishing House, 2011), 379.

27. Walker, *A History of the Christian Church*, 264.

28. "Birth of the Black Plague: The Mongol Siege on Caffa," (warhistoryonline, July 28, 2018), accessed April 6, 2023, https://www.warhistoryonline.com/instant-articles/mongol-siege-caffa-black-plague.html.

29. Kelly DeVries, *Infantry Warefare in the Early Fourteenth Century Discipline, Tactics, and Technology* (Woodbridge, Suffolk UK, Rochester, NY: The Boydell Press, 1996), 178.

30. Costain, *The Three Edwards The Pageant of England*, 303.

31. Thornton, *English Spirituality*, 168.

32. Jones, *Hermits and Anchorites in England 1200–1550*, 24, 28.

33. Ibid., 193, 197.

34. G. W. Bromiley, D. M. Beegle, and W. M. Smith, "English Versions," *The International Standard Bible Encyclopedia, Revised*, Geoffrey W. Bromiley ed. (Grand Rapids, MI: Wm. B. Eerdmans, 1979–1988).

35. Jones, *Hermits and Anchorites in England 1200–1550*, 114.

36. Bromiley, Beegle, and Smith, "English Versions."

37. Thornton, *English Spirituality*, 221.

38. Alec Gilmore, "Rolle, Richard," *A Concise Dictionary of Bible Origins and Interpretation* (London; New York: T&T Clark, 2006). Logos.

39. George Thomas Kurian, ed., "Rolle Richard," *Nelson's New Christian Dictionary: The Authoritative Resource on the Christian World* (Nashville, TN: Thomas Nelson Publishers, 2001). Logos.

40. Thornton, *English Spirituality*, 218.

41. Kurian, "Rolle Richard."

42. Jones, *Hermits and Anchorites in England 1200–1550*, 114.

43. Ibid., 220.

44. Thornton, *English Spirituality*, 220.

45. Ibid., 18, 221.

46. Jones, *Hermits and Anchorites in England 1200–1550*, 26.

47. Ibid., 197.

48. Aubigne, *The Reformation in England Volume One*, 76.

49. Volz, *The Medieval Church*, 218–219.

50. "The Hundred Years' War," accessed March 9, 2023, http://web.cn.edu/kwheeler/hundred_years.html.

51. Cross, and Livingstone, *The Oxford Dictionary of the Christian Church*, 232–233.

52. DeVries, *Infantry Warefare in the Early Fourteenth Century Discipline*, 155.

53. "King Edward III of England (1312–1377) [Edward of Windsor; Hundred Years' War]," accessed April 5, 2023, https://www.luminarium.org/encyclopedia/edward3.htm.

54. Simon Schama, *A History of Britain At the Edge of the World? 3500 BC–1603 A.D.* (New York, NY: Hyperion, 2000), 239.

55. Costain, *The Three Edwards The Pageant of England*, 323.

56. John M'Clintock and James Strong, eds., "Bradwardine, Thomas," *Cyclopedia of Biblical, Theological and Ecclesiastical Literature* (New York: Harper Brothers, Publishers, 1895). e-Sword.

57. Thornton, *English Spirituality*, 73.

58. Aubigne, *The Reformation in England Volume One*, 76.

59. Ibid., 75.

60. Cross and Livingstone, *The Oxford Dictionary of the Christian Church*, 232–233.

61. DeVries, *Infantry Warefare in the Early Fourteenth Century Discipline*, 155.

62. "King Edward III of England (1312–1377) [Edward of Windsor; Hundred Years' War]."

63. DeVries, *Infantry Warefare in the Early Fourteenth Century Discipline*, 156.

64. Ibid., 157.

65. Ibid., 158.

66. Ibid., 186–187.

67. Costain, *The Three Edwards The Pageant of England*, 309.

68. DeVries, *Infantry Warefare in the Early Fourteenth Century Discipline*, 167.

69. Ibid., 176.

70. "The History of the Welsh Dragon–Symbol of Wales," https://www.historic-uk.com/HistoryUK/HistoryofWales/The-Red-Dragon-of-Wales/.

71. Cantor, *The Civilization of the Middle Ages*, 518.

72. Gies and Gies, *Cathedral, Forge, and Waterwheel Technology and Invention in the Middle Ages*, 208.

73. DeVries, *Infantry Warefare in the Early Fourteenth Century Discipline*, 178.

74. Ibid., 181.

75. Ibid., 186.

76. Walker, *A History of the Christian Church*, 268.

77. Thornton, *English Spirituality*, 63.

78. Ibid., 84.

79. Ibid., 66.

80. Ibid., 64.

81. Ibid., 84.

82. Ibid., 64

83. Will Durant, *The Story of Civilization: 4 The Age of Faith* (New York: MJF Books, 1950), 74.

84. M'Clintock and Strong, "Cyclopedia of Biblical, Theological and Ecclesiastical Literature."

85. "Crimea - History | Britannica," accessed April 2, 2023, https://www.britannica.com/place/Crimea.

86. "Genoa Summary | Britannica," accessed April 6, 2023, https://www.britannica.com/summary/Genoa-Italy

87. "Birth of the Black Plague."

88. "Crimean or Giray Khanate (Tartars)," accessed April 6, 2023, https://byzantinebronzes.ancients.info/page45.html.

89. "Birth of the Black Plague."

90. Schama, *A History of Britain At the Edge of the World? 3500 B.C.–1603 A.D.,* 226.

91. Costain, *The Three Edwards The Pageant of England,* 338.

92. Time-Life Books, *What Life Was Like in the Age of Chivalry Medieval Europe AD 800–1500,* 137–138.

93. Strayer and Munro, *The Middle Ages 395–1500,* 474.

94. Schama, *A History of Britain At the Edge of the World? 3500 B.C.-1603 A.D.,* 225.

95. Ibid., 232.

96. Roger Euan Cameron, "St George's College, Windsor Castle, in the Late-Fifteenth and Early-Sixteenth Centuries," https://pure.royalholloway.ac.uk/ws/portalfiles/portal/26067599/St_George_s_College_Windsor_Castle_in_the_Late_Fifteenth_and_Early_Sixteenth_Centuries.pdf, 12.

97. "St. George's Chapel, 1348–1975 | History Today," https://www.historytoday.com/archive/st-george%E2%80%99s-chapel-1348-1975.

98. "St George's College, Windsor Castle, in the Late- Fifteenth and Early-Sixteenth Centuries."

99. "St George's Chapel, 1348–1975 | History Today."

100. Schama, *A History of Britain At the Edge of the World? 3500 B.C.-1603 A.D.,* 224.

101. "St George's Chapel, 1348–1975 | History Today."

102. "St George's College, Windsor Castle, in the Late-Fifteenth and Early-Sixteenth Centuries."

103. "History and Antiquities Windsor Castle and the Royal College and Chaple of St. George with the Institution, Laws, and Ceremonies of the Most Noble Order of the Garter," (Joseph Pote, Bookfeller, 1749. https://www.academia.edu/28855591/The_History_and_Antiquities_of_Windsor_Castle_and_the_Royal_College_and_Chapel_of_St_George, 85.

104. Schama, *A History of Britain At the Edge of the World? 3500 B.C.–1603 A.D.*, 224.

105. Ibid., 215.

106. Costain, *The Three Edwards The Pageant of England*.

107. Time-Life Books, *What Life Was Like in the Age of Chivalry Medieval Europe AD 800–1500*, 11.

108. Ibid., 138–140.

109. Costain, *The Three Edwards The Pageant of England*, 337.

110. Ibid., 340.

111. Cantor, *The Civilization of the Middle Ages*, 482.

112. Holder, *Crisis and Renewal The Era of the Reformations*, Kindle location, 325.

113. Ibid., 329–333.

114. Costain, *The Three Edwards The Pageant of England*, 340.

115. Ibid., 341.

116. Schama, *A History of Britain At the Edge of the World? 3500 B.C.–1603 A.D.*, 236.

117. Holder, *Crisis and Renewal The Era of the Reformations*, Kindle locations, 309–310.

118. Schama, *A History of Britain At the Edge of the World? 3500 B.C.–1603 A.D.*, 235.

119. Allan C. Flisher, Jr. et al., "York and the Northeren Counties," *This England*, eds., Melville Bell, Grosvenor and Franc Shor (Washington, D. C.: National Geographic Society, 1966), 386–417, 390.

120. John D. Woodbridge and Frank A. James III, *Church History Volume Two From Pre-Reformation to the Present Day* (Grand Rapids, MI: Zondervan, 2013), 48.

121. Walker, *A History of the Christian Church*, 256.

122. Woodbridge and James, *Church History Volume Two From Pre-Reformation to the Present Day*, 48.

123. Strayer and Munro, *The Middle Ages 395–1500*, 474.

124. Time-Life Books, *What Life Was Like in the Age of Chivalry Medieval Europe AD 800–1500*, 140.

125. Strayer and Munro, *The Middle Ages 395–1500*, 462; Costain, *The Three Edwards The Pageant of England*, 341.

126. Ibid., 341.

127. Schama, *A History of Britain At the Edge of the World? 3500 B.C.–1603 A.D.*, 241.

128. Kuh, "The Age of Chivalry," 273.

129. Ibid., 274.

130. Strayer and Munro, *The Middle Ages 395–1500*, 474–475.

131. Cantor, *The Civilization of the Middle Ages,* 518.

7

John Wycliffe

English Roots

John Wycliffe (1324–1384) held the position of master of Balliol College at Oxford University from 1360–1366 and Warden of Canterbury Hall from 1365–1367.[1] In 1365, Pope Urban V tried to get possession of England due to their default of 1000 marks per year, as promised by King John in 1213.[2] None of the last five popes asked for the tribute, which had been paid only sometimes,[3] mostly in stipends to absent holders of English benefices.[4] In 1366, Wycliffe wrote a tract justifying King Edward III's refusal to pay Urban V the debt of tribute granted by John to the Holy See.⁵ According to *Foxe's Book of Martyrs*, Wycliffe addressed his tract to the pope. Then, Edward called a parliament. Parliament declared King John forfeiting England to the Pope an illegal act.⁶

Wycliffe earned his BA in theology around 1369⁷ while Edward III's body, hygiene, and spirit crumbled after the death of Queen Phillipa from dropsy at Windsor Castle.⁸ He drank too much and allowed Alice Peters, "a haughty round-hipped hussy, to lead him" in public. Phillipa knew about one of her household ladies' affairs with her husband. Although Perrers was mentioned in the will, she received nothing. Clergy denounced people gawking at shameless hussies at the tournaments, but the king enjoyed the spectacle. As Perrers' influence over Edward grew, she publicly interfered with royal and justice decisions.⁹ The Black Prince contracted an illness in Spain. In 1370, while besieging and destroying Limoges, he was already an invalid and returned to England in 1371.¹⁰

Wycliffe earned his doctorate in theology around 1372.¹¹ After Wycliffe earned his doctorate, he attacked friars as an embarrassment and a source of heresies.¹² He became a celebrated Oxford theology professor.[13] He taught large classes on the complete rule of the Church by the secular ruler and morally and practically supported one another.[14] He maintained that Scripture is error-free and argued for a Bible written in English.[15]

While Wycliffe taught large classes in Oxford in 1373, Anchoress Julian of Norwich (ca. 1342–1423) lived in Conisford parish in Norwich, one of England's most prominent cities near the wharf on the river Wensum.[16] While deathly ill from the Black Plague, at age thirty, she experienced sixteen showings revealing the love of Christ, sin, and following God, with graphic scenes from the Crucifixion.[17]

In Oxford, in 1374, Edward III appointed Wycliffe as his clerk and rector of the parish church in Lutterworth, overlooking Speed River near Oxford,[18] where he worked until he died.[19] Edward hired Wycliffe to assist with diplomacy with the pope over royal authority for the local hiring of the clergy.[20]

Wycliffe modeled his poor preachers on Francis of Assisi's brown robed friars, who begged and did low-level jobs while serving the poor and the sick.[21] Lollards or mumblers taught that God created all people equally and property belonged to the righteous instead of the rich and powerful; the male priesthood needed to be replaced by one composed of both sexes preaching the Bible.[22] Lollards inspired the English people to restore an intensified significant personal engagement in spirituality denied by centuries-old Church legalism and its desire to subjugate its members with theological definitions.[23] Wycliffe's friendship with Edward III's son, John of Gaunt, armed with his limited circle of high-ranking knights, supported his reform movement[24] and helped repair his reputation of high-handedness and neglect of established rights.[25] Wycliffe lectured in Oxford, *On Civil Lordship* in 1376:

> "God is the great overlord. He gives all positions, civil and spiritual, as fiefs to be held on condition of faithful service. They are stewardships, not property. God gives the use but not the ownership. If the user abuses his trust, he forfeits his tenure. Hence, a bad ecclesiastic loses all claim to office, and the temporal possessions of unworthy clergy may well be taken from them by the civil rulers, to whom God has

given the lordship of temporal things, as He has that of things spiritual to the church."[26]

Wycliffe wrote several commentaries solely on the Ten Commandments from Exodus 20 and Deuteronomy 5:6–21.[27] He advised in *Seven Works of Mercy* that everyone should know and keep them. In *Form of Confession,* he directs his readers to confess sins that violate the Ten Commandments.[28] In the *Dialogue between a Wise Man and a Fool,* "the Wise Man urges the Fool to believe and keep the commandments, while the fool protests that he would prefer a good tale." In *Of Wedded Men and Wives,* proper teaching should replace idle stories.

Wycliffe wrote five commentaries on the Lord's Prayer.[29] He maintained that all the Ten Commandments appear in the Lord's Prayer. When asking God for "our daily bread," we ask for bodily nourishment to keep God's commandments, which spiritually nurture one's soul.[30] The words of the Lord's Prayer follow a blueprint of "sorrow, dread, desire, and hope," plunging people into action.[31]

In Wycliffe's other books, he endorsed Christ's commandments to love God above all and our neighbor as ourselves (Matt. 22:37–39, Mark 12:29–31, Luke 10:27, James 2:8), and Paul's view that loving one's neighbor fulfilled the law in Rom. 13:10, and Gal. 5:14.[32] *The Lantern of Light, On Love,* and *The Five Questions of Love* prepared the reader for martyrdom.[33] Another topic resolved around why subjects should pay for the sins of their rulers. Were inferiors responsible for preventing corruption by exposing sin when they observed sinful rulers?[34] Salvation originated from God as opposed to the clergy.[35] Wycliffe saw Christianity as "the church that shall be saved" with an unknowable membership.[36]

After struggling with illness for many years, the Black Prince died in 1376.[37] For the first time, the burgesses and knights elected a speaker, Peter de la Mare, in the "Good Parliament of 1376" for a debate. Members of Parliament testified against elderly King Edward III's councilors as disloyal and unprofitable to the kingdom. Indignant John of Gaunt accepted the inquiry on the conduct and impeachment of the government officials who were found guilty and removed from office. The July 10 Parliament denied the government's request for funds.[38]

Lollard priests preached in favor of English nationalism due to Rome draining their treasuries.[39] In 1376, Pope Gregory XI wrote letters to Edward III, the Archbishop of Canterbury, the Bishop of London, and the University of Oxford, asking for Wycliffe's arrest and trial.[40] Wycliffe completed a book-by-book commentary on the complete Old and New Testaments.[41]

On February 19, 1377, in four friars, each from a different mendicant order, the Duke and the Marshal of England, Lord Percy, escorted Wycliffe into the long aisle of the packed St. Paul's Lady Chapel in London.[42] The duke and bishop of London, William Courtenay, hotly debated on allowing the feeble old scholar a chair during the inquiry. The duke's guard held off the Londoners as they tried to break into the inner chamber. Wycliffe remained composed as his guards escorted him out of the cathedral through another door.[43] Gaunt and other nobles rendered Wycliffe's trial before Courtenay null and void.[44] Gregory XI responded by sending Edward III five bulls ordering Wycliffe's arrest and prosecution.[45] Edward died of a stroke[46] on Trinity Sunday, June 8, and England mourned his death.[47] Twenty-four knights dressed in black slowly marched, carrying his body.[48] Ten-year-old Richard II became England's King in 1377.[49] The first literary reference to Robin Hood appeared in the Sloane manuscripts in 1377.[50] William Langland parroted Wycliffe's criticisms in his poem *Piers Plowman*.[51] Wandering priests pushing for pure democracy or sometimes socialism repeated Lollard preacher John Ball's: "When Adam delved and Eve span. Who was then the gentleman?"[52]

The English court of 1378 continued to protect Wycliffe, frustrating the archbishop of Canterbury and the Bishop of London's legal proceedings against him.[53] His English and Latin tracts and treaties advised judging priests to the pope by biblical standards and stripping faithless, secular clergy from their power and property because corrupt clergy lost claim to even spiritual matters.[54] When Gregory XI died in 1378, the cardinals elected one Roman pope, Urban VI, and another French pope, Clement VII, known as the "Great Schism," split Europe and magnified the Anglo-French conflict.[55]

People responded to the Hundred Years War (1337–1454) against France by insisting on speaking English rather than French.[56] During the Great

Schism, both English Kings Richard II and Henry V sided with the Roman popes.[57] The Avignon and Roman popes excommunicated each other.[58] In 1379, the *Power of the Papacy* Wycliffe criticized heretical beliefs, immoral acts, and transubstantiation.[59] The bread and wine did not become the body and the blood upon the moment of consecration by the ordained priest. People suddenly doubted the sacraments of baptism and confession. They questioned the Church's use of images and the penitence gained from pilgrimages.[60] Wycliffe also criticized extravagant rituals, prayers to saints, and the worship of relics.[61]

The scarcity of labor due to the Black Death elevated the status of the serfs. As the English language and education increased in popularity, an awareness of lay people's rightful place in society arose.[62] Workers resented the 1351 Statute of Laborers, which denied profits from the labor shortage.[63] Heavy war taxes also factored into the cause of the revolt, among many others that broke out across Europe.[64] Gaunt's government levied the 1380 poll tax to support the French treat, which was a flat rate per household regardless of wealth.[65] Although only two groups, counting as forty Bristol clergy and artisans, identified as Lollards.[66] Lollard preaching nevertheless aided in stimulating the Peasant Revolt of 1381.[67] Preachers explained the Black Death as a time of reckoning since God reached into castles and left nobility in the grave.[68]

The government botched assessing and collecting the poll tax, so they sent out royal commissioners to collect more money. The revolt started in Kent, followed by Essex, then Canterbury, and spread across England.[69] Over 60,000 people participated, including churchmen, peasants, merchants, and soldiers.[70] Wat Tyler and priest John Ball's supporters occupied London.[71] Peasants targeted lawyers, demolishing manorial records.[72] Peasants burned John of Gaunt's palace and threw much of the castle's contents into the Thames.[73] The crowd massacred foreign lawyers and merchants.[74] Ball led the protesters in the song, "When Adam delved and Eve span, Who was then the gentleman?"[75]

When King Richard II left the London Tower to confer with rebels, another group cut off the heads of Simon Sudbury, archbishop of Canterbury, the treasurer, and other members of the King's Council on Tower Hill.[76] The next day, a riot festered when the king's escort stabbed Tyler amidst a yelling match. Fourteen-year-old Richard rode into the mob, asking, "Sirs, will you shoot your king? I will be your chief and captain; you will get from me all that you seek." The peasants went home.

The frightened nobility retaliated by hunting and terminating rebels for many years.[77] The rebel leaders died swinging from the gallows. Farmers retaliated by forming gangs who lived by robbing people on the highways.[78] In danger of being charged with vagrancy, the canon that once only applied to anchorites now regulated the hermit's life.[79] Although English soldiers suppressed the revolt, wealthy townsfolk eventually drew up sharecropping deals with ex-serfs shifting from cereal crop farming to grazing.[80]

Wycliffe maintained that the Bible needed translation so that it could be preached. Objectors argued that people interpreting the Bible for themselves undermined the accepted function of a priest.[81] In 1382, William Courtenay, the archbishop of Canterbury, condemned twenty-four of Wycliffe's points and fired him from his teaching position.[82] Poor Lollards were arrested.[83] Gaunt withdrew his support from the Lollard movement.[84]

Wycliffe either supervised or wrote the first Middle English Bible, handwritten and translated from the Latin Vulgate, which appeared in 1382. Many scholars contend that Wycliffe inspired the translation bearing his name. Woodbridge and James credit five fellow scholars who "penned the Lollard Bible."[85] Sharon Rusten and E. Michael explained that the leader of the Lollards, Nicholas of Hereford (d. 1420), finished the translation in 1382.[86]

The first version was translated directly into Middle English without considering the difference between Latin and English, so his secretary, John Purvey, released an amended version written in an easier-to-understand Bible in 1395.[87] The *Chronicle of the Augustine Canon* by Henry Knighton records the Wycliffe translation as controversial, questioning if English was suitable for conveying Scripture to uneducated readers. While rejecting the sacraments due to the priest's sins, Lollards preached that the Church should not receive donations, preached against intercessory prayer, and advocated that friars should perform manual labor instead of begging without an ecclesiastical license.[88] Barefoot, meandering in pairs, Lollards dressed in long robes with a staff in hand[89] spread their doctrine through preaching faith based on personal experience and promoting people to read the Bible.[90] The Bible "became the driving force of people's lives" and affected thought, deeds, and actions as more literate people read the Word of God and preached it to the illiterate.[91] Wycliffe died peacefully in 1382. Knighton records that dukes, earls, and knights protected and set up schools to train additional Lollards to preach.[92]

Geoffrey Chaucer began writing *Canterbury Tales* in 1387.[93] He used Pope Innocent III as a model for the *Man of Laws Tale* based on the pope's reputation as a canonist and his dim view of a legalist.[94] In 1388, under pressure from Parliament, the king's council morally and practically supported one another by ordering that Wycliffe's heretical writings be seized.

---

1. Cross and Livingstone, "Wycliffe, John," *The Oxford Dictionary of the Christian Church*.

2. *Lights and Shadows of the Reformation*.

3. Aubigne, *The Reformation in England Volume One*, 81.

4. Costain, *The Three Edwards The Pageant of England*, 409.

5. Addis and Arnold, "Wycliffites," 886.

6. John Foxe, *Foxe's Book of Martyrs* (London, England: John Day, 1563). e-Sword.

7. Hanson, "Wycliffe."

8. Costain, *The Three Edwards The Pageant of England*, 389–390.

9. Ibid., 390.

10. "Edward, the Black Prince (1330–1376) and Richard II," https://archives.history.ac.uk/richardII/black_prince.html.

11. Hanson, "Wycliffe, John."

12. Addis and Arnold, "Wycliffites."

13. Clouse, *The Church from Age to Age*, 421.

14. Christopher Allmand, *Henry V* (Berkeley and Los Angeles, CA: The University of California Press, 1992), 284.

15. Woodbridge and James, *Church History Volume Two From Pre-Reformation to the Present Day*, 48.

16. Jones, *Hermits and Anchorites in England 1200–1550*, 27.

17. Tim Perrine, "Work Info: Revelations of Divine Love" (Christian Classics Ethereal Library), Tim Perrine, "Work Info: Revelations of Divine Love" (Christian Classics Ethereal Library), accessed June 8, 2020, https://www.ccel.org/ccel/julian/revelationshttps://www.ccel.org/ccel/julian/revelations.

18. Costain, *The Three Edwards: The Pageant of England*, 409.

19. Hanson, "Wycliffe, John."

20. Allmand, *Henry V*, 280.

21. Costain, *The Three Edwards The Pageant of England*, 408.

22. Allmand, *Henry V*, 281.

23. Ibid., 282.

24. Schama, *A History of Britain At the Edge of the World? 3500 B.C.–1603 A.D.*, 238.

25. Costain, *The Three Edwards The Pageant of England*, 410.

26. John Wycliffe, as quoted in Walker, *A History of the Christian Church*, 268.

27. J. Patrick, Hornbeck II, al eds., *Wycliffite Spirituality*, trans. J. Patrick Hornbeck II, et al., The Classics of Western Spirituality (New York; Mahwah, NJ: Paulist Press, 2013), 8. Logos.

28. Ibid., 9.

29. Ibid., 36.

30. Ibid., 10.

31. Ibid., 13.

32. Ibid., 8.

33. Ibid., 14.

34. Ibid., 17.

35. Harrison and Sullivan, *A Short History of Western Civilization*, 313.

36. Hornbeck, *Wycliffite Spirituality* 43.

37. "Edward, the Black Prince (1330–1376) and Richard II."

38. Schama, *A History of Britain At the Edge of the World? 3500 B.C.–1603 A.D.*, 244.

39. Costain, *The Three Edwards The Pageant of England*, 406.

40. Addis and Arnold, "Wycliffites," 886.

41. Hornbeck, *Wycliffite Spirituality*, 30.

42. Costain, *The Three Edwards The Pageant of England*, 411.

43. Ibid., 412.

44. Walker, *A History of the Christian Church*, 268.

45. Ibid., 269.

46. Schama, *A History of Britain At the Edge of the World? 3500 B.C.–1603 A.D.*, 244.

47. Costain, *The Three Edwards The Pageant of England*, 405.

48. Schama, *A History of Britain At the Edge of the World? 3500 B.C.–1603 A.D.*, 244–45.

49. John D. Gurst, *Saga of a Sceptred Isle*, printed, 15"x10", inside "This England" National Geographic Society cover, 1966.

50. "Robin Hood - Fact or Fiction?," (Historic UK), https://www.historic-uk.com/HistoryUK/HistoryofEngland/Robin-Hood/.

51. Hornbeck, *Wycliffite Spirituality*, 32.

52. Strayer and Munro, *The Middle Ages 395–1500*, 477.

53. Walker, *A History of the Christian Church*.

54. Clouse, *The Church from Age to Age*, 421.

55. Allmand, *Henry V*, 233.

56. Robert McCrum, William Cran, and Robert MacNeil, *The Story of English* (New York, NY: Elisabeth Sifton Books, Viking, Viking Penguin Inc., 1986), 78.

57. Allmand, *Henry V*, 234.

58. Holder, *Crisis and Renewal The Era of the Reformations*, Kindle location, 350.

59. Woodbridge and James, *Church History Volume Two From Pre-Reformation to the Present Day*, 48.

60. Allmand, *Henry V*, 281.

61. Harrison and Sullivan, *A Short History of Western Civilization*, 313.

62. Allmand, *Henry V*, 282.

63. Strayer and Munro, *The Middle Ages, 395–1500*, 478.

64. Gies and Gies, *Cathedral, Forge, and Waterwheel Technology and Invention in the Middle Ages*, 172.

65. Schama, *A History of Britain At the Edge of the World? 3500 B.C.–1603 A.D.*, 247.

66. Allmand, *Henry V*, 299.

67. Cantor, *The Civilization of the Middle Ages*, 500.

68. Schama, *A History of Britain At the Edge of the World? 3500 B.C.–1603 A.D.*, 247.

69. Strayer and Munro, *The Middle Ages 395–1500*, 478.

70. "Wat Tyler and the Peasants Revolt," Historic UK, https://www.historic-uk.com/HistoryUK/HistoryofEngland/Wat-Tyler-the-Peasants-Revolt/.

71. Aubigne, *The Reformation in England Volume One*, 238.

72. Gies and Gies, *Cathedral, Forge, and Waterwheel Technology and Invention in the Middle Ages*, 173.

73. "Wat Tyler and the Peasants Revolt."

74. Strayer and Munro, *The Middle Ages 395–1500*, 478.

75. Aubigne, *The Reformation in England Volume One*, 93; Hale, *The Civilization of Europe in the Renaissance,* American ed. (Atheneum Macmillan Publishing Company, 1994), 468.

76. "Wat Tyler and the Peasants Revolt."

77. Strayer and Munro, *The Middle Ages 395–1500*, 479.

78. Costain, *The Three Edwards The Pageant of England*, 342.

79. Jones, *Hermits and Anchorites in England 1200–1550*, 28.

80. Gies and Gies, *Cathedral, Forge, and Waterwheel Technology and Invention in the Middle Ages*, 173.

81. Allmand, *Henry V*, 281.

82. Woodbridge and James, *Church History Volume Two From Pre-Reformation to the Present Day*, 48.

83. Walker, *A History of the Christian Church*, 270.

84. Allmand, *Henry V*, 283.

85. Woodbridge and James, *Church History Volume Two From Pre-Reformation to the Present Day*, 48.

86. Sharon with Rusten and E. Michael, *The Complete Book of When and Where in the Bible and Throughout History* (Wheaton, IL: Michael E Rusten, 2005), 194.

87. Youngblood, "Wycliffe's Versions."

88. Hornbeck, *Wycliffite Spirituality*, 2.

89. Walker, *A History of the Christian Church*, 269.

90. Cantor, *The Civilization of the Middle Ages*, 500.

91. Allmand, *Henry V*, 281.

92. Hornbeck, *Wycliffite Spirituality*, 3.

93. Kuh, "The Age of Chivalry," 373.

94. Miller, *Chaucer Sources and Backgrounds*, 484.

8
Mystic Writings and the Aftermath of Wycliffe

English Roots

A small group of Lollard Knights held positions at Richard II's court,[1] so the Lollard movement grew during his reign.[2] In 1393, while

Richard II wrote The Second Statute of Praemunire, disputing the jurisdiction between the rights of an English king and the pope,[3] Julian of Norwich wrote about her visions, which she had twenty years ago, starting with "A Vision of the Universe,"[4] "The Motherhood and Fatherhood of God,"[5] "The Working of the Trinity in Our Salvation," which was a common subject of both devotions and sermons,"[6] and "God Cares for Us Like a Mother for an Erring Child."[7]

Thornton explains her mystic experience as a combination of imagining a body from ordinary prayer, "ghostly bodily likeness" where imagination and intellect fuse into a "three-point meditation leading into contemplation," or it may have been a "ghostly sight" which is an intuitive perception of divine truth. After recovering, Julian spent the next twenty years recording her meditation with God[8] while living as a strict anchoress where two servants cared for her until she died of old age.[9] Julian authored the first English text written by a female.[10] God granted her grace for comfort, so she concentrated on Christ's Passion and trusted in the Lord who rescued her from the enemy, and in the morning, all was well.[11] Julian of Norwich synthesized Anselm's concept of Christ's judgment through His sacrifice, love, and hope.[12] She related all sixteen showings to her first vision and used her church training to assist in interpreting how Jesus was sent to rectify the problem of sin.[13] Thornton says that Julian, like Anselm, combined an Augustine-Victorine doctrine with St. Bernard's Christology, "English Benedictine optimism," and St. Bonaventure's idea of "three-in-one."[14]

Across the English Channel, Czech scholars resented German imperialism and their universities. Upon Richard II's marriage to Anne, the daughter of Charles IV, King of Bohemia, King Charles founded the University of Prague in 1347[15] by freeing the Bohemian Church from German influence by creating the position of archbishop in Prague and coordinating the Slavonian Monastery of Emmaus.[16] The Monastery of Emmaus restored the Moravian[17] (southeast of Bohemia sharing similar histories)[18] traditions of transforming the hearts of their people through the Gospels, a Slavonian Bible, and services once enjoyed in 863.[19] Czech scholars absorbed intellectually refreshing Oxford theology by authors like Grosseteste and Bradwardine.[20]

In 1349, the first Bridgettine abbess, St. Catherine, famous for her devotions and revelations, campaigned in Rome for Church reforms.[21] Bridget of Sweden (1303–1373), with the help of her daughter St. Catherine of Sweden (1331–81), formed both female and male Cistercian monasteries devoted to prayer, meditation, and literature in 1350.[22] Catherine spoke of her visions of Christ as a child, and her power for healing inspired mystics in every European country. Brethren of the Common Life and Sisters of the Common Life developed their piety on prayer, love, and direct communion with God.[23] They believed Anselm's premise that one could lose one's faith because one starved it by prayer swallowed by doctrine. Prayer was the "proper way to learn theology."[24] Catherine and Bridgit formed communities in Germany, Belgium, the Netherlands, and Luxembourg rose from pooling resources, confessing sins, and caring for the unfortunate.[25]

Because of Richard II's royal marriage to Anne of Bohemia arranged by Pope Urban VI, opportunities opened up for students from Prague the freedom to attend Oxford in 1382.[26] Twenty-four of Wycliffe's stances were declared heretical. Hermit William Swinderby's preaching, which promoted Wycliffe's stances, gained popularity in Leicester, England.[27]

The Lynn, Norfolk's five-time mayor and six-time Member of Parliament, John Burnham's (d. 1413) daughter Margery (1373–1438) married John Kempe, burgess of Lynn, in 1393.[28] Margery received a vision of Christ shortly after giving birth to her first child.[29]

While Swinderby preached at Almeley in the 1390s before Sir John of Oldcastle (1370–1417) inherited Almeley manor in Herefordshire,[30] anchoress Amy Palmer preached Lollardy from her cell[31] and harbored known Lollards in St. Peter, Northampton.[32] According to Jones, her followers condemned brutal priests, clerical property, images, and pilgrimage, arguing that any layperson could function as a priest and "that Christian worship was better undertaken privately in bedrooms or fields rather than pretentiously in a church building." The bishop removed Palmer to a more secure cell in a Banbury, Lincoln, Apr 27, 1394, prison and was ordered to deliver her to London.[33] Palmer called the bishop and his clerks "disciples of the Antichrist."[34]

In January 1395, Wycliffe supporters attached a twelve-point Lollard bill to Westminster Hall, where Parliament was in session, and to the doors of St. Paul's Cathedral, "Transubstantiation was a fake miracle; today's priesthood was less than Christ ordained and lacked the power to absolve sins; pilgrimages and prayer in front of crosses and images were idolatry; they condemned war; recommended to abolish many religious foundations; and questioned the Church's right to own land."

Thomas Arundel, the new 1396 archbishop of Canterbury, petitioned Parliament "to bring England in line with general European practices" that the death penalty be applied to heretics.[35] Around that time, documents containing St. Bridget[36] of Sweden's visions of Jesus and Mary[37] ignited the English cult of St. Bridget.[38]

After Richard had been secretly murdered,[39] two days after the Feast of St. Edward the Confessor on Oct. 13, 1339, as part of King Henry IV's coronation ceremonies, his son Henry of Lancaster became Prince of Wales, Duke of Cornwall, Earl of Chester, and heir upon the King's death.[40] The House of Commons accepted the change in the crown, and Henry sat on his throne in the center of a full parliament. Parliament granted Archbishop Thomas Arundel of Canterbury's request for the prince to bear the title of Duke of Aquitaine.[41]

In 1400, Oldcastle fought for England,[42] led by Prince Henry, in the ill-fated[43] Scottish campaign.[44] Descended from princes, Glyn Dwr, to honor Wales, proclaimed himself to be the Prince of Wales. On Sept. 16, 1400, he called his friends, financial supporters, and relatives. On the 18th, they set fires in Ruthin, attacked Denbigh and spots in Flintshire, and did the same as they traveled south, conquering Oswestry and Welshpool.[45] Owain Glynder raised the red dragon standard, symbolizing a national revolt.[46] By Sept. 24. Hugh Burnell's forces captured and executed many rebels, yet the revolt spread.[47]

Henry IV's (1399–1413) 1401 Parliament passed De Haerectico Comburendo. This statute condemned the Lollard as a "false and perverse people... who usurp the office of preaching... and stir people to sedition" and should burn at the stake.[48] Welsh scholars left Oxford to return to Wales. Armed laborers did the same.[49] Soldiers thought to harbor Lollard sympathies marched off to join in wars against the Welsh.[50]

Oldcastle and Prince Henry became friends as they fought in the Welsh Wars.[51]

In 1406, the Scotts paid Thomas Warde of Trumpington, who looked exactly like Richard II, to incite people against King Henry at Bermondsey, Westminster, and Whitelock abbeys and urged the Scots and Welsh to invade. Many believed Warde's impersonation of Richard II, and others felt their testimony.[52] Meanwhile, west of the coast of Asia, independent of China, Koreans tinkered with the first metal moveable type printing press made from bronze.[53]

An anonymous monk who wrote *The Cloud of Unknowing* was the first English theologian to write about God in Middle English.[54] The monk wrote instructions on letting go of all knowledge of God to experience God purely with love.[55] He believed that God speaks through Scripture. Christians receive grace through the sacraments. God became incarnate of Christ. His goal was to help others experience God in the fullness of Christ.[56]

Scholars who study modern-day prayer include William Meninger, Thomas Keating, and Basil Pennington, who call this practice "Centering Prayer" or "Contemplative Meditation."[57] One begins with a one-syllable word like "love" and focuses on that word to stop thinking and start loving.[58] The monk warned that if one does not believe that "God is love that moves the sun and other stars as well as the love that is closer to you than your very breath," one should stop reading his guide immediately.[59]

When Archbishop Arundel became chancellor of England (1407–1409), he flushed out Lollards from Oxford by regulating preaching and teaching at the University.[60] In 1408, the "Constitutions of Oxford" prohibited anyone from translating or reading any part of the Bible in English without the permission of a bishop or a local church council.[61]

An English mystic and an Augustine canon of Thurgarton, Hilton Walker, from 1343–1396, viewed the Church as the mother[62] who controlled a joyful life for a favored family.[63] He wrote about Christocentric piety in *The Scale of Perfection*, among many other compositions.[64] He saw redemption as an endless struggle in response to God's grace and love.[65] Souls reform in faith and then reform in feeling, which starts with prayer by stepping up a ladder. Improving faith may be quick and easy, but reforming feeling is a drawn-out procedure.⁶⁶ Humble knowledge of the Scriptures is where prayer starts. Necessary obedience where one sees washing dishes as a true manifestation of love.

Hilton explained that Bernardine Margery Kempe's visions typified the simple kind of meditation of God through the grace of the Holy Spirit and permitted her to feel the love, passion, and works of Christ. Those who coldly contemplate Christ regularly are higher on the ladder than those who occasionally experience a Godly moment and then forget, explains the English inclination for constant remembrance of the Gospel and Christ's Passion over meditation. The final phase of Christian mysticism is knowing God's love.⁶⁷ Meditation started with a simple personal prayer. The second phase began the Lord's Prayer in Latin, baptism of the Holy Spirit combined with the sacraments, and ended in the morning, noonday, and evening offices. A greater love for God characterizes the third stage achieved through praying the Lord's prayer, the Ave Maria, hymns, or psalms.⁶⁸

By 1408, Margery Kempe suffered madness and then received several visions of signs of Christ's love.⁶⁹ Margerie's prayers mimicked Anselm's, addressing her prayers to Christ, judge, advocate, and redeemer whom angels and saints encompass.[70] The Kempe couple took a pilgrimage to Canterbury.[71] Most people knew Margaery as a spiritual advisor.[72] Whenever Margery visited a new location, she saw the local anchorite or anchoress. She routinely donated small sums to passing hermits who stood by castle doors.[73]

Margery credited St. Bridget's revelations and listened to the first section of Hilton's *The Scale of Perfection*, which introduced an anchoress to the contemplative life. Hilton's book *Epistle on Mixed Life*[74] introduced Margery to how a layperson pursued a contemplative life while actively working in an occupation. Her inward fire copied Rolle's Latin guide for spiritual life, *The Fire of Love*,[75] and recollections on Christ's wounds stemmed from Rolle's *Meditations on the Passion*. Her sources encouraged her to visualize a biblical scene, choose a character from the narrative, and meditate on how the character saw what happened in Scripture for deeper understanding.[76]

Under Chancellor Arundel's leadership, by June 1409, Oxford condemned seven works by Wycliffe.[77] In 1410, during his first session in the House of Commons, Oldcastle promoted two unsuccessful bills, one curtailing clergy income and the other repealing heresy. Arundel retried Bardley, the second Lollard heretic to die burned at Smithfield in front of Prince Henry, Prince John, and the Duke of York. Oldcastle and Lollard clergy authored letters congratulating Bohemian noble Wok of Waldstein and scholar and John Huss follower for opposing the Prague clergy. They also sent letters to Bohemia's King Wladislas advocating backing the reformers. Arundel arrested and prosecuted anyone connected to Oldcastle.

Prince Henry awarded Oldcastle command of the expedition, aiding the French Burgundian party against the Orléanist party.[78] Lists condemning Wycliffe's errors were based on Lollard preacher's creative interpretations changed over time as recorded by transcripts from clergy-led inquisitions.[79] In 1411, the Wycliffe error list contained two hundred heresies.[80]

Henry V (1413–1422) confessed to the anchorite at Westminster Abbey as he prepared for his coronation.[81] On Oldcastle's first day back in Parliament (the first parliament of Henry V) in May 1413, Arundel presented a heretical book belonging to

Oldcastle procured in a London raid. Aug 21, Henry granted Arundel permission to prosecute him.[82]

Bishop Officers summoned Margery to appear in Norwich, where she visited William Southfields and Julian of Norwich.[83] She spent many days sharing her revelations, hoping that Julia could point out any trickery since visions demand careful discernment and Julian, an anchoress and a visionary, was an expert.[84] The Kempe couple took vows of chastity before the Bishop of Lincoln, Philip Repington, in 1413. After publicly scolding Abbot Arundel for his followers' actions, Margery took a pilgrimage to the Holy Land from 1413–1417.[85] While Margery wintered in Venice,[86] by the end of 1413, Henry V had Richard II reburied.[87]

Oldcastle was tried at St. Paul's on Sept. 23, 1413. Two days later, he was excommunicated with the orders to be burned in forty days. London Lollards aided in his escape on Oct. 19. He hid at William Parchmyner's house near Clerkenwell. From there, he sent messages to Lollards throughout England to meet at night on Jan. 9–10, 1414, in St. Giles Fields. Knights disguised as actors would kidnap or murder the King on Twelfth Night, Jan. 6, at Eltham Palace.[88]

Margery started habitually screeching on Mount Calvary, Jerusalem, and continued wailing for the next ten years.[89] She called her crying "the gift of tears."[90]

By 1415, the list citing Wycliffe's errors had expanded to three hundred and five.[91] Accounts placed Margery in Leicester, Bristol, and York, all associated with the Wycliffite heresy.[92] Margery's condemnation of all pleasure prompted charges of Lollardy, and she was later formally accused,[93] investigated for heresy, and detained at Leicester, York, Cawood, Beverley, and London in 1417.[94] Margerie's orthodox answers cleared her of heresy charges.[95] Meanwhile, the Scotts claimed Richard II still lived and planned to invade England and, in 1419, repeated the rumor.[96] People believed that the Lollards were somehow connected.[97]

1418–1426, Margerie's health failed; from 1418 to 1422, she suffered revelations about the next Lynn Prior. In 1420, she visited Richard of Caister's (d. March 29, 1420) grave, as the young priest had read to her for seven years. A Franciscan friar who arrived at Lynn complained about her crying during his sermons.[98] Thornton describes Margery utilizing St. Victor's five-step process of symbolic interpreting the world, meditation on Christ, prayer on genuine theological questions, progress in knowing and loving God, and ends in the mystical "loving contemplation."[99]

Even letter writing was a specialized line of work. Paid secretaries wrote the wealthy gentry's letters in Norfolk.[100] Margery tried dictating her recollections to her son or husband, but they lacked the writing skills for anyone to decipher her two books. Afterward, she sought out clergy to revise her work. The priest procrastinated for four years or more. However, her mystical experiences and journeys did get written in the *Book of Margery Kempe* toward the end of her life as she recalled events in no particular order in her memoirs.[101]

To secure political and religious unity, Henry V dealt with the Southampton Lollards rising with the execution of Oldcastle,[102] finishing the political importance of the Lollards in 1417.[103]

In 1420, the Archbishop of York traveled to All Saints North Street Parish in York to seal Emma Rawghton permanently into a cell attached to the side of the church. Anchoress Rawghton experienced seven visions from the Virgin Mary in 1421.[104] A short time later, Richard de Beauchamp, 13th Earl of Warwick

(1382–1439),[105] consulted her for advice since his wife had only birthed three daughters and needed a son as an heir.[106] She told Henry V's knight that if he built a church in Warwickshire, his wife would give birth to a son, and he would get custody of the infant king of England and France.

Henry V donated a gift to the Westminster anchorite for his queen's 1420 coronation and remembered him in his will the following year.[107] Beauchamp applied for a license to build at Guy's Cliffe in 1423. Henry de Beauchamp was born on March 22, 1425. Rawghton's cell was sealed on April 2, 1425. In 1430, the Earl of Warwick paid the endowment for the church at Guy Cliffe.[108]

Lollard disagreements with some of the Church's beliefs[109] spread in an underground movement centered in London, Kent, and Oxford, which survived persecution and possibly regained popularity during the reign of King Henry VIII (June 28, 1491–January 28, 1547).[110] The last recorded Lollard investigation was in the 1520s.[111] With Henry VIII's Dissolution of the church, solitaries were formally removed from their chapels, and cells drew a pension that helped pay for secular life.[112] Two Norwich anchoresses joined the nuns of Carrow Priory in a privately owned house in the city, but most must have returned to the secular world.[113]

---

1. Allmand, *Henry V*, 283.

2. Walker, *A History of the Christian Church*, 270.

3. Evans and Wright, *The Anglican Tradition: A Handbook of Sources*, 117.

4. Ibid., 110.

5. Ibid., 111.

6. Ibid., 113.

7. Ibid., 115.

8. Thornton, *English Spirituality*, 201–202.

9. James William, "Revelations of Divine Love–Julian (of Norwich)" (Harvard College Library, 1923), accessed June 8, 2023, https://books.google.com/books?id=2o8NAAAAYAAJ&printsec=frontcover&hl=en#v=onepage&q&f=false. Google Books.

10. Daniel DeForest London, *The Cloud of Unknowing Distilled* (Hannacroix, NY: Apocryphile Press, 2021), Kindle location, 139. Kindle.

11. Julian, of Norwich, "Revelations of Divine Love," 106–110.

12. Thornton, *English Spirituality*, 162.

13. Denys Turner, *Julian of Norwich: Theologian* (New Haven, CT: Yale University Press, 2011), accessed June 9, 2023, https://ebookcentral-proquest-com.ezproxy.regent.edu/lib/regent-ebooks/reader.action?docID=3420686.

14. Thornton, *English Spirituality*, 204.

15. Hornbeck, *Wycliffite Spirituality*, 33.

16. Edmund De Schweinitz, *The History of the Church Known as the Unitas Fratrum or The Unity of the Brethren* (Bethlehem, PA: Moravian Publication Office, 1885), 19. Logos.

17. Ibid., 9.

18. Ibid., 5.

19. Ibid., 9.

20. Hornbeck, *Wycliffite Spirituality*, 33.

21. Cross, and Livingstone, "Bridget."

22. Kurian, "Bridget (Birgitta) of Sweden, St."

23. Harrison and Sullivan, *A Short History of Western Civilization*, 312.

24. Thornton, *English Spirituality*, 160.

25. Harrison and Sullivan, *A Short History of Western Civilization*, 312.

26. Volz, *The Medieval Church*, 222.

27. Jones, *Hermits and Anchorites in England 1200–1550*, 233.

28. Kempe, *The Book of Margery Kempe*, xiv.

29. "The Book of Margery Kempe: Introduction | Robbins Library Digital Projects," accessed June 10, 2023, https://d.lib.rochester.edu/teams/text/staley-book-of-margery-kempe-introduction.

30. "Oldcastle, Sir John (c.1370–1417), of Almeley, Herefs. and Cobham, Kent. | History of Parliament Online," https://www.historyofparliamentonline.org/volume/1386-1421/member/oldcastle-sir-john-1370-1417.

31. Jones, *Hermits and Anchorites in England 1200–1550*, 237.

32. Ibid., 239.

33. Ibid., 237–40.

34. Ibid., 239.

35. Allmand, *Henry V*, 284.

36. Margery Kempe, *The Book of Margery Kempe*, ed. and trans. B. A. Windeatt (London, England: Penguin Classics, 2005), xxii. Kindle.

37. Kurian, "Bridgettines."

38. Kempe, *The Book of Margery Kempe*, xxii.

39. Strayer and Munro, *The Middle Ages 395–1500*, 481.

40. Allmand, *Henry V*, 16.

41. Ibid., 17.

42. "Sir John Oldcastle: English Soldier: Britannica," accessed June 22, 2023, https://www.britannica.com/biography/John-Oldcastle.

43. Allmand, *Henry V*, 18.

44. "Sir John Oldcastle: English Soldier: Britannica."

45. Allmand, *Henry V*, 18.

46. "The History of the Welsh Dragon–Symbol of Wales."

47. Allmand, *Henry V*, 21.

48. Volz, *The Medieval Church*, 222.

49. Allmand, *Henry V*, 20.

50. Ibid., 288.

51. "Sir John Oldcastle: English Soldier: Britannica."

52. Ibid., 309.

53. Gies and Gies, *Cathedral, Forge, and Waterwheel Technology and Invention in the Middle Ages*, 98–9.

54. London, *The Cloud of Unknowing Distilled*, Kindle location, 120, 127.

55. Ibid., Kindle location, 153–56, 162.

56. Ibid., Kindle location, 164–68,

57. Ibid., Kindle location, 158.

58. Ibid., Kindle location, 216–230.

59. Ibid., Kindle location, 266–270.

60. Allmand, *Henry V*, 289.

61. Youngblood, "Wycliffe's Versions."

62. Thornton, *English Spirituality*, 185.

63. Ibid., 184.

64. Kurian, "Hilton Walker."

65. Thornton, *English Spirituality*, 178.

66. Ibid., 178–79.

67. Ibid., 182.

68. Ibid., 183.

69. Cross and Livingstone, "Kempe Margery."

70. Thornton, *English Spirituality*, 163.

71. Cross and Livingstone, "Kempe Margery."

72. Jones, *Hermits and Anchorites in England 1200-1550*, 25.

73. Ibid., 23.

74. Kempe, *The Book of Margery Kempe*, xxiii.

75. Ibid., xxiv–v.

76. Ibid., xxv.

77. Youngblood, "Wycliffe's Versions."

78. "Oldcastle, Sir John (c.1370–1417), of Almeley, Herefs. and Cobham, Kent.: History of Parliament Online."

79. Hornbeck, *Wycliffite Spirituality*, 4, 46.

80. "Oldcastle, Sir John (c.1370–1417), of Almeley, Herefs. and Cobham, Kent. | History of Parliament Online."

81. Jones, *Hermits and Anchorites in England 1200-1550*, 25.

82. "Oldcastle, Sir John (c.1370–1417), of Almeley, Herefs. and Cobham, Kent. | History of Parliament Online."

83. Kempe, *The Book of Margery Kempe*, ix.

84. Jones, *Hermits and Anchorites in England 1200–1550*, 107.

85. Cross and. Livingstone, "Kempe Margery."

86. Kempe, *The Book of Margery Kempe*, x.

87. Allmand, *Henry V*, 436.

88. "Oldcastle, Sir John (c.1370–1417), of Almeley, Herefs. and Cobham, Kent. | History of Parliament Online."

89. Kempe, *The Book of Margery Kempe*, xiv.

90. Cross and Livingstone, "Kempe Margery."

91. Hornbeck, *Wycliffite Spirituality*, 4, 46.

92. "The Book of Margery Kempe: Introduction | Robbins Library Digital Projects."

93. Cross and Livingstone, "Kempe Margery."

94. Kempe, *The Book of Margery Kempe*, x, xiv.

95. Ibid., xxix.

96. Allmand, *Henry V*, 309.

97. Ibid., 310.

98. Kempe, *The Book of Margery Kempe*, x, xiv.

99. Thornton, *English Spirituality*, 223.

100. Kempe, *The Book of Margery Kempe*, xvii.

101. Ibid., xviii, xix.

102. Allmand, *Henry V*, 436.

103. Walker, *A History of the Christian Church*, 270.

104. Jones, *Hermits and Anchorites in England 1200–1550*, 127.

105. Ibid., 25.

106. Ibid., 126.

107. Ibid., 25.

108. Ibid., 126.

109. Allmand, *Henry V*, 293.

110. Woodbridge and James, *Church History Volume Two From Pre-Reformation to the Present Day*, 48, 219–220.

111. Hornbeck, *Wycliffite Spirituality*, 1.

112. Jones, *Hermits and Anchorites in England 1200–1550*, 253.

113. Ibid., 254.

9

ENGLISH ROOTS

SUMMARY

IN AN ARTICLE PUBLISHED in *Christian Century* (1978), Matthew Fox summed up this study's chapter titled, "English Roots Leading Up to the Moravians," when he pointed out that Christian orders practiced Christianity spiritually differently during the Middle Ages as they coped with a secular world. The people who practiced spirituality in the twelfth and thirteenth centuries understood that "courage, not comfort," was "the key to the Christian way, and it is this that the cross signifies in creation-centered spirituality."[1]

God reworks the aftermath of atrocities for good. The Roman Catholic Church backing William the Conqueror of Normandy revolved around his pious donations and their wish to reform the Angle-Saxon Church. Sometimes, loyalty to church policies can cause problems for hundreds of years. Anselm's devotion to the pope as the Church's supreme leader circumvented William the Conqueror's bid for an independent church of England. The piety of Williams, archbishop of Canterbury, secured the pope's authority in England until King Henry VIII. Instead, nationalism, which would split the Church of England from the Roman Catholic Church, began as a reaction to King John's incompetence, resulting in lands lost in France.

The fall and rise of monasteries and religious orders show that the accumulation of money eventually destroys religious organizations despite starting with humble Christ-centered ambitions. When one religious movement becomes corrupt, reformers strive for a new Christian order that will return to the faithful service of God. The Ten Commandments slowly grew in a Christian understanding of Peter Lombard's symbolism, like a well-nurtured plant foundation of morality to be contemplated in many of Wycliffe's writings. What Wycliffe wrote to defend the English king and reform the Catholic church was rejected by the Catholic church. Oxford produced chaplains for kings, scholars, and theologians whose insights would shape reformations and revivals in the backdrop of peace, war, prosperity, famine, and disease.

King Henry II's founding of Oxford to support funding England and competition against Paris helped maintain a practical form of Catholic Christianity enjoyed by the converted Celts and Saxons, which still survives in the Anglican church. This spirituality grows within peasants and priests from hearing or reading Scripture, prayers, and contemplation. This formula has worked and will always work because, as Heb. 13:8 noted, "Jesus Christ is the same yesterday, today, and forever."

Although God remains a steadfast constant, the faithful refine meditating on Scripture through prayer diversely. Margery Kempe cultivated techniques accredited to a multitude of Christian mystics from throughout England's history. Her inner relationship with the almighty triune God amplified without undermining her orthodoxy. The next chapters examine how the Holy Spirit either transformed a single person or affected entire communities based on God's pleasure.

---

1. Matthew Fox, "Spirituality for Protestants – Religion Online," *Christian Century* August 2-9: 731–36, accessed June 23, 2023, https://www.religion-online.org/article/spirituality-for-protestants/.

10

Across the English Channel

Fueling the Moravian Revival

Like in England, sovereign authority united law, theology, state, and the church in Europe.[1] Heredity determined secular titles except for archbishops and the King of Bohemia.[2] In 1212, Premysl Otakor I received The Gold Bull of Sicily decreeing Bohemia a kingdom, their princes' hereditary kings, inseparable from the Holy Roman Empire.[3] Bohemian noble estates elected their king.[4] From 1254 to 1273, German princes built up small local independent states. Eastern Germany, centered in Bavaria, produced powerful states while the lords in the east succumbed to Leagues.[5]

In 1312, Henry VII became the first crowned Holy Roman Emperor since Fredrick II (d. 1250).[6] Charles IV had Prague's first bishop by 1344. In 1348, Charles named their realm the Crown of Bohemia, which included Moravia, Siclisea, and Lustatia. Charles University was the first university built north of the Alps. The electors crowned him Roman Emperor in 1355.[7]

Under the Golden Bull of 1356,[8] seven electors, the prince— Archbishop of Mainz, Cologne, Trier, the Duke of Saxony, Count Palatine of the Rhine, Margrave of Brandenburg, and the king of Bohemia[9] voted on the German Holy Roman Emperor who became King of the Romans. After the pope crowned the King of the Romans, he became the Holy Roman Emperor.[10] The Holy Roman Emperor controlled three hundred territories, dutchies, and free imperial cities ruled by archbishops, bishops, counts, dukes, city councils, and imperial knights.[11] His lands spread across modern Austria, Belgium, the Czech Republic, Germany, Liechtenstein, Luxemburg, the Netherlands, Slovakia, Slovenia, Switzerland, and sections of Denmark, Italy, Poland, and France.[12] Like a Bishop in an Episcopal Diocese, the Holy Roman Emperor traveled throughout his jurisdiction, leading his assemblies.[13]

---

1. Avis, "Great Britain," 5.

2. Kilsdonk, "The Thirty Years War(s)," 15.

3. "History of the Czech Republic: Embassy of the Czech Republic in Tehran," accessed July 12, 202, https://www.mzv.cz/teheran/en/information_about_the_czech_republic/history/index.html.

4. Kilsdonk, "The Thirty Years War(s)," 15.

5. Strayer and Munro, *The Middle Ages 395–1500*, 325.

6. "History of the Holy Roman Empire," accessed July 12, 2023, http://www.holyromanempireassociation.com/history-of-the-holy-roman-empire.html.

7. "History of the Czech Republic: Embassy of the Czech Republic in Tehran."

8. "History of the Holy Roman Empire,"

9. Kilsdonk, "The Thirty Years War(s)," 15.

10. "King of the Romans," accessed July 12, 2023, http://www.holyromanempireassociation.com/king-of-the-romans.html.

11. "History of the Holy Roman Empire."

12. "Holy-Roman-Empire-1250-Map-1.Jpg (1561×1972)," accessed July 12, 2023, https://www.globalsecurity.org/military/world/europe/images/holy-roman-empire-1250-map-1.jpg.

13. "History of the Holy Roman Empire."

11

JOHN HUSS

FUELING THE MORAVIAN REVIVAL

JOHN HUSS (1369–1415) LIVED outside the Holy Roman Empire.[1] Huss studied to become a priest at the University of Prague and lectured there in 1398. In 1401, he packed[2] the Bethlehem Church, where he served as a minister on Sundays and festival days, preaching in Czech and German.[3]

Huss' rash sermons attacked the weaknesses of the lazy and the wealthy.[4] He quoted the Bible as his only source of religious truth in his sermons, held Communion often, and lifted the morals of the clergy and the congregation of the Bethlehem Chapel, where he served as a chaplain in Prague.[5] Huss first read Wycliffe when his friend Jerome of Prague returned from Oxford with copies of his work.[6] As Huss digested Wycliffe's writings, his approval of the English reformer's opinions grew.[7] The 1403 cathedral chapter in Prague banned possessing and preaching forty-five of Wycliffe's articles.[8] Huss responded by incorporating Wycliffe's writings into his own books and sermons. German soldiers overwhelmed the land. German nobles possessed offices of state in the city.[9]

While the rector at the University of Prague, Huss hotly disputed a charter change at the Czech university that favored the German's voting power to three-fourths, exceeding their population. Over fifteen hundred masters and students deserted the University of Prague to start a new university in Leipzig in 1409 due to financial disputes.[10] In a subsequent sermon, Huss questioned why Bohemian bishops had to be fluent in German and against German nobles seizing public office. People credited Huss for the win when King Wenceslaus altered the charter to reverse the voters favoring the Bohemians in a three-to-four ratio.[11] Huss grew into the new leader of the Bohemian reform *devotio moderna* (new devotion), which believed in frequent communion and moral reform.[12]

In 1410, Pope Alexander V ordered Zbynek, archbishop of Prague, to close chapels where Wycliffe's views were preached, such as Huss'. As Huss loudly protested, the archbishop seized two hundred Wycliffe writings from the chapel. The archbishop burned the writings on a bonfire in his palace's courtyard. Afterward, Huss defended a Wycliffe tract on the Trinity.[13] Wycliffe's heresy or church reforms fueled the Bohemian national rebellion against Germany.[14]

Alexander V died in 1410, and Pope John XXIII became the pope.[15] Catholic Church representative, Zbinco excommunicated Huss in 1410 on the grounds of possessing Wycliffe's documents. Huss refused Pope John XXIII's citation, and the University appealed to the Pisan pope, who upheld the charges of "rebellion and disobedience." The people in Prague responded by burning the papal decree. Huss invited Pope John to try him in Prague. Rome placed an interdict prohibiting rites and service in the city in response.[16] In 1411, Huss "admitted that he and his friends had been reading Wycliffe's writing for over twenty years."[17]

Drummers preceded the preachers, selling indulgences for the forgiveness of sins and freedom from Hell at the Prague market.[18] Huss attacked papal indulgences authorized by John XXIII to finance a crusade against Ladislaus, king of Naples, in 1412[19] but maintained his only agreement with Wycliffe came purely from Scripture and argued that he remained a good Catholic.[20] Huss fled and then wrote *On the Church*, which agreed with Wycliffe by denying the bull of Pope Boniface *UM Sanctum* that the true church of Christ differed from the Church of Rome because the pope and the cardinals were stained by error and sin.[21] From 1412–1414, influential nobles protected Huss,[22] who continued to write the majority of his Bohemian and Latin compositions[23] and preach in fields and villages in rural Bohemia.[24] Huss also revised a fourteenth-century anonymously written Bohemian Bible. His many hymns appeared in the Unity of Brethren Hymnal.[25]

A party of thirty-five, including King Henry V, his embassy, clergy from Canterbury and York, and representatives from England's colleges, traveled in a seven-horse-drawn wagon caravan to the Council of Constance (1414–1418) to shut down the "Great

Schism," end the Bohemian rebellion and reform the Church.[26] Sigismund, the King of Bohemia (Germany and Hungary), King of the Romans, and the Holy Roman Emperor[27] granted England the right of nationhood separate from the Germans if the English voted on the emperor's side.[28] England, France, Germany, and Italy voted as nations.[29]

The Great Scism, brought about by too many popes dissolved in 1415. The Council of Constance deposed Pope John XXIII on May 29; Pope Gregory XII resigned on July 4. The Council dissolved the papacy from absolute power to a "constitutional monarchy."[30]

Oxford professor Dr. Abendon preached powerfully against the greed and worldliness of foreign bishops and clergy at the Council.[31] Due to quarrels among the nations, no other reform could be agreed upon.[32] The Council decreed that bread without the blood of Christ would be served for Communion to the laity.[33]

The Council of Constance condemned two hundred sixty-seven Wycliffe's teachings errors and burned his heretical books. So, the church exhumed his body from consecrated ground and burned it.[34]

As Sigismund promised Huss safe conduct, he attended the Council to explain his views. He was immediately arrested[35] and jailed in a dungeon on an island near a sewer in the Rhine for three and a half months. The pope's soldiers transferred Huss to the castle tower on Lake Geneva. The Council examining *On The Church* condemned Huss as a heretic, which was decided before his appearance.[36] They ordered Huss to burn at the stake on July 6, 1415.[37] His executioners threw Huss' ashes into the Rhine.[38]

---

1. Kilsdonk, "The Thirty Years War(s)," 13.

2. J. E. Hutton, "The Burning of Huss," *The History of The Moravian Movement*, 2nd ed. (1909). e-Sword.

3. *Lights and Shadows of the Reformation*.

4. Hutton, "The Burning of Huss."

5. Volz, *The Medieval Church*, 222.

6. Ibid., 223.

7. Hutton, "The Burning of Huss."

8. Volz, *The Medieval Church*, 222.

9. Hutton, "The Burning of Huss."

10. Volz, *The Medieval Church*, 131.

11. Hutton, "The Burning of Huss."

12. Clouse, *The Church from Age to Age*, 424.

13. "Introduction," *The Church by John Huss*.

14. Cantor, *The Civilization of the Middle Ages*, 500.

15. Woodbridge and James, *Church History Volume Two From Pre-Reformation to the Present Day*, 45.

16. Volz, *The Medieval Church: From the Dawn of the Middle Ages to the Eve of the Reformation*, 223.

17. Clouse, *The Church from Age to Age*, 384.

18. Hutton, "The Burning of Huss."

19. "Huss and the Church | Online Library of Liberty," https://oll.libertyfund.org/page/huss-and-the-church.

20. Woodbridge and James, *Church History Volume Two From Pre-Reformation to the Present Day*, 48.

21. Clouse, *The Church from Age to Age*, 384.

22. "Introduction," *The Church by John Huss*.

23. Schweinitz, *The History of the Church Known as the Unitas Fratrum or The Unity of the Brethren*, 45.

24. "Introduction," *The Church by John Huss*.

25. Schweinitz, *The History of the Church Known as the Unitas Fratrum or The Unity of the Brethren*, 45.

26. Allmand, *Henry V*, 236, 238-39.

27. Woodbridge and James, *Church History Volume Two From Pre-Reformation to the Present Day*, 46.

28. Allmand, *Henry V*, 241.

29. "Council Of Constance: Encyclopedia.Com," https://www.encyclopedia.com/philosophy-and-religion/christianity/roman-catholic-and-orthodox-churches-councils-and-treaties/council-constance.

30. Walker, *A History of the Christian Church*, 276.

31. John Henry Blunt, *A Key to the Knowledge of Church History* (London: Oxford, and Cambridge: Rivingtons Waterloo Place, 1877). e-Sword.

32. Walker, *A History of the Christian Church*, 276.

33. Evans, and Wright, *The Anglican Tradition: A Handbook of Sources*, 118.

34. "Wycliffe, John," The Episcopal Church, accessed July 7, 2023, https://www.episcopalchurch.org/glossary/wycliffe-john/.

35. Clouse, *The Church from Age to Age*, 384.

36. Hutton, "The Burning of Huss," *A History of the Moravian Church*.

37. Volz, *The Medieval Church*, 207, 224.

38. Woodbridge and James, *Church History Volume Two From Pre-Reformation to the Present Day*, 50.

12

The Hussites

Fueling the Moravian Revival

People in the Middle Ages and during the Renaissance traditionally considered warfare as a conflict between God and the devil.[1] On Sept. 7, fifty-eight barons declared in a manifesto that anyone charging Bohemians with heresy was "a son of the Devil and the father of lies." The Council of Constance placed Prague under an interdict. Utraquists retaliated by serving mass to the Prague laity.[2] Spain became a nation when their delegates joined the council in Oct. 1416.[3] The Bohemians rebelled. Their martyr Huss symbolized Bohemian nationalism. News arrived that the Council convicted

Jerome of Prague, and he, too, had been burned at the stake.[4] In Nov. 1417, cardinals, with six representatives from each nation, elected Roman Martin V (1417–1431).[5] Two years later, Jan Zelivsky led a procession through the Prague streets to the new town hall at Charles Square, demanding the release of Hussite prisoners. Someone threw a stone from the town hall's window, causing a riot. The crowd stormed the hall. They threw the judge, the burgomaster, and five other Prague Council members out the windows onto the pikes of the army below.[6] Armed conflicts erupted throughout Bohemia.[7]

The Hussites defeated five consecutive crusades between 1420 and 1431.[8] After fifteen years of civil war, they produced factions[9] claiming Huss as their religious heir. The moderate Calixtines stood for "cup," and the Utraquists, standing for the word "both," wanted to remain under the Catholic Church but insisted on both bread and wine during Communion.[10]

Taborites drew their name from Mount Tavor, a haven South of Prague.[11] The Taborites completely separated from the Catholic Church, maintaining the Bible as the one source of religious truth.

They opposed penance, prayer to the saints, relics, transubstantiation, and veneration of images. Under the leadership of Taborite generals John Zizka and Procopius the Great, the groups combined forces and repelled Sigismund's army.

In 1420, the two Hussite groups authored the Four Articles of Prague: Free preaching of the Word of God, communion with bread and wine for clergy and laity, reform of morals, and reduction of wealth and power for the clergy.[12]

The Koreans perfected their brass printing press, and European progress in improving the printing press followed in the Netherlands and the Rhineland headed by a silversmith named Johann Gutenberg. Meanwhile, 1420 bookbinders started to use woodblock printing for their titles. Gutenberg solved the problem when striking a clay letter ruined the letter next to it by fashioning individual letters from a lead-tin alloy in 1426.[13]

Eventually, the Utraquists defeated the Taborites. Bohemia remained governed by the Unity of the Bohemian Brothers, who slowly evolved into the Moravians.[14] Pope Martin V died, and Eugene IV (1431–1447) replaced him. The legislative body started to work coherently by reconciliation with the Hussites in 1433.[15]

---

1. Kilsdonk, "The Thirty Years War(s)," 18.

2. Woodbridge and James, *Church History Volume Two From Pre-Reformation to the Present Day*, 50.

3. "Council Of Constance: Encyclopedia.Com."

4. Woodbridge and James, *Church History Volume Two From Pre-Reformation to the Present Day*, 50–51.

5. Walker, *A History of the Christian Church*, 276.

6. ER, "The Defenestration of Prague of 1618" (Naked History, May 19, 2017), accessed July 19, 2023, https://www.historynaked.com/defenestration-prague-1618/.

7. Woodbridge and James, *Church History Volume Two From Pre-Reformation to the Present Day*, 50–51.

8. "History of the Czech Republic: Embassy of the Czech Republic in Tehran."

9. Clouse, *The Church from Age to Age*, 358.

10. Volz, *The Medieval Church*, 224.

11. Woodbridge and James, *Church History Volume Two From Pre-Reformation to the Present Day*, 51.

12. Volz, *The Medieval Church*, 224.

13. Gie and Gies, *Cathedral, Forge, and Waterwheel Technology and Invention in the Middle Ages*, 242.

14. Volz, *The Medieval Church*, 224.

15. Walker, *A History of the Christian Church*, 277.

13
Spirituality, Sugar and Gold, the Slave Trade, Print Industry, and the Protestant Reformation

Christianity's feudal system had mostly replaced the ancient labor force of slavery with serfs, peasants, nuns, monks, and hermits, except for the international port of Bristol England which had been selling Irish and English slaves since the 1100s[1] and the Italian city-states. Italian merchants continued their tenth-century industry of selling infidels and Jews as slaves to the Egyptian Sultanate.[2]

1434 Portuguese captain Gil Eanes collected the reward from Prince Henry the Navigator after he braved tall tales of the boiling ocean at the Equator and the reality of "prevailing northerlies" preventing southern travel south on Africa's west coast. He rounded the enormous bulge of northwest Africa and returned since his fast new small sailing ship called a caravel could "beat to the windward."[3] One of Henry's ships returned home with the first shipment of gold and slaves from New Guinea.[4]

In 1441, a Dutch[5] priest[6] of the Brethren of the Common Life, Thomas a Kempis, published a spiritual instruction manual, *The Imitation of Christ*,[7] translated from Netherlandish into Latin.[8] The devotional booklet promoted humbleness, passivity, and contemplation to prepare one's soul for the purity needed to unite with God while reading and studying Scripture equipped one's inner spirit.[9] Four hundred copies of his Middle Ages manuscript still survive,[10] and next to the Bible, it is the most-read devotional worldwide.[11] The Brethren of Common Life's many mystic communities lived in communal piety.[12] Pope Martin V's 1441 bull excommunicated Gazaria, Calaffa a Genoese city-state on the Black Sea as their laws allowed the sale of both Christian and Muslim slaves.[13]

Portuguese traded for gold dust with Africans as their ships crept closer to the Equator. They learned that African slavery always existed as a commercial institution controlled by local rulers and occasionally aided by Arab traders. Enslaved captives, people with lost tribal status, and strangers were both currency and exchangeable commodities.[14] Both Portuguese and African slaves could earn their freedom back, becoming free slaves. They often married and ended up with property.[15]

Henry the Navigator built the first Portuguese fortified trading post on the island of Arguin in 1448 as the armed Africans repelled Portuguese landing parties in canoes. By negotiating with local West African rulers Portugal created a Royal monopoly that included Safi (Morrocco) where Africans traded wool for salt and wool cloth. Along New Guinea and the Ivory Coast, Portuguese ships exchanged cloth, wheat, and horses for cotton, silk, gold, and seven to eight hundred slaves.[16] The first slave-operated sugar mill was built on the island of Maderia in 1452 under Portuguese management. Maderia soon became Europe's biggest supplier of sugar.[17]

Woodblock printing of religious pictures with short texts popularized newly invented playing cards, posters, calendars, concise Latin grammars, and booklets called the "Poor Man's Bible," which Low Countries and the Rhineland printers mass produced. This led to the copper plate engravings. By 1450, south Germans and northern Italians duplicated more copies than when using a woodblock technique.[18] That year, Gutenberg invented the printing press at Mainz,[19] and in 1455, the Gutenberg Bible was printed. In 1457, the first Italian press churned out books, followed by presses in Paris and London.[20]

One to three percent of Europe's population served as friars, monks, nuns, or priests. Neither Wycliffe's nor Huss' reforms by their successors improved the run-of-the-mill sermons. Bishops served as landlords. Abbots could call their tenets to fight for their property.²¹ Knights carried relics in their sword hilts, and pilgrims wore relics in small bags tied around their necks or in jeweled arm cuffs. Spirits of the deceased infused bones, clothing, and hair from saints with mystical healing wealth or blessings.²² Brotherhoods of Christian laymen organized to do religious or charitable service became known as a "confraternity."²³

In 1471, King Cazimir of Poland, Vladislav Jagellon's son, had been elected King in Bohemia. The power of Estates multiplied as the power of royalty grew smaller. Struggles and conflicts broke out between royal towns and landowning aristocrats. The Catholic minority tried to regain her former control from the Hussite Church.²⁴

Carrying a written prayer while traveling to every destination and meditating on the rosary became popular based on the efforts of a French Cologne Confraternity founded in 1472.²⁵ The Catholic Reformation created the Blessed Sacrament or Rosary societies for the elite to wipe out the village's Holy Spirit organizations in Southern Europe.

Thornton credits the Dominican Order for the rosary and defines it as a devotion that produced

Church unity between the pope, priest, and peasant.[26] One privately meditated on symbols of whip and torches of the Mount of Olives, and crucifixions colored wooden engravings, paper embossed in lead molds: some substituted clubs, nails, latter, and sponges. Confraternities and random people tried to relive Christ's passion daily.[27]

Cologne University developed the first censorship by requiring authors to obtain a license from the pope to publish and the right to punish anyone who published or read unauthorized material in 1475.[28] Closely tied to the Spanish monarchy, the Spanish Inquisition was formed in 1478 to route out Judaism and secret Muslims.[29]

By 1480, every city in Europe owned a printing press. A scribe could copy a manuscript for one guilder. A press charged three guilders for every five pages, including typesetting and ink. An unlimited supply could be printed after the initial cost for the price of paper and ink.[30] Continental Rabbis printed new Hebrew Bibles between the 1480s and the 1490s.[31]

Once a year from 1482-1485, King Ferdinand who reigned in Castile from 1474 to 1504 (also known as Fredrick II king of Aragon from 1452-1516), and

Queen Isabella attacked the last Moor strongholds of Granada and Malaga for their silk markets and to protect Spanish shipping in the Straights of Gibraltar. When besieged Malaga fell in 1487, Spain enslaved between eleven and fifteen thousand citizens because they fought fiercely. As more Muslim ports lost against the Catholic adversary the Granada inhabitants headed for Africa.[32]

After pursuing humanistic and biblical studies at the Latin School of Deventer between 1478 and 1483, Desiderius Erasmus resided at the Brethren of Common Life hostel from 1485–1487 while studying St. Jerome of Stridon, who first translated the Vulgate and classical authors at a monastery.[33]

The Portuguese trained the noble Congo ambassadors in their language and Catholicism from 1483 to 1485 to expand the Catholic Church. The nobles reported back to King Nzinga who sent them back to Lisbon in 1487.[34] 1490 Portuguese missionaries sailed the Congo River, baptized Nzinga as Joao I, and founded the national Catholic Church by 1491.[35] The missionaries baptized Joao's son Nzinga Mbemba as Dom Affonso.[36]

Their attempt to spread Catholicism succeeded. Mwene Soyo, ruler of Congo's Soyo providence unearthed a black stone carved with a cross that legitimized their king's Christian conversion.[37] The four branches of the Kimpasi cross denoted the cycle of human existence. One underwent a symbolic death and resurrection to become a Kimpasi.[38] The Portuguese allied with the triumphant Congolese (Bakongo) and found more common religious ground. Congo armies reported ghostly symbols and signs in the sky. The Portuguese like other European soldiers regularly saw angels amidst battle.[39] Alonso employed a few Portuguese and Bakongo converts to create a school with a class of four hundred noble children. After four years of training, the graduates taught others throughout the Congo. Only Portuguese clergy could perform the sacraments. However, the Bakongo taught and recruited new members.[40]

Censorship in the print industry began in Italy in 1491 in the diocese of Treviso.[41] The Moor capital of Granada surrendered without a fight to Spain on Jan 2, 1492[42] By 1493, the translated Latin version of Christopher Columbus' letter to the Queen of Spain was printed in eleven editions, purchased, and read to an excited European public about his discoveries in the West Indies.⁴³

Holy Emperor Fredrick III sought finances from his dukes to fund his war against Hungary. Then, he elected his son Maximilian I as Germany's king in 1486, uniting his duke's insistence on participating in an Imperial Court. Fredrick refused, but after he died in 1493, Maximilian I convened the Diet at Worms in 1495. The king and dukes passed four bills creating⁴⁴ administrative circles called the Imperial Kreise or circle estates, the Reichstag, or the general diet, which acted like England's parliament. They were empowered to defend themselves and to form smaller, regional assemblies to resolve how to sustain peace convened at the emperor's invitation. The elector vote counted as one.⁴⁵ They could meet and discuss Imperial affairs without the emperor.⁴⁶

The other two legislative bodies voted on proposals based on an electoral system: the higher one's title, the higher one's votes. An assembly of all Imperial princes acted as another voting entity comparable to the House of Lords. Their decision counted as a vote by the emperor. Members of the Imperial Free Cities voted in an independent second assembly,[47] which was added after the Diet at Worms.[48]

In 1496, Mainz's archdiocese required publishing licenses to be obtained from the pope. Unauthorized reading or production of printed materials would be punished by excommunication or a fine to curtail the spread of unorthodox religious philosophies.[49]

In 1499, Lord Mountjoy invited Erasmus' student William Blount to England, where he met Oxford professor John Colet, bishop of Winchester Richard Fox, and Sir Thomas More (1478–1535), whom each became one of the twenty members of Erasmus' circle. Erasmus' circle was devoted to Erasmus and his expertise with Latin and Greek texts. As "humanists," they sought to reform Christianity by reviving the "purity" from its earliest roots. Erasmus roomed with Mountjoy. Chancellor of Cambridge University and bishop of Rocester John Fisher secured a position at Cambridge where Erasmus taught Greek and the writings of St. Jerome. He dedicated *Adages* to More in his introduction.[50] In *Adages* and *In Praise of Folly*, he summoned Christians to a Scriptural, practical, theologically sound learned piety that emulated Jesus' ethics and self-sacrifice.[51]

Pope Alexander VI extended the censorship practiced in Cologne and Mainz to include all of Germany.[52]

Venice, Italy, won the title of "printing capital of Europe with 2,789 published titles by 1500. Europe boasted 40,000 of most Latin editions of books ranging from science by Grosseteste, Aquinas, and Bacon to encyclopedias and Bibles. They printed ninety-four Latin, fifteen German, and eleven Italian Bibles. Printing presses churned out fifteen to twenty million copies.[53]

In 1504, Erasmus published biblical criticism, arguing with Colet over the nature of Christ's agony in the Garden of Gethsemane. By 1505, he returned to England and translated Greek poets and dramas from More's house as he prepared to translate St. Jerome's sacred letters. William Warham became his most consistent patron.[54] OP M. von Weida of Leipzig published a partial German version of St. Gertrude's and Mechthild of Hackenborn's visions in 1505.[55]

By 1506, Erasmus chose to study in Italy, where he gained the admiration and support of scholars William Latimer and diplomat Cuthbert Tunstall.[56] Starting in 1506, Pope Julius II employed the Swiss as personal bodyguards at the Vatican.[57] Dom Affonso became Mani-Congo (King) either in 1506 or 1507.[58] In 1509, after Henry VIII[59] of the Welsh House of Tudor[60] accepted the throne, Mountjoy and Warham coaxed Erasmus back to Cambridge.[61] In 1510, Ferdinand V began signing royal orders for slaves to be sent and sold to the Spanish Canary Islands along the South American coast, which resulted in Spain's first 1515 shipment of West Indian Sugar. By 1518, the kings in the different provinces of Spain lived off the trade from the orders for four thousand slaves to work the sugar plantations.[62]

The young priest Ulrich Zwingli joined the 1512 Swiss mercenaries hired by Italy. Zwingli witnessed savage looting following their victory over the French at the 1513 Battle of Novara.[63] He struggled with the tragedy experienced by defeated soldiers[64] after the 1515 Battle of Marignano.[65] Meanwhile, the Habsburg government in the Netherlands resisted a Frisian peasant revolt initiated by Pier Gerlofs Donia, which Wijerd Jackama continued. The peasants sacked cities and sank one hundred thirty-two ships.[66] Zwingli went on to serve as a priest in the canton of Schwyz, the home of one of Switzerland's most famous pilgrimage sites, the Benedictine Abby, dedicated to the Virgin Mary in Einsiedeln. He wrote a second satire, a portrait of righteous Swiss countrymen exploited by French politics, the empire, and the papacy in *The Labyrinth* in 1516.[67]

Erasmus released *Novum Instrumentum,* his revised Greek New Testament (March 1516). He had compared his translation against authentic Greek transcripts as Jerome and Augustine instructed and doublechecked his translation against ancient Latin versions.[68] Erasmus' students at Cambridge included Augustinian Miles Coverdale, William Tyndale, and Thomas Cranmer.[69] Bohemia elected Lous Jagellon, who continued to lose power to the Bohemian princes.[70] Ferdinand II of Aragon (Ferdinand V king of Castile) died, and at the persistence of his surviving grandfather, Maximilian, Charles I enlarged Spain's borders based on his pedigree as he received the crown.[71]

To debate Roman Church policy, Augustine monk Martin Luther posted ninety-five theses on the door of the Whittenburg Church in 1517.[72] German dukes saw Luther's Reformation as a tool to oppose Charles I's bid for Holy Roman Emperorship and the

Habsburg family. Frankfurt and Strasbourg became Protestant strongholds.[73]

At the request of King Manuel of Portugal, Pope Leo X's May 5, 1518, bull on accepting four new cardinals also promoted King Affono's son Prince Henry of Congo to the rank of bishop.[74]

In 1519, Charles I won over contenders Francis I of France, Henry VIII, and Fredrick the Wise of Saxony, who protected Luther, and the Holy Roman Empire election to govern as Charles V. In a Leipzig debate against Johann Eck, Luther said John Huss' views were "plainly Christian and evangelical."[75] Zwingli responded to Luther's remarks by describing Luther as the "new Elijah."[76]

Zwingli's favorite Dutch scholar from his University days was Erasmus, who republished his Greek New Testament in 1519.[77] In his new introduction *Annotations*, Erasmus explained his translation's purpose was to become the basis for translating the New Testament into the local spoken language as Scripture reveals "the living image of Christ's holy mind and Christ himself speaking, healing, dying and rising."[78] Zwingli copied it to carry with him to memorize the Scripture.[79] He caught the plague while consoling his sick and dying congregation, which wiped out over a fourth of Zurich's population between 1590 and 1520. Zwingli wrote the *Plague Song,* which said to God, "Do as you will, for I lack nothing. I am a vessel to be restored or destroyed." Zwingli recovered.[80]

Luther's contraband publications captivated England's curious and devout the year Pope Leo X excommunicated Luther. Luther countered by burning the papal bull along with a book of canon law in 1520.[81] Leo X called Henry VIII the "Defender of the Faith" after Henry published *Assertion of the Seven Sacraments* protesting Luther.[82] Meanwhile, Cologne and Louvain made bonfires out of Luther's pamphlets. By 1521, Charles V prohibited the possession, reading, or printing of any publication by Luther,[83] while Mexico City became the capital of New Spain in South America.[84] Spain replaced her enslaved workforce of 50,000 every twenty years in her American silver mines and sugar plantations.[85]

While laying low at Wartburg Castle in 1522, Martin Luther published his everyday common tongue[86] German New Testament based on the original Greek by Erasmus and proofread by a Greek scholar, Philip Melanchthon, in Sept. 1522. Luther's German used by housewives and children playing[87] outdid fourteen previous German Bible translations and facilitated standardizing the German language.[88] The literate read out loud and preached Luther's Bible. Private reading of the Bible was unprofitable as only a few people could read.[89] It sold out and was republished in 1523.[90]

Princes in the German Holy Roman Empire Electors of Saxony, Brandenburg, and Palatine converted to Lutheranism.[91] The Habsburgs finally quelled the Frisian Nethread peasant revolt by capturing and decapitating rebel leaders.[92]

Members attending the Gloucestershire churches in England warned Tyndale against further preaching from Scripture, which may "cost him his life."[93] The Bishop of London, Cuthbert Tunstall, rejected Tyndale's request for patronage of the new English Bible based on Greek in 1524.[94]

A German noble, Casper von Schwenkfeld (1490–1548) strayed from his Spirit-filled Lutheran Reformation preachings in northern Germany by explaining that the Lord's Supper nourished the soul according to the feeding of the five thousand from

John 6:1-15, 22-59.[95] The indwelling of the Holy Spirit of Jesus' followers in John 14:22–24, and on those who live according to the Spirit are alive as opposed to choosing to follow the desires of flesh leading to death in Rom. 8 deified Christ's flesh.

Schwenkfeld opposed the over-attention to liturgy and administrative details enforced by clergy and the Bible only as the Protestant religion.[96] He began teaching that God creates Himself inside of good humans without Scripture since God is the only bona fide source of actual knowledge.[97] His followers wrote hymns on God's breath in piety, inner Christian life, personal union with Christ, regeneration, sanctification, devotion, and resigning to God's will under persecution.[98]

During the following year, Tyndale relocated to Cologne, Germany. After authorities raided Peter Quentell's printing house as they finished the first part of Matthew,[99] Tyndale escaped down the Rhine to Worms, where he published his first complete English New Testament translation.[100] The first Lutheran hymnal included twenty-four of Luther's hymns,[101] while the Council of Zurich abolished mass in 1525.

In 1526, Tyndale's New Testament crossed into England, smuggled in cotton bales, and sold for a week's wages.[102] Canterbury's Archbishop Warham bought all the copies, and Tunstall burned them in front of St. Paul's Cathedral. This financed Tyndale's second edition.[103] Tyndale continued to smuggle in copies of his New Testament as rapidly as the British people bought them, and authorities set them on fire.[104]

The Habsburg dynasty succeeded to the Bohemian throne, reintroduced the Catholic faith, and began to form a multinational empire by including the Crownlands of Bohemia.[105] Charles V's troops fended off the Ottoman Turks at the Battle of Mohacs in Hungary, and his unpaid Imperial troops marched on Italy. By 1527, Imperial troops sacked Rome and took Pope Clement VII prisoner.[106] In 1529, Charles V granted Mexico's conqueror Hernan Cortes (1485-1547) hereditary lordship over Oaxaca.[107]

Coverdale worked with Tyndale to translate the five books of Moses in Hamburg, Germany, in 1529.[108] Just north of Moravia, Schwenkfeld was exiled as a heretic from Silesia.[109] In England, More attacked Tyndale's New Testament for advocating heretical Lutheranism.[110] Tyndale published his translated first five books of the Old Testament in 1530.[111]

In 1530, Pope Clement VII crowned Charles V as Holy Roman Emperor.[112] Then, in 1531, Cranmer met Zwingli's Zurich successor, Swiss reformer, Henry Bullinger.[113] The Portuguese attempted their first Brazilian colony in 1532.[114] Anne Boleyn married Henry VIII in 1533.[115]

With the aid of Wittenberg translators, who met weekly,[116] Luther published the complete Old Testament in German based on a 1492 Hebrew Bible in 1534.[117] Before its completion, whenever Luther's team translated a book from the Old Testament, they published each book separately.[118] In Antwerp, George Joyce revised and published Tyndale's New Testament, causing Tyndale to re-revise his newest issue. Queen Boleyn requested a copy.[119]

By 1534 in England, Lutheran ideas mixed with the Lollards supporting King Henry VIII, which veered toward Wycliffe's conception of creating an exclusively English church. Canterbury's Archbishop Cranmer also favored an independent Church of England.[120] Representatives of the Holy Roman

Empire charged, stripped Tyndale of office, and sentenced him to death for being a Lutheran at the Castle of Vilvoorde in Belgium.[121] Charles V ordered Tyndale burned at the stake as representing the "heretical Church of England."[122]

Parliament passed the Act of Supremacy on Nov. 3, granting Henry and his heirs the Supreme Head of the Church of England, allowing him to overturn the Pope and divorce Catherine, and complete authority to rectify abuses and heresies.[123] Thus, in 1535, Henry executed Carthusian monks John Fisher and Sir Thomas More for denying his supremacy.[124] Meanwhile, between 1535 and 1536, Southwark, English printers assembled and bound an English Bible dedicated to Henry VIII by Coverdale, who had collected, written, and translated it abroad in Germany.[125] On Oct. 6, 1536, Tyndale was strangled and then burned on the bonfire.[126]

Charles V and Francis I (1515–1547) fought from 1536 to 1538[127] as the Holy Empire defended French advances in Italy. Between 1536 and 1537, everyone who was anyone in Zurich talked about a new French theologian, John Calvin, who had recently published an exposition on Christian doctrine.[128] On

Oct. 12, 1537, Henry VIII's third wife, Queen Jane Seymour, bore Henry a son named Edward VI, who was baptized by his godfather Cranmer.[129] The Queen caught puerperal fever and died twelve days later.[130]

The first edition of the Great Bible was known as Cromwell's Bible after Thomas Cromwell, Secretary of State, became the first authorized English Bible in 1538–1539.[131] Archbishop Cranmer revised, edited, and wrote the preface in Coverdale's Bible, known as Cranmer's, and the second edition of the Great Bible in April 1540. The crown published two additional revised editions during the same year and ordered its purchase by clergy so that a copy would be chained inside each church.[132] Unbound copies sold for ten shillings, while bound editions sold for twelve shillings.[133] Much of Catholic England recoiled in dread at the vernacular readings.[134] As crowds gathered around people who could read the Bible, people started to argue about religion and the need for clergy and judges.[135]

On Sept. 27, 1540, Pope Paul III approved a new military order, the Society of Jesus, led by Ignatius of Loyola, to defend the Venetian Republic from the Turks. His Jesuits spent two years as novices before vowing poverty, chastity, and obedience, followed by ten years studying philosophy, theology, and ministry. Subsequently, they swore allegiance to the pope.[136] Good Jesuit soldiers obeyed without thought. Serving God is always justified by any means. Jesuits founded European schools and universities, committed to missionary work, and to stop Protestantism.[137]

Intending to force governments to conform with God's law,[138] the leaders of Geneva approved Calvin's Ecclesiastical Ordinances, empowering pastors and twelve lay elders to enforce the law in 1541,[139] In July 1542, Pope Paul III introduced the Roman Inquisition to impede the rise of Protestantism.[140] Polish astronomer Nicolaus Copernicus (1473-1543) presented evidence that the sun is the center of the universe due to the earth revolving around the sun defying Aristotelian physics, astronomical observation, theories of knowledge, and Scriptural interpretation in his six books *On the Revolutions of the Heavenly Spheres*.[141] His heliocentric model still matched ancient Greek Ptolemy's circles spinning within circles. However, he removed Ptolemy's abstract points in space where an observer might witness uniform planetary motion and placed Mercury and Venus nearer to the sun than the Earth. He proposed that the Earth spun on its axis as it circled the sun.[142] Meanwhile, Luther's complete German translation of the Bible became available in 1543.[143]

Henry VIII's Oct. 1, 1543 edict forbade all public Bible reading in any assembly or church unless authorized by the king. Violators would spend one hundred months in prison. Henry outlawed private reading by both genders of the lower classes. Only the upper class could read the Bible in houses, gardens, and orchards.[144]

Luther's 1544 treatise, "Short Confession on the Holy Sacrament" viciously assaulted Schwenkfeld's Sacramentarians labeling them as "blasphemers, soul-murderers, and bedeviled all over." God judged Zwingli's death as he turned hypocritical professing the belief in the "salvation of pious heathen." He criticized Melanchthon's and Brucer's 1543 reformation of Cologne's omission of Luther's precepts on communion might "aid or comfort" the Sacramentarians.[145]

Cranmer's 1547 *Book of Homilies* forced the clergy to preach Reformed doctrine. He released the first *Book of Common Prayer* in 1549.[146] Although Luther died in 1546, in 1549, Calvin and others from South Germany signed the Zurich Consensus, claiming that the different views on communion should not divide Protestantism.[147]

In 1549, Portuguese King John III (1502-1557) invested in transporting over a thousand colonists under governor-general Martin Alfonso de Sousa to develop slave-driven sugar plantations in Brazil.[148] From then on, Europe profited from sales of New Guinea slavers, licenses authorizing the transaction, which were eventually sold as stock, money from the plantation and mine owners on receipt of their property, and the sales in Europe from the goods shipped from the Americas.[149]

Cranmer published the Forty-two Articles outlining the Protestant faith just before Edward VI died in 1553.[150] That year, English Protestant refugees hastily evacuated the reign of Bloody Mary. Many found shelter in Geneva, Switzerland, where French scholars labored over a French translation of the Bible.[151]

As Pope Paul IV began his reign in 1555, the Roman Inquisition shifted into a "witch-hunt mentality."[152] Mary burned sixty-seven protestants, including Cranmer, despite his recantation.[153] The 1555 Peace of Augsburg recognized Lutheranism legally holding equal rights to Catholicism and which territories within the Holy Empire depended on the whims of each prince, bringing on sixty-three years of peace in Germany.[154] Ruling members of the Diet had the right to require their subjects to follow their version of religion or emigrate.[155] Heretics could now own land,[156] but only if they were Lutheran.[157] Most Utraquists became Lutherans.[158]

In 1556, Jesuits operated seventy-four colleges on three continents.[159] Concurrently, Philip II of Spain issued an edict, continuing Charles V's edict outlawing Protestant books, sects, and preaching in the Spanish-owned Netherlands enforced by the Spanish Inquisition on the increasing Protestant population.[160]

In 1557, Calvin's brother-in-law, English Puritan William Whittingham translated a new version of the English New Testament. In 1558, many English refugees returned to England upon the execution of Queen Mary Tudor.[161] In 1559, Calvin opened the Genevan Academy, spreading Calvinism to the British Isles and the rest of Europe.[162] Many princes embracing Calvinism in the Holy Empire, including the once-Lutheran Brandenburg and Palatine, pointed to the Peace of Augsburg as their precedent.[163] Under Edward VI, Cranmer reduced the hours of prayer to two since the Church of England now had only two services. Congregations now read The Lord's Prayer and scriptural lessons in English; everything else was in Latin. Lessons read on Sundays started in 1559.[164]

---

1. "Bristol and the Transatlantic Traffic in Enslaved Africans," (British Museums Collections, nd.), acessed August 8, 2024. https://collections.bristolmuseums.org.uk/stories/transatlantic-traffic-enslaved-africans/.

2. Basil Davidson, *The African Slave Trade Precolonial History 1450-1850* (Boston, MA; Toronto: Atlantic Monthly Press Book Little Brown and Company, 1961), 22.

3. Samuel Eliot Morison, *The European Discovery of America: The Southern Voyages A. D. 1492-1616* (Oxford, NY: Oxford University Press, 1974), 4-5.

4. Michael C Meyer and William H.Breezley ed., *The Oxford History of Mexico* (New York, NY: OxfordUniversity Press, 2000), 32.

5. "Thomas à Kempis Writes 'The Imitation of Christ,' One of the Most Widely Published of Religious Texts : History of Information," accessed June 29, 2023, https://www.historyofinformation.com/detail.php?id=3235.

6. Thomas à Kempis, *The Imitation of Christ Translated from Latin to Modern English*, trans. Aloysius Croft and Harold Bolton (Oak Harbor, WA: Logos Research Systems, 1996), v. Logos.

7. Harrison and Sullivan, *A Short History of Western Civilization*, 312.

8. Kempis. *The Imitation of Christ*, v.

9. Clouse, *The Church from Age to Age*, 425.

10. "Thomas à Kempis Writes 'The Imitation of Christ,' One of the Most Widely Published of Religious Texts: History of Information."

11. Kempis. *The Imitation of Christ*, v.

12. Harrison and Sullivan, *A Short History of Western Civilization*, 312.

13. Davidson, *The African Slave Trade Precolonial History 1450-1850*, 22-23.

14. Paul Johnson, *A History of the American People* (New York, NY: HarperCollins Publishing, 1997), 4-5.

15. Paul Johnson, *A History of the American People*, 5.

16. Meyer and Breezley, *The Oxford History of Mexico*, 32.

17. Johnson, *A History of the American People*, 5.

18. Gies, and Gies, *Cathedral, Forge, and Waterwheel Technology and Invention in the Middle Ages*, 241.

19. Ibid., 241.

20. Ibid., 245.

21. Hale, *The Civilization of Europe in the Renaissance*, 133.

22. Time-Life Books, *What Life Was Like in the Age of Chivalry Medieval Europe AD 800–1500*, 31.

23. "The Free Dictionary by Falax," Windows 10 (Feasterville, PA: Farlex, 2023), accessed April 7, 2023, thefreedictionary.com/confraernity.

24. "History of the Czech Republic | Embassy of the Czech Republic in Tehran."

25. Aries and Duby, *A History of Private Life Revelations of the Medieval World*, 612.

26. Thornton, *English Spirituality*, 142.

27. Aries and Duby, *A History of Private Life Revelations of the Medieval World*, 622.

28. Hale, *The Civilization of Europe in the Renaissance*, 472.

29. Woodbridge and James, *Church History Volume Two From Pre-Reformation to the Present Day*, 204–05.

30. Gies, and Gies, *Cathedral, Forge, and Waterwheel Technology and Invention in the Middle Ages*, 245.

31. Tuchman, *Bible and Sword*, 93.

32. Meyer and Breezley, *The Oxford History of Mexico*, 29.

33. Woodbridge and James, *Church History Volume Two From Pre-Reformation to the Present Day*, 98.

34. Isaac Samuel, "The Kingdom of Kongo and the Portuguese: diplomacy, trade, warfare and early Afro-European interactions (1483- 1670)" (African History Extra, 2022), https://www.africanhistoryextra.com/p/the-kingdom-of-kongo-and-the-portuguese.

35. "Crucifix from the Kingdom of Kongo," *Campus Crucifixes* (RaclinMuseum of Art, University of Notre Dame, 1980), https://campuscrucifixes.nd.edu/campus-crucifixes/crucifix-from-the-kingdom-of-kongo/.

36. Davidson, *The African Slave Trade Precolonial History 1450-1850*, 121.

37. Samuel, "The Kingdom of Kongo and the Portuguese: diplomacy, trade, warfare and early Afro-Europeaninteractions (1483-1670)."

38. "Kongo crucifix (N 20196,)"(Tribal Art, Digital Consult, 2024), https://www.tribal-art-gallery.com/tribal-art/Usual-items-tribal-art/Kongo-crucifix/20196.

39. Davidson, *The African Slave Trade Precolonial History 1450-1850*, 121.

40. Samuel, "The Kingdom of Kongo and the Portuguese: diplomacy, trade, warfare and early Afro-European interactions (1483-1670)."

41. Hale, *The Civilization of Europe in the Renaissance*, 472.

42. Meyer and Breezley, *The Oxford History of Mexico*, 29.

43. Gies, and Gies, *Cathedral, Forge, and Waterwheel Technology and Invention in the Middle Ages*, 246.

44. "History of the Holy Roman Empire."

45. Kilsdonk, "The Thirty Years War(s)," 14.

46. Ibid., 15.

47. Ibid., 14.

48. "History of the Holy Roman Empire."

49. Hale, *The Civilization of Europe in the Renaissance*, 472.

50. "Erasmus Circle in England (Act. 1499–1521)," *Oxford Dictionary of National Biography*, accessed July 4, 2023, https://doi.org/10.1093/ref:odnb/96813.

51. Woodbridge and James, *Church History Volume Two From Pre-Reformation to the Present Day*, 98.

52. Hale, *The Civilization of Europe in the Renaissance*, 472.

53. Gies, and Gies, *Cathedral, Forge, and Waterwheel Technology and Invention in the Middle Ages*, 246.

54. "Erasmus Circle in England (Act. 1499–1521)."

55. Cross and Livingstone, "Gertrude, St. 'the Great,'" 674.

56. "Erasmus Circle in England (Act. 1499–1521)."

57. Woodbridge and James, *Church History Volume Two From Pre-Reformation to the Present Day*, 152.

58. Davidson, *The African Slave Trade Precolonial History 1450-1850*, 121.

59. "Erasmus Circle in England (Act. 1499–1521)."

60. "The History of the Welsh Dragon—Symbol of Wales."

61. "Erasmus Circle in England (Act. 1499–1521)."

62. Davidson, *The African Slave Trade Precolonial History 1450-1850*, 46-48.

63. Woodbridge and James, *Church History Volume Two From Pre-Reformation to the Present Day*, 152.

64. Gonzalez, *The Story of Christianity Volume II The Reformation to the Present Day*, 57–8.

65. Woodbridge and James, *Church History Volume Two From Pre-Reformation to the Present Day*, 152.

66. "History of the Holy Roman Empire."

67. Woodbridge and James, *Church History Volume Two From Pre-Reformation to the Present Day*, 152.

68. Ibid., 98.

69. William P. Haugaard, "The Bible in the Anglican Reformation," *Anglicanism and the Bible*, The Anglican Studies Series (Wilton, CT: Morehouse Pub Co, 1984), 30. PDF.

70. "History of the Czech Republic | Embassy of the Czech Republic in Tehran."

71. "History of the Holy Roman Empire."

72. Woodbridge and James, *Church History Volume Two From Pre-Reformation to the Present Day*, 114–115.

73. "History of the Holy Roman Empire."

74. Davidson, *The African Slave Trade Precolonial History 1450-1850*, 126.

75. Clouse, *The Church from Age to Age*, 432.

76. Woodbridge and James, *Church History Volume Two From Pre-Reformation to the Present Day*, 153.

77. Ibid., 129.

78. Ibid., 98.

79. Gonzalez, *The Story of Christianity Volume II The Reformation to the Present Day*, 57.

80. Woodbridge and James, *Church History Volume Two From Pre-Reformation to the Present Day*, 150.

81. Haugaard, "The Bible in the Anglican Reformation," 30.

82. Walker, *A History of the Christian Church*, 358.

83. Hale, *The Civilization of Europe in the Renaissance*, 472.

84. Meyer and Breezley, *The Oxford History of Mexico*, 113.

85. Davidson, *The African Slave Trade Precolonial History 1450-1850*, 59; Johnson, *A History of the American People*, 9.

86. Woodbridge and James, *Church History Volume Two From Pre-Reformation to the Present Day*, 128.

87. "Martin Luther, translator of the Bible," *Musee protestant*, https://museeprotestant.org/en/notice/martin-luther-translator-of-the-bible/.

88. Mary Jane Haemig, "Luther on Translating the Bible," *Word & Word*, Vol. 31, num. 3, Summer 2011 (Luther Seminary: Faculty Productions), 255–262, 260, accessed on February 2, 2024, https://digitalcommons.luthersem.edu/cgi/viewcontent.cgi?article=1094&context=faculty_articles

89. Ibid., 261.

90. Woodbridge and James, *Church History Volume Two From Pre-Reformation to the Present Day,* 129.

91. Kilsdonk, "The Thirty Years War(s)," 15.

92. "History of the Holy Roman Empire."

93. Peter J. Gurry "The Life and Legacy of William Tyndale," *Text&Canon Institute,* May 3, 2022 (AZ: Pheonix Seminary). https://textandcanon.org/the-life-and-legacy-of-william-tyndale/.

94. Clouse, *The Church from Age to Age,* 440.

95. "The Schwenkfelder Story," (Schwenkfelder Library and Heritage Center), https://www.schwenkfelder.org/the-schwenkfelder-story.

96. Philip Schaff, *The Creeds of Christendom, with a History and Critical Notes: The History of Creeds,* Vol. 1 (New York: Harper & Brothers, Publishers, 1878), 866, Logos.

97. Hodge, Charles. *Systematic Theology*. Vol. 1 (Oak Harbor, WA: LogosResearch Systems, Inc., 1997), 83. Logos.

98. Philip Schaff, *The Creeds of Christendom, with a History and Critical Notes: The History of Creeds,* Vol. 8 (New York: Harper & Brothers, Publishers,1878), 80, Logos.

99. Gurry, "The Life and Legacy of William Tyndale."

100. "William Tyndale: the most dangerous man in Tudor England," *Anglican Focus*, Friday 1 October 2011, accessed February 3, 2024, https://anglicanfocus.org.au/2021/10/01/william-tyndale-the-most-dangerous-man-in-tudor-england/

101. Clouse, *The Church from Age to Age*, 440.

102. "William Tyndale: the most dangerous man in Tudor England."

103. Haugaard, "The Bible in the Anglican Reformation," 34.

104. MacGregor, *The Bible in the Making*, 119.

105. "History of the Czech Republic: Embassy of the Czech Republic in Tehran."

106. Haugaard, "The Bible in the Anglican Reformation," 39.

107. Meyer and Breezley, *The Oxford History of Mexico*, 24.

108. Haugaard, "The Bible in the Anglican Reformation," 39.

109. "The SchwenkfelderStory."

110. Ibid., 34.

111. MacGregor, *The Bible in the Making*, 119.

112. "Dwarfing of Italy, 1494–1527: Hapsburg-Valios Wars."

113. J. H. Merle d' Aubigne, *The Reformation in England Volume Two*, trans. H. White M. A. (London, England: Carlise, PA: The Banner of Truth Trust, 1972), 355.

114. Johnson, *A History of the American People*, 8.

115. Tuchman, *Bible and Sword*, 95.

116. "Martin Luther, translator of the Bible."

117. Tuchman, *Bible and Sword*, 93.

118. Haemig, "Luther on Translating the Bible," 255–256.

119. MacGregor, *The Bible in the Making*, 120.

120. Gonzalez, *The Story of Christianity Volume II The Reformation to the Present Day*, 90.

121. Gurry, "The Life and Legacy of William Tyndale,"; "William Tyndale: the most dangerous man in Tudor England."

122. Tuchman, *Bible and Sword*, 96.

123. Walker, *A History of the Christian Church*, 359.

124. Ibid., 359–60.

125. Haugaard, "The Bible in the Anglican Reformation," 40, 39.

126. "William Tyndale: the most dangerous man in Tudor England."

127. Walker, *A History of the Christian Church*, 361.

128. Aubigne, *The Reformation in England Volume Two*, 355.

129. Ibid., 353–54.

130. Ibid., 354.

131. Tuchman, *Bible and Sword*, 128.

132. Geddes MacGregor, *The Bible in the Making*, 128.

133. Ibid.,129.

134. Tuchman, *Bible and Sword*, 96-97.

135. Geddes MacGregor, *The Bible in the Making*, 131.

136. Woodbridge and James, *Church History Volume Two From Pre-Reformation to the Present Day*, 207.

137. Ibid., 208.

138. Gonzalez, *The Story of Christianity Volume II The Reformation to the Present Day*, 86.

139. Ibid., 82–83.

140. Woodbridge and James, *Church History Volume Two From Pre-Reformation to the Present Day*, 205.

141. Ibid., 339.

142. Curt Suplee, *Milestones of Science* (Washington D. C.: National Geographic, 20000), 60.

143. Woodbridge and James, *Church History Volume Two From Pre-Reformation to the Present Day*, 129.

144. Geddes MacGregor, *The Bible in the Making*, 132.

145. Philip Schaff, *The Creeds of Christendom, with a History and Critical Notes: The History of Creeds*, Vol. 7 (New York: Harper & Brothers, Publishers,1878), 654–655. Logos.

146. Mark Galli and Ted Olsen. "Martyrs: Thomas Cranmer, Reform and Reversals," *131 Christians Everyone Should Know* (Nashville, TN: Broadman & Holman Publishers, 2000), 373. Logos.

147. Gonzalez, *The Story of Christianity Volume II The Reformation to the Present Day*, 84.

148. Johnson, *A History of the American People*, 9.

149. Davidson, *The African Slave Trade Precolonial History 1450-1850*, 48, 51.

150. Bray, *Anglicanism: A Reformed Catholic Tradition*, 15.

151. MacGregor, *The Bible in the Making*, 132.

152. Woodbridge and James, *Church History Volume Two From Pre-Reformation to the Present Day*, 205.

153. Tuchman, *Bible and Sword*, 99.

154. Peter Wilson, "The 30 Years' War (1618–48) and the Second Defenestration of Prague," (2018), accessed July 8, 2023. https://www.gresham.ac.uk/watch-now/30-years-war-1618–48-and-second-defenestration-prague, 3.

155. From the Reformation to the Thirty Years War (1500–1648)." https://ghdi.ghi-dc.org/sub_document.cfm?document_id=4501, 3.

156. Kilsdonk, "The Thirty Years War(s)," 15.

157. "Holy-Roman-Empire-1250-Map-1.Jpg (1561×1972)."

158. Clouse, *The Church from Age to Age*, 424.

159. Woodbridge and James, *Church History Volume Two From Pre-Reformation to the Present Day*, 208.

160. Joshua J. Mark, "Eighty Years' War," *World History Encyclopedia*, https://www.worldhistory.org/Eighty_Years'_War/.

161. MacGregor, *The Bible in the Making*, 133.

162. Gonzalez, *The Story of Christianity Volume II The Reformation to the Present Day*, 85.

163. Kilsdonk, "The Thirty Years War(s)," 15.

164. J. H. Maude, The History of the Book of Common Prayer, ed. Leighton Pullan (London; Rivingtons: Oxford Church Text Books, 1900), 73. Logos.

14

Power Wealth War and Seeds of Toleration

Fueling the Moravian Revival

In April 1560, the fruit of the Protestant English exiles under Whittingham blossomed into the first publication of the Geneva Bible. This edition featured biblical text divided into numbered verses. It was smaller than other editions.[1] Scholarship rivaled the Great Bible.[2] The Hebrew translation of the Old Testament was closer to the original manuscripts.[3] Scotland abolished the papacy and required every household with enough income to purchase a copy.[4]

A hundred-year cold spell began in 1560, producing shorter crop growing seasons. The average human height declined an inch.[5] The Holy Roman Empire's "Germany" sat in Europe's center. The emperor reigned over princes and landowning nobility. His lands included Germany and extended from large parts of Poland, the Czech Republic, Austria, and chunks of Hungary.[6] Bohemia's agriculture and mines paid a vast portion of the Imperial Empire's bills.[7] Meanwhile, the king of Bohemia's four states, Lusatia, Moravia, and Silesia, boasted of their local capital, local laws, and national assembly.[8] The Bohemian Diet in Prague limited voting to the 1,400 landowners, but the money of burgher and peasant representatives influenced decisions. Nobles attended Lutheran services along with the residents who were not Calvinists. Most peasants went to mass.[9] Tycho Brahe (1546-1601) watched the partial 1560 solar eclipse. King Fredrick II of Denmark financed the building of two private observatories.[10] Jesuits obtained permission to settle in Prague in 1561.[11]

The 1563's Thirty-Nine Articles[12] restored bread and wine served to the laity during Communion in England.[13]

In 1564, Rome created a list of banned books listed in the Tridentine Index to avoid if one prized their body and soul. Publication required either government or ecclesiastical permission.[14] The House of Orange oversaw the Protestant Dutch and Flemish uprisings against Spanish rule. Duke Alva of Spain quelled the initial riots in 1566.[15] In 1567, Presbyterian Scotland crowned James I king.[16] By 1567, the Spanish Inquisition executed thousands in the Netherlands.[17] Scientist Thomas Digges envisioned the universe stretching out into infinity.[18]

The 1568 unauthorized Geneva Bible became a favorite edition in English homes.[19] The Dutch Revolt against Spain from 1568–1609 ignited the Eighty Years' War that founded the Dutch Republic[20] and was fought in seventeen providences of Spain and the Netherlands.[21] The 1572 Archbishop of Canterbury, Matthew Parker, published *De*

Antiquitate Britannicae Ecclesiae, contending ancient Irish and Welsh Celtic roots fashioned the Church of England independent and unique from the Roman Catholic Church.[22] The church maintained the authority to reform itself.[23]

The Bohemian Brethren (Unitas Fratrum), the Utraquists, and Lutheran Estates signed Bohemia king Maximilian II's "The Bohemian Confession of 1575." Calvinists added their names to the confession afterward.[24]

Rudolf II succeeded Holy Roman Emperor Maximilian II in 1576. He favored classical Greek philosophy over Christianity and resided in a secluded location in Bohemia.[25] After he left Venice and settled in Prague, Bohemia blossomed into a predominant European cultural center.[26] Alva wiped out a thousand houses and eight thousand people in Antwerp, defeated the Flemish, and reinstated Belgium to Spanish rule.[27] In 1577, Tycho witnessed a supernova and studied a comet. He expected the comet to be in the imperfect realm between Earth and the moon, just as Aristotle had taught. It was the sole place where such phenomena could occur. He measured the comet to be much farther away and heading through sections of space that Ptolemy and Copernicus assured contained solid crystal-like spheres. The sphere did not exist. Tycho lashed out at Fredrick II and gained employment as the imperial mathematician for Rudolf II in Prague.[28]

Charles V's son Philip II of Spain forbade The Dutch from shipping the spices gained from the Portuguese spice monopoly from Lisbon to the rest of Europe when he succeeded to the Portuguese throne in 1580.[29]

In 1581, Church of England priest Richard Hooker preached to crowds at Paul's Cross outside St. Paul's Cathedral, London, which included members of the Queen's court.[30] In 1585, Queen Elizabeth appointed Hooker over Puritan Walter Travers as the vicar to the legal profession, Master of the Temple centered in Inns of Court. Hooker preached that God's promise may differ from one's perception, and even some "Roman Catholics may be saved."[31] God willed salvation for all, yet God also willed that people live according to the grace that God had offered[32] during the Temple's morning service. Travers preached Presbyterian predestination and tore apart Hooker's morning sermon at the Temple's afternoon services every Sunday.[33] Meanwhile, England sent an army of six thousand to Holland to aid in their clash against Spain.[34]

In March 1586, the Archbishop, backed by the Privy Council,[35] terminated the Temple Sunday controversy by charging Travers with unlawful debate on religion contrary to statute and preaching on defective orders as his Presbyterian ordination was held in Antwerp. Hooker began *Of the Laws of Ecclesiastical Polity* on the dangers of Puritanism undermining *The Book of Common Prayer* and the Church of England[36] because *The Book of Common Prayer's* liturgy and sacraments formed the basis of Anglican theological understanding.[37] The ordained took responsibility for preaching God's Word, administrating sacraments, and accepting Christ as one's Lord and Savior as learned from the past.[38] One's participation in Christ defied a logical understanding but is a coherent personal experience transmitted through Scripture and the sacraments, maintaining individuality within the community.[39]

The bishop of London and the Archbishop of Canterbury attempted to ensure political and religious orthodoxy by licensing books.[40] London printing presses boasted of turning out two hundred fifty sheets an hour. Printers and bookshops filled St. Paul's Cathedral's churchyard in London. The church cleared the burial chapel's underground vault of bones and two privies to expand retail space for book merchants.[41] Traveling vendors hawked booklets, chapbooks, and pamphlets at fairs and markets. Officials suspected they dealt in papist works from secret Catholic presses and bootleg printing houses.[42]

The Bohemian Utraquists, who had not embraced Lutheranism, renounced their Hussite traditions in 1587.[43] The English Army failed in the Netherlands against Spain during the same year.[44] Most of Europe accepted the Gregorian calendar based on the season, but England continued to base their calendar on the vernal equinox.[45]

In 1588, Parliament outlawed Catholic priests.[46] Johannes Kepler began his Lutheran seminary studies at the German University of Tubingen. Kepler's math professor, a famous astronomer Michael Maestlin (1550-1631) lent Kepler his annotated copy of Six Books Concerning the Revolutions of Heavenly Orbs. Kepler envisioned the Trinity as visible by the world's shape of a geometric sphere. The Earth's center symbolized God. The Earth's circumference demonstrated God's son Christ, and intervening space demonstrated the Holy Spirit.[47] English volunteers and mercenaries joined Maurice of Nassau, who began his first ten-year victory streak in the Netherlands as Captain and Admiral General in 1590.[48] In 1591, Hooker resigned from the Temple to focus on his writing.[49]

The London bishop and the Canterbury Archbishop issued over three thousand new book titles from 1593 to 1603.[50] The year Bohemian Utraquists reconciled with the Catholic Church,[51] Hooker published his first four books of *Laws* in March 1593.[52] Later, Hooker published his fifth law book, which is as long as his first four books, in 1597.[53] In the Netherlands, Maurice of Nassau secured Holland from Spanish troops by 1600,[54] the year Hooker died.[55] Answering Tycho's invitation, Kepler joined his court at Castle Benarky near Prague.[56] Tycho mathematically eliminated Kepler's hypothesis of an elliptical path and Copernicus' revolving planet by theoretically placing the Earth back in the center with the sun and the moon revolving around it, while everything else in space circled the sun.[57] Kepler succeeded him upon his death as imperial mathematician to Rudolf II. Tycho's astronomical observations became a crucial source allowing Kepler to back up his solar hypothesis with data.[58]

On March 24, 1603, Queen Elizabeth died in her sleep after a forty-four-year reign. Puritans interrupted the royal caravan to present James I with the "Millenary Petition," signed by a thousand Puritans. They hoped their new king would abolish the bowing in the name of Jesus, exchanging rings at marriage, the sign of the cross during baptism, wearing surplices, and authorizing shorter services with less music.[59]

In 1603, the beloved Amsterdam preacher Jacob Arminius (1560–1609), fiercely debated Professor Franciscus Gomarus (1563–1641) over issues of Scripture.[60] In a battle to define predestination, Arminius insisted that God's offer of grace was universal and that everyone held the autonomy to respond to God in faith. Following Calvin's doctrine, Gomarus maintained that God was the author of all things, including sin.[61] Faith resulted from predestination, and that God determined one's faith.[62]

The year the Catholic Church authorized the cult of St. Gertrude,[63] King James addressed the Puritan concerns in January 1604's Hampton Court Conference by siding with episcopacy. He threatened to drive out the Puritans if they refused to conform to the Church of England. He authorized a new Bible.[64] The King James version would be true to England's previous versions written by Cambridge, Oxford, and Westminster committees.[65] Over one-third of the new Bible retained the previous work of Tyndale.[66] In 1605, Kepler proved the planet Mars travels around the sun in an elliptical orbit.[67]

While William Shakespeare wrote *Anthony and Cleopatra* in 1606, three ships financed by the London Company sailed to the West Indies. In April 1607, the London Company landed north of Spanish-owned Florida and far south from the lands claimed by the French. They named the river flowing into the Chesapeake Bay, the James River, and their settlement Jamestown, honoring their king.[68]

In Europe, Spanish troops forced Maurice of Nassau from Belgium's coast. Spain began a three-year and seventy-one-year siege on Ostend. Then, in 1607, Spain took the town after losing 60,000 men, while the

Dutch lost 30,000.[69] Dutch optician Hans Lippershey patented the first telescope in 1608.[70]

Bohemian Protestants comfortably comprised most of Bohemia's population.[71] In 1608, Rudolf's brothers, led by Archduke of Austria Matthias von Habsburg,[72] demanded Rudolf's resignation. The three estates consisting of spiritual and temporal lords, knights, and burghers held diets at the Castle of Prague, agreeing that the Bohemian Confession was the same as the Augsburg Confession codified at the General Diet in 1575 signed by both the Unitas Fratrum and the Utraquists parties so they should enjoy complete freedom to practice their religion.[73] They wanted the right to build churches and their own graveyards. Meanwhile, the Catholics could freely partake in communion of "one kind" according to their tradition without altering the Catholic institution.[74] The invasion of Bohemia forced Rudolf to consent to the diet's wishes that communion included both bread and wine.[75]

In 1609, Rudolf issued and Emperor Matthias approved the "Letter of Majesty" written to quell the Jesuit sects,[76] activities of falsely controlling both Protestants in Bohemia and the Holy Roman Empire's estates.[77] Meanwhile, in the Netherlands, Arminius asked the Holland and West Friesland estates to call a national synod to mend the divide caused by his debate. He explained his ideas before the United Netherlands' States General. He died before the synod concluded.[78] Court preacher John Wtenbgaert and University Leyden's theology professor candidate Simon Episcopius rose to leadership in Arminius' Remonstrant party[79] while Spain and the Dutch agreed on a truce.[80] Armed British warships secured the Bermudas allowing them to start their first West India plantations.[81]

In the 1609 edition of the *Atsronomia Nova* Kepler published his 1605 finding proving the planet Mars travels around the sun in an elliptical orbit leading to his first two laws of planetary motion the same year that Galileo built his telescope using two convex lenses. Galileo published his observations of Jupiter's four moons in *Siderius Nuncius* in 1610, which in the Aristotelian cosmos was impossible.[82] Kepler responded by writing two articles on Jupiter's moons and a theoretical paper on telescope optics.[83] Galileo reported mountains on the moon, Venus mimicking the moon as it passed through phases from crescent to full, and spots on the sun. By recording the changing sunspot patterns, he calculated that the sun rotated on its access once every 27 days.[84]

Led by Johan van Oldenbarnevelt (a Dutch statesman), 1610,[85] Arminius' followers published the *Remonstrance* pleading for toleration and stated the five points of Arminianism: Salvation is given to believers who persevere in their faith; "Christ died for all; a person must be born of the Holy Spirit prior to doing good; "grace is not irresistible," and it is possible to fall from grace.[86]

In 1610, six English committees submitted their Authorized King James Version to London for final review.[87] England published the King James Bible.[88] In 1611, the Dutch purchased islands across from the Portuguese Island off the Gold Coast and started constructing strategically located forts masquerading as factories but instead, the Dutch stockpiled supplies to support attacks on the Portuguese.[89] Shakespeare wrote his last play, *The Tempest*,[90] based on a severe thunderstorm at the apex of the Bermuda Triangle five hundred miles east of what would be Charlestown, which left three survivors from the wreck of Jamestown's first supply ship *Sea Venture* who were rescued in 1612.[91] As the King James Bible eloquence standardized English, Shakespeare's mastery of lower- and upper-class English dialect heard in his Stafford theater and its written availability began to unify the language.[92]

The University of Prague faculty condemned Kepler for befriending Calvinist and Catholics and disdained Kepler's reconciling theology.[93] Both he and Galileo contended Augustine's observation that God adjusted the writing in Scripture to the limits of human understanding. The Bible is not a science textbook, yet accurately reports the natural world as perceived by its authors, making it infallible.[94] Emperor Rudolf II died in 1612.[95] The new Holy Roman Emperor kept Kepler as the royal mathematician but relocated him to Linz.[96] Matthias became both Emperor and Bohemian king and named his cousin Ferdinand von Habsburg to succeed him.[97]

The 1616 Spanish Inquisition ruled his theory "philosophically absurd" and heretical. The Catholic Congregation of Index ruled that Copernicus' heliocentric theory of the universe was "contrary to Scripture, and not physically the case." They placed Copernicus' book on the Index "suspended until corrected."⁹⁸ As the elector of Palatine, a territory on the Rhine River, Fredrick could cast two votes for the emperor. Ferdinand II was elected king of Bohemia on June 5, 1617.⁹⁹

Dutch Remonstrant historian and founder of international law, Hugo Grotius, published a 1617 paper challenging Anselm's view that Christ's death satisfied the injured honor of God and the Calvinist view that Christ's sacrifice was *sufficient* for all but efficient only for the elect. Grotius answered, "Why, if Jesus died for the sins of all," as explained by the Arminians, "then why is everyone not saved?" He answered, "Christ's death is a divine tribute to the broken law. God may offer pardon to all who will receive it on such terms as He chooses, for example, on the condition of faith and repentance."¹⁰⁰

Jesuits preserving the Catholic faith in Bavaria and Habsburg ignited southern Europe's Catholic and northern Protestant European states¹⁰¹ and publicized that agreements with heretics were meaningless. Catholic fanatics were promoted as regents, while Protestant estate leader Count Heinrich Matthias von Thurn visited Vienna, complaining that they violated the guarantee allowing the construction of Unitas

Fratrum and the Utraquists churches.[102] Regents ordered the Klostergrab church torn down and terminated further erection of Braunau church. The regents arrested church members when they refused to turn in their keys at another church. The Protestant Estates held a diet in 1617 and requested action from the emperor.[103]

Ferdinand II ordered the demolition of Protestant churches located on Catholic Crown lands in Bohemia during the early spring.[104] On May 23, 1618, King Ferdinand sent two representatives to the Habsburg governing Prague assembly. Thousands attended the rally outside Prague's royal castle, protesting Ferdinand and Emperor Matthias.[105] Bohemian aristocrats forced entry into a Habsburg meeting chamber inside Prague Castle,[106] found the emperor's representatives guilty at a mock trial,[107] and threw two Habsburg councilors, Vilem Slavata and Jaroslav Borita von Martinitz and Secretary Philip Fabricius, out a third-story window.[108] Landing in a heap of horse manure in the courtyard saved all three from the fifty to seventy-foot fall.[109] Catholics hailed their survival as a miracle.[110] The three escaped to Vienna and reported to Ferdinand.[111]

In 1618, England formally entered the slave trade when King James I allocated the Company of Adventurers of London Trading into Parts of Africa, composed of twenty merchants, a monopoly charter. Other companies gained monopolies afterward.[112]

Under Oldenbarnevelt, Holland rejected the Netherlands' 1618 national Synod's authority, contending that each province had the right to decide on religious affairs.[113] Over 100 reformed Calvin German, Swiss, English, and Scottish delegates[114] attended the Synod of Dort from Nov. 13, 1618, to May 9, 1619.[115] Soldiers ejected the three Arminian representatives.[116] Oldenbarnevelt headed the rally for a merchant-backed country, and Grotius backed the Arminian Remonstrant party. Maurice of Nassau led the national party[117] while striving to elevate his family, the House of Orange, to the monarchy sided with the Gomarists.[118] The Calvinists countered the Arminian five points with the "Five Points of Calvinism" or "TULIP," standing for total depravity, unconditional election, limited atonement, irresistible grace, and perseverance of the saints.[119] They adopted the Heidelberg Catechism and the Belgic Confession. Maurice violently arrested, convicted, and beheaded seventy-one-year-old Oldenbarnevelt, overthrowing his "states-rights" party on May 13, 1619, and sentenced Grotius to life imprisonment.[120] The synod deposed over two hundred pastors from their pulpits and exiled and imprisoned eighty others.[121]

Ferdinand II was elected as the Holy Roman Empire in 1619. On May 27, the Bohemian Estates disposed of Ferdinand and elected Fredrick V, Elector Palatine, as the King of Bohemia.[122] Fredrick was a young, good-looking Calvinist Prince, active in the Evangelical Union. Still, in his need, neither the Calvin community nor the Evangelical Union rose to defend him.[123] Meanwhile, Latin scholars digested Kepler's *Harmonies of the World* which bound twenty years of research explaining all harmonics came from dividing polygons. As planets traveled into angles mirroring regular polygons their harmonics shaped the soul.[124]

On Nov. 8, 1620, Ferdinand II combined forces with the German Catholic League,[125] Bavaria, Spain, and the papacy.[126] Their twenty-seven thousand soldiers devastated the Czech's fifteen thousand mercenaries during the Battle of White Mountain. The Imperial forces lost seven hundred while the Czechs lost four thousand.[127] On November 21, the

Pilgrim Fathers, who escaped from England and sailed from Holland on the *Mayflower*, landed in New England.[128]

Ferdinand II reclaimed his position as Holy Roman Emperor. He seized the Protestant lands and proclaimed Bohemia a Habsburg hereditary possession.[129] Jesuits poured into Bavaria triggering 150,000 protestants to flee. Ferdinand conquered Palatine.[130] Fredrick V found shelter in Holland. The Bohemian leaders were publicly executed in 1621.[131] The Habsburgs transferred all official offices to Vienna. Bohemians either converted to Catholicism or emigrated.[132] The Dutch established the West India Company to connect trade from New Guinea to their West India settlement.[133]

That same year, politician Lord High Chancellor Francis Bacon (1561-1629) was convicted of taking bribes under King James and expelled from court. Bacon now had time to write treatises against Aristotle's use of "abstract principles" as a basis for "laws governing the real world." He promoted "deductive reasoning" by observing and documenting enough data, that principles would "emerge by themselves."[134] Kepler published *Epitome of Copernican Astronomy,* a theoretical textbook combining Copernicus' astronomy with his planetary motion and harmonics.[135]

An estimated 4.5 to 8 million died during the Thirty Years War (1618–1648)[136] on Czech, Denmark, and German soil. England and the Netherlands financially supported the Protest Union.[137] Prince Christian IV, Duke of Holstein, King of Denmark (1577–1648) and Norway (1588–1648) cultivated sovereignty and riches by overseeing ships' entry into the Baltic Sea. With England's and Netherlands' funds, Protestant German princes joined Christian's campaign against the Catholic Danes to thwart the new tilt of power gained by Ferdinand.[138]

Alliances changed as each European kingdom's goals evolved.[139] Every German prince sided with some other king in each step of each war, starting with the 1621 Polish-Swedish war[140] over the crown of Sweden,[141] which lasted until 1629, while the Dutch Republic resumed its war with Spain.[142] Spain supported the Catholic League.[143] Poland-Lithuania, the Ottoman Empire, the Dutch Republic, Italian states, and the papacy sent finances and military support. Across the English Channel, King James died in 1625. Charles I succeeded his father to an impoverished English throne due to the influx of gold from America and Parliament's refusal to convene. Charles married Roman Catholic Princess Henrietta-Marie de Bourbon.[144] While Charles I ascended the English throne, William Lauf preached about the King as God's earthly lieutenant at Chapel Royal, Whitehall, in 1625.[145]

Upon the 1625 death of Maurice, Arminian Remonstrants returned to the Netherlands.[146] Competing with the English lucrative West India slave-operated-ventures as they had expanded to St Christopher in 1623, Barbados in 1625, now controlled the Leeward Islands, French battleships secured Guadeloupe settling the island for their initial plantation.[147] Denmark declared war on the Holy Roman Empire from 1625–1629, and Sweden fought the Empire (1630–1648). In 1630, Puritans crossed the Atlantic to establish a community that would serve as an example for their English counterparts.[148]

Anglican Archbishop of Armagh James Ussher (1581-1656) published *A Discourse of the Religion Anciently Professed by the Irish and the British* in 1631 to promote the validity of the Anglican church against

Catholicism. Puritans and Presbyterians criticized English Celtic roots as "popularism" against arranging people according to their social class, which directly conflicted with Anglican elitism.[149]

Despite the Catholic Church's 1632 injunction that prohibited further discussion of the earth's motion, Galileo published *Dialogue on the Two Chief World Systems, Ptolemaic and Copernican* favoring Copernican.[150] King Charles II granted the Charter of Maryland in June 1632 to George Calvet Baron of Baltimore, who had died two months earlier in April. His son Cecelius.[151] gained the charter for the lands between the Chesapeake Bay and the Potomac River as a refuge for Catholics.[152]

England inched toward civil war. In 1633, Charles appointed William Laud as archbishop of Canterbury, who inflamed the Calvinistic Puritans with his High Anglican sacramentalism stressing ceremonies and his theological acceptance of Arminianism.[153] Cambridge, MA, and ordained mystic Jeremy Taylor (1613–1667) won Laud's patronage after Laud heard him preach. Laud appointed Taylor as a Fellow at All Soul's College, Oxford, his personal chaplain, and Charles I's chaplain.[154]

The 1633 Inquisition tried Galileo for violating the 1632 Church ruling. The prosecution charged heresy. Galileo recanted and the Inquisition sentenced him to life in prison, which they lowered to a life sentence of house arrest due to his old age.[155] Between 1633 and 1688, the Cambridge Platonists read and republished widely read Catholic medieval mysticism classics and pseudo-Dionysius the Areopagite (Acts 17:34).[156] They promoted tolerance between the High Anglicans and the Puritans, maintaining the reason arbitrated both naturally derived through human reason and revealed religion through prophets and mystics.[157] In 1634, a Remonstrant Brotherhood was established in the Netherlands.[158]

The Franco-Spanish War from 1635 to 1659, the Portuguese War of Independence from 1640 to 1668, and the Neapolitan Revolt in 1647 prevented Spain's aid to Austria.[159] The Dutch confiscated Elmina Castle from Portugal on the Gold Coast in 1637 with only one last fort to conquer.[160] In the summer of 1637, Charles I ordered the Scotts to perform church services with a new Anglican prayer book. In 1641, Parliament passed an act prohibiting their dissolution without their consent. Under the charge of high treason, Parliament imprisoned Archbishop Laud in the Tower of London for opposing Puritans.[161]

Oliver Cromwell led Puritan Parliament forces in the 1642–1653 English Civil War,[162] which remained separate from the Thirty Years War.[163] Axim, the last Portuguese stronghold along the Gold Coast fell to the Dutch in 1642.[164] The Swedish-Danish War of 1643–1645 coincided with French civil wars and uprisings. France and Sweden started a political-military coalition in the 1640s.[165] Agriculture ceased, causing famine. Universities closed.[166] The German princes continued to fight for and against the Empire.[167] Germans had lost 50% of their population in some places.[168] Emperor Ferdinand III negotiated peace while France and Sweden tasted victory.[169]

Uneducated George Fox set out on a holy quest, hoping to locate the "true church" in 1643 England.[170] He defined a "true church" where Christ's light shined from inside each (Matt. 5:14-16, 2 Cor. 4:6), creating a church void of schism and heresy where no one ever is persecuted (Acts 4:32-33).[171] Parliament tasked an assembly to form a creed acceptable to Calvin Scotts and English Puritans to reform the Church of England at Westminster while the Civil War continued.[172]

In 1644, Jeremy Taylor was imprisoned for supporting Charles I against Parliament. The 1645 Parliament ordered Laud executed. On Taylor's release, Taylor became chaplain to Richard Vaughan, Second Earl of Carbery, and his household at Golden Grove in Wales.[173]

Fox's quest failed, and he abandoned his "true church" quest in 1646.[174] After a mystical conversion where Christ's "Inner Light" reveals revelations, which leads all believers,[175] for God speaks directly to the human soul.[176] He began to preach in 1647: 2 Cor. 13:5, (determine if you choose God as Jesus lives within,) John 1:12, (God gifted all who receive Him "the right to become children of God.") Heb. 12:2, "looking to Jesus, the founder and perfecter of our faith, who for the joy that was set before him endured the cross, despising the shame, and is seated at the right hand of the throne of God," Heb. 11:1–40, (faith conquers all,) and Heb.12:1–3, (lay aside sin because saints surround you.)[177] His followers, the Friends of Truth, abandoned concepts of clergy and rituals and endorsed pacifism.[178] Informally, men, women, and children would sit silently waiting for the Holy Spirit to speak and then share their prayers and revelations.[179] England's archbishops screamed "enthusiasm," defined as "a vain belief in private revelation" and "divine favor," whenever someone insisted that the Holy Spirit gave them certain directions.[180] The Church of England adopted the 1646 Westminister Confession.[181]

The Peace of Westphalia declared a "Christian and Universal Peace... Benefit, Honor, and Advantage each other," bringing peace in the Roman Empire and France,[182] ending the Dutch revolt and the Thirty Years War in 1648.[183] The Austrian Habsburgs retained the position of Holy Roman Emperor and the region they conquered from the Bohemians,[184] but the treaty limited their lands to Austria and Hungary.[185] German princes and the church sought to avoid future wars by becoming devout, compliant followers of God.[186] The Peace of Westphalia granted regions almost complete independent governance[187] and guaranteed a prince's right to determine the religion of his country.[188]

On Jan. 27, 1649, a parliament composed of Independents found Charles I guilty of high treason and executed him in front of the Banqueting House of Whitehall Palace on Jan. 30. On May 19,[189]

Cromwell became Great Britain's Lord Protector under England's first constitution until his death in 1658. His reign tolerated every religion, excluding Catholics. Even Jews would not be prosecuted if caught practicing their faith and were allowed English residency.[190]

Written records show that hotter temperatures increased throughout the world starting in 1650.[191] The judge trying Fox for blasphemy in 1650 admonished Fox for trembling at "the Word of God.' His followers were now dubbed Quakers. He spent six years in and out of prison.[192] The Presbyterian Church of Scotland adopted the Westminster Confession as their standard.[193] From 1657–1658, Taylor oversaw a small congregation of Episcopalians in London.[194]

The Sign of the Ship in St. Paul's Churchyard published a 1658 revised English edition of his earlier 1650–1654 Latin copies of the *Annals of the World* by Archbishop of Armagh and Primate of Ireland Ussher two years after his death. Ussher concluded after he labored through Biblical chronology that Earth was created on October 22, 4004 B. C. according to the Julian calendar, or September 21, using the Gregorian calendar.[195]

English religious freedom ended with Charles II's restoration to the throne in 1660. That year, politician John Milton (1608–1674) hid, fearing that his past loyalty to Cromwell would get him killed. Bedford native John Bunyan (1628–1688), a part-time home-church Puritan preacher, was arrested and jailed for preaching without a license as he disagreed with the Church of England and lacked education. He spent his next twelve years making shoelaces to support his second wife and six children and published fifty-eight books.[196] As the planet began to warm on April 23, 1661, Charles II of England's coronation at Westminster Abbey[197] triggered the European Age of Enlightenment.[198]

In June 1661, Isaac Newton (1643-1727) studied Copernicus, Kepler, and Galileo at Trinity College at Cambridge. French mathematician and scientist Rene Descartes (1596-1650) led philosophers to view nature as a complex, "impersonal inert machine."[199] Descartes' philosophy to doubt everything called "Cartesianism" was to doubt everything except for a subject's existence which led to, "I think, therefore I am." God existed because the mind could not comprehend divine perfection. Thoughts exist due to "adequate cause" and God was the only cause great enough to produce thought. Many French Universities asserted Aristotelianism as the best philosophy suited to Christianity. "Cartesianism" would only lead to heresy. Descartes accepted the Queen of Sweden's invitation for him to relocate to her country's northern province.[200]

Overcoming many years of blindness, by dictating his poem to others, Milton published *Paradise Lost* in 1667.[201] In Germany, Johann Jakob Christoffel von Grimmelshausen published the first German novel, *The Adventures of Simplicissimus*, in 1668. It was about growing up during the Thirty Years War and serving as a soldier. In 1945 public opinion surveys, Germans felt the Thirty Years War had been worse than the Black Death or Nazism after WWII.[202]

William and Mary, King and Queen of England, Ireland, and Scotland ended the London-based Royal African Company's monopoly that propelled Bristol from merchants who profited from West Indian sugar for refining and tobacco that needed processing to Bristol's official entry into England's slave trade in 1698. They sold guns, tools, soap, candles boots, and clothing for slaves in the British colonies. Their ships to

Bristol additionally supplied their local industry with cocoa for chocolates and rum. Only a small number of domestic slaves, musicians, and seamen were sold in Bristol. They shipped African slaves directly to the Caribbean Islands, Virginia, North, and South Carolina.[203] Industry farming, building construction, cooking, and heating during the Middle Ages caused a scarcity of timber for the wood fires fueling paper and gunpowder mills, distilleries, pottery, glass making, cannon foundries, and sugar refineries.[204]

---

1. MacGregor, *The Bible in the Making*, 133.

2. Ibid., 134.

3. Ibid., 133.

4. Ibid., 134.

5. ScienceNow, "Climate Shifts Sparked 17th-Century Conflicts," *Wired*, https://www.wired.com/2011/10/climate-change-war/.

6. Kilsdonk, "The Thirty Years War(s)," 6, 12.

7. "The Defenestration of Prague: May 23, 1618," *Catholic Textbook*, https://www.catholictextbookproject.com/post/the-defenestration-of-prague-may-23-1618.

8. Will and Ariel Durant, *The Story of Civilization: 7 The Age of Reason Begins* (New York, NY: MJF Books, 1961), 541.

9. Hale, *The Civilization of Europe in the Renaissance*, 472.

10. Suplee, *Milestone of Science*, 62.

11. "The Bohemian Religious Peace," 2.

12. Jeremy Thompson, "Creeds and Confessions, Anglicanism," *Lists from Church History*, Faithlife Biblical and Theological Lists (Bellingham, WA: Faithlife, 2022). Logos.

13. Evans and Wright, *The Anglican Tradition: A Handbook of Sources*, 118.

14. Hale, *The Civilization of Europe in the Renaissance*, 472.

15. "The Dutch War of Independence | Military History Matters," https://www.military-history.org/battle-maps/the-dutch-war-of-independence.htm.

16. Woodbridge and James, *Church History Volume Two From Pre-Reformation to the Present Day*, 265.

17. Mark, "Eighty Years' War."

18. Woodbridge and James, *Church History Volume Two From Pre-Reformation to the Present Day*, 338.

19. MacGregor, *The Bible in the Making*, 135.

20. Wilson, "The 30 Years' War (1618–48) and the Second Defenestration of Prague," 1.

21. Mark, "Eighty Years' War."

22. Bernard McGinn, ed., *Celtic Spirituality*, trans., Oliver Davies, The Classics of Western Spirituality (New York; Mahwah, NJ: Paulist Press, 1999), 7.

23. Paul Avis, *The Anglican Understanding of the Church: An Introduction*, 2nd ed. (London: SPCK, 2013), 24. Logos.

24. "From the Reformation to the Thirty Years War (1500–1648)," 1.

25. "History of the Holy Roman Empire."

26. "History of the Czech Republic | Embassy of the Czech Republic in Tehran."

27. "The Dutch War of Independence | Military History Matters."

28. Suplee, *Milestone of Science*, 62.

29. Morison, *The European Discovery of America: The Southern Voyages A. D. 1492-1616*, 333, 728.

30. John E. Booty and Owen C Thomas, William J. Wolf eds., *The Spirit of Anglicanism Hooker, Maurice, Temple* (Wilton, CT: Morehouse-Barlow Co. Inc., 1979), 4.

31. Booty and Thomas, *The Spirit of Anglicanism Hooker, Maurice, Temple*, 5.

32. Ibid., 4.

33. Ibid., 5.

34. "The Dutch War of Independence | Military History Matters."

35. Booty and Thomas, *The Spirit of Anglicanism Hooker, Maurice, Temple*, 5.

36. Ibid., 6.

37. Ibid., 17.

38. Ibid., 41.

39. Ibid., 40.

40. Denise Dersin, ed., *What Life Was Like In The Realm of Elizabeth England AD 1533–1603*, 5th printing (Alexandria, VA: Time-Life Books, 1998), 96.

41. Ibid., 94.

42. Ibid., 96–7.

43. Durant, *The Story of Civilization: 7*, 541.

44. Dersin, *What Life Was Like In The Realm of Elizabeth England AD 1533–1603*, 105.

45. Mattingly, *The Armada*, xv.

46. Dersin, *What Life Was Like In The Realm of Elizabeth England AD 1533–1603*, 105.

47. Robert S. Westman, "Johannes Kepler" (Britannica, 2024), https://www.britannica.com/biography/Johannes-Kepler.

48. "The Dutch War of Independence | Military History Matters."

49. Booty and Thomas, *The Spirit of Anglicanism Hooker, Maurice, Temple*, 6.

50. Dersin, *What Life Was Like In The Realm of Elizabeth England AD 1533–1603*, 96.

51. Durant, *The Story of Civilization: 7 The Age of Reason Begins*, 541.

52. Ibid., 7.

53. Booty and Thomas, *The Spirit of Anglicanism Hooker, Maurice, Temple*, 7.

54. "The Dutch War of Independence | Military History Matters."

55. Booty and Thomas, *The Spirit of Anglicanism Hooker, Maurice, Temple*, 7.

56. Westman, "Johannes Kepler."

57. Suplee, *Milestone of Science*, 62.

58. Westman, "Johannes Kepler."

59. Woodbridge and James, *Church History Volume Two From Pre-Reformation to the Present Day*, 265.

60. Gonzalez, *The Story of Christianity Volume II The Reformation to the Present Day*, 229.

61. Clouse, *The Church from Age to Age*, 531.

62. Gonzalez, *The Story of Christianity Volume II The Reformation to the Present Day*, 230.

63. Cross and Livingstone, "Gertrude, St. 'the Great,'" 674.

64. Woodbridge and James, *Church History Volume Two From Pre-Reformation to the Present Day*, 265–66.

65. McCrum, *The Story of English*, 112.

66. Haugaard, "The Bible in the Anglican Reformation," 32.

67. Westman, "Johannes Kepler."

68. McCrum, *The Story of English*, 106.

69. "The Dutch War of Independence | Military History Matters."

70. Suplee, *Milestone of Science*, 64.

71. Kilsdonk, "The Thirty Years War(s)," 22.

72. "The Defenestration of Prague."

73. "The Bohemian Religious Peace," 1.

74. Ibid., 4.

75. Ibid., 1.

76. Kilsdonk, "The Thirty Years War(s)," 21.

77. Ibid., 22.

78. Clouse, *The Church from Age to Age*, 531

79. Walker, *A History of the Christian Church*, 399.

80. "The Dutch War of Independence | Military History Matters."

81. Davidson, *The African Slave Trade Precolonial History 1450-1850*, 48, 58.

82. Suplee, *Milestone of Science*, 64; Westman, "Johannes Kepler."

83. Westman, "Johannes Kepler."

84. Suplee, *Milestone of Science*, 64.

85. Walker, *A History of the Christian Church*, 400.

86. Clouse, *The Church from Age to Age A History from Galilee to Global Christianity*, 531.

87. McCrum, *The Story of English*, 112.

88. McCrum, The Story of English, 109.

89. Davidson, *The African Slave Trade Precolonial History 1450-1850*, 54.

90. Ibid., 113.

91. Ibid., 109.

92. Ibid, 113, 98, 100–5.

93. Westman, "Johannes Kepler."

94. Woodbridge and James, *Church History Volume Two From Pre-Reformation to the Present Day*, 340.

95. "History of the Holy Roman Empire."

96. Westman, "Johannes Kepler."

97. "Defenestration of Prague of 1618-World History Online."

98. Woodbridge and James, *Church History Volume Two From Pre-Reformation to the Present Day*, 340-341.

99. "Defenestration of Prague of 1618-World History Online."

100. Walker, *A History of the Christian Church*, 401.

101. Igor Radulovic, "The Thirty Years War (5 Greatest Battles)," *The Collector*, November 12, 2021, accessed July 8, 2023, https://www.thecollector.com/thirty-years-war-5-greatest-battles/

102. Kilsdonk, "The Thirty Years War(s)," 22.

103. Ibid., 23.

104. Donald A. Hempsoon III, "Out the Window: Religion, Politics, and a Defenestration in Prague," *Origins*, accessed July 19, 2023, https://origins.osu.edu/milestones/may-2018-out-window-religion-politics-and-defenestration-prague?language_content_entity=en.

105. "Defenestration of Prague of 1618-World History Online."

106. Wilson, "The 30 Years' War (1618–48) and the Second Defenestration of Prague," 1.

107. Hempsoon, "Out the Window."

108. Wilson, "The 30 Years' War (1618–48) and the Second Defenestration of Prague," 1; Hempsoon, "Out the Window;" Radulovic, "The Thirty Years War (5 Greatest Battles)."

109. Hempsoon, "Out the Window."

110. Clouse, *The Church from Age to Age*, 539.

111. Hempsoon, "Out the Window."

112. Davidson, *The African Slave Trade Precolonial History 1450-1850*, 54-55.

113. Walker, *A History of the Christian Church*, 400.

114. Clouse, *The Church from Age to Age*, 532.

115. Walker, *A History of the Christian Church*, 400; Clouse, *The Church from Age to Age*, 532.

116. Woodbridge and James, *Church History Volume Two From Pre-Reformation to the Present Day*, 257.

117. Walker, *A History of the Christian Church*, 400.

118. Clouse, *The Church from Age to Age*, 532.

119. Woodbridge and James, *Church History Volume Two From Pre-Reformation to the Present Day*, 258.

120. Clouse, *The Church from Age to Age*, 532.

121. Woodbridge and James, *Church History Volume Two From Pre-Reformation to the Present Day*, 258.

122. "Defenestration of Prague of 1618-World History Online."

123. Clouse, *The Church from Age to Age*, 539.

124. Westman, "Johannes Kepler."

125. Radulovic, "The Thirty Years War (5 Greatest Battles)."

126. Clouse, *The Church from Age to Age*, 539.

127. Radulovic, "The Thirty Years War (5 Greatest Battles)."

128. Carol Smith and Roddy Smith. *Quicknotes Christian History Guidebook* (Uhrichsville, OH: Barbour Publishing, Inc., 2001), 374.

129. Hempsoon, "Out the Window."

130. Clouse, *The Church from Age to Age*, 539.

131. "Defenestration of Prague of 1618-World History Online."

132. "History of the Czech Republic: Embassy of the Czech Republic in Tehran."

133. Davidson, *The African Slave Trade Precolonial History 1450-1850*, 55.

134. Suplee, *Milestone of Science*, 70.

135. Westman, "Johannes Kepler."

136. Lawrence Mello, "LibGuides: Primary Sources: Wars and Conflicts: Thirty Years War," accessed July 8, 2023, https://libguides.fau.edu/wars-conflicts/thirty-years-war.

137. Radulovic, "The Thirty Years War (5 Greatest Battles)."

138. Clouse, *The Church from Age to Age*, 539.

139. Kilsdonk, "The Thirty Years War(s)," 5.

140. Ibid., 19.

141. Ibid., 5.

142. Wilson, "The 30 Years' War (1618–48) and the Second Defenestration of Prague," 5.

143. Radulovic, "The Thirty Years War (5 Greatest Battles)."

144. Dale T. Irvin and Scott W. Sunquist, *History of the World Christian Movement: Modern Christianity from 1454–1800* (Maryknoll, NY: Orbis Books, 1970), www.maryknollsociety.org, Kindle location, 7458–60. Kindle.

145. Avis, *The Anglican Understanding of the Church: An Introduction*, 32.

146. Walker, *A History of the Christian Church*, 400.

147. Davidson, *The African Slave Trade Precolonial History 1450-1850*, 48, 58.

148. Smith and Smith, *Quicknotes Christian History Guidebook*, 374.

149. McGinn, *Celtic Spirituality*, 8.

150. Woodbridge and James, *Church History Volume Two From Pre-Reformation to the Present Day*, 341.

151. "The Maryland State House," *The Rotunda and the Dome The First Lord Baltimore George Calvert (1578/79–1632)* (Annapolis, MD: Maryland State Archives, 2007), accessed June 17, 2024. https://msa.maryland.gov/msa/mdstatehouse/html/rotunda_gcalvert.html.

152. Ushistory.org, "Maryland—The Catholic Experiment," *U. S. History Online Textbook* (2024), accessed June 17, 2024. https://www.ushistory.org/us/5a.asp.

153. Woodbridge and James, *Church History Volume Two From Pre-Reformation to the Present Day*, 266.

154. Alister E. McGrath, ed. *The SPCK Handbook of Anglican Theologians* (London: SPCK, 1998), 208.

155. "Galileo Galilei," (NASA), accessed August 2, 2024, https://gsfc.nasa.gov.

156. Evelyn Underhill, *The Mystics of the Church* (New York: George H. Doran Company, 1925), 221. Logos.

157. Cross and Livingstone, "Cambridge Platonists."

158. Woodbridge and James, *Church History Volume Two From Pre-Reformation to the Present Day*, 258.

159. Wilson, "The 30 Years' War (1618–48) and the Second Defenestration of Prague," 5.

160. Davidson, *The African Slave Trade Precolonial History 1450-1850*, 54.

161. Irvin and Sunquist, *History of the World Christian Movement: Modern Christianity from 1454–1800*, Kindle location, 7468.

162. Woodbridge and James, *Church History Volume Two From Pre-Reformation to the Present Day*, 268.

163. Wilson, "The 30 Years' War (1618–48) and the Second Defenestration of Prague," 5.

164. Davidson, *The African Slave Trade Precolonial History 1450-1850*, 54.

165. Wilson, "The 30 Years' War (1618–48) and the Second Defenestration of Prague," 5.

166. Woodbridge and James, *Church History Volume Two From Pre-Reformation to the Present Day*, 260.

167. Kilsdonk, "The Thirty Years War(s)," 6.

168. Mello, "LibGuides: Primary Sources: Wars and Conflicts: Thirty Years War."

169. Wilson, "The 30 Years' War (1618–48) and the Second Defenestration of Prague," 5.

170. Nathan P. Feldmeth, "Fox, George," *Pocket Dictionary of Church History: Over 300 Terms Clearly and Concisely Defined*. The IVP Pocket Reference Series (Downers Grove, IL: IVP Academic, 2008), Logos; Kurian, "Fox, George,"; Rusten, "George Fox Begins to Preach."

171. "William Penn, "Chapter 1," *A Brief Account of the Rise and Progress of the People Called Quakers*, transcribed by David Price (London: Harris & Crofield, 1834). e-Sword.

172. Rusten, "Westminister Confession is Completed."

173. McGrath, ed. *The SPCK Handbook of Anglican Theologians*, 208.

174. Feldmeth, "Fox, George."

175. Woodbridge and James, *Church History Volume Two From Pre-Reformation to the Present Day*, 398.

176. Rusten, "George Fox Begins to Preach."

177. Kurian, "Fox, George,"; William Penn, "Sermon."

178. Feldmeth, "Fox, George,"; Kurian, "Fox, George."

179. William Penn, "Chapter 1."

180. Woodbridge and James, *Church History Volume Two From Pre-Reformation to the Present Day*, 397–398.

181. Rusten, "Westminister Confession is Completed."

182. "Avalon Project - Treaty of Westphalia," accessed July 11, 2023, https://avalon.law.yale.edu/17th_century/westphal.asp.

183. Wilson, "The 30 Years' War (1618–48) and the Second Defenestration of Prague," 1.

184. Ibid., 6.

185. "History of the Holy Roman Empire."

186. Wilson, "The 30 Years' War (1618–48) and the Second Defenestration of Prague," 6.

187. "History of the Holy Roman Empire."

188. Woodbridge and James, *Church History Volume Two From Pre-Reformation to the Present Day*, 260.

189. Ibid., 270.

190. Ibid., 269.

191. ScienceNow, "Climate Shifts Sparked 17th-Century Conflicts."

192. Kurian, "Fox, George."

193. Rusten, "Westminister Confession is Completed."

194. McGrath, *The SPCK Handbook of Anglican Theologians*, 208.

195. James Ussher, *The Annals of the World*. Revised and updated by Larry and Marion Pierce (Green Forest AR: Master Books, 2003), 21, 891.

196. Rusten, "1667 Milton Writes Paradise Lost"; "1678 John Bunyan Publishes Pilgrim's Progress,"; "A Tinker's Pilgrimage."

197. Woodbridge and James, *Church History Volume Two From Pre-Reformation to the Present Day*, 271.

198. ScienceNow, "Climate Shifts Sparked 17th-Century Conflicts."

199. Richard S. Westfall, "Isaac Newton English physicist and mathematician" (Britannica, 2024), accessed July 30, 2024, https://www.britannica.com/biography/Isaac-Newton.

200. Gonzalez, *Church History An Essential Guide*, 238-239; Walker, *A History of the Christian Church*, 427.

201. Rusten, "1667 Milton Writes Paradise Lost."

202. Wilson, "The 30 Years' War (1618–48) and the Second Defenestration of Prague," 2.

203. "Bristol and the Transatlantic Traffic in Enslaved Africans."

204. Brenda Ralph Lewis, ed. *Great Civilizations* (Bath, BA; HE, UK: Parragon Publishing, 2003), 56; Gies and Gies, *Cathedral, Forge, and Waterwheel Technology and Invention in the Middle Ages*, 290.

15
Pietism, Moravians, Quakers, Welch, and the Great Awakening
Fueling Revivals

JOHANN ARNDT (1555-1621) HAD preached that "Christianity was more than the forgiveness of Christ but Christ living within."[1] Pietism began as an internal Lutheran renewal of Christian piety.[2] Born and raised in Alsace, Philip Jakob Spencer (1635–1705) studied at the best Protestant Universities, earned his doctorate, and pastored in Frankfurt in 1666, where he started Bible study and devotional groups which he named "colleges of piety"[3] to discuss sermons and devotions for the replenishment of the larger church.[4] Written as a preface for a new collection of sermons by Arndt, Spencer published *Pia Desideria* (1675) outlining his program to develop piety, which became Pietism's fundamental charter.[5] He advocated more use of the Bible, further studied by small groups, an emphasis on laity in ministry, the correlation between life and doctrine, restraint in theological disputes, relatable sermons, and reform in pastoral training to include piety and devotions.[6]

In 1676, Scottish Quaker Robert Barclay (1648–1690) published *An Apology for True Christian Divinity: Being an Explanation and Vindication of the Principle and Doctrines of the People Called Quakers.*

His introduction to Charles II explained that the peaceful Quakers believed according to the Bible and had "no conspiracies against the monarchy."[7] On February 18, 1678, Bunyan published his allegory of Christian life, *Pilgrim's Progress*.[8]

By 1680, Charles II owed Admiral William Penn Sr. money loaned to him during the English-Dutch War. Over three hundred Quakers died since Charles' coordination; thousands remained in prison. In June 1680, Charles signed over land in the colonies to Quaker William Penn. On March 4, 1681, William Penn Jr. and the Quaker founder George Fox named the land after his father.[9] Meanwhile, Puritans continued to leave England in hopes of religious freedom. Among the shiploads, candle-maker, and soap boiler Josiah Franklin settled in Boston with his first wife and seven children to practice their Puritan faith.[10] In 1682, Penn established Pennsylvania to create a society based on religious tolerance.[11]

After he transferred to Dresen in 1686, Spencer met August Hermann Franke (1663–1727).[12] A year later, Franke felt the agonizing conviction of sin and then conversion into living a genuine holy life.[13] Roman Catholic King James II (reigned 1685-1689) tried to reestablish Catholicism in England, which caused the Glorious Revolution of 1689,[14] which led to Parliament's 1689 Toleration Act excluding Catholics and Unitarians.[15]

In 1691, Spencer transferred to Berlin, where he served as a preacher for St. Nicolaus and a church inspector for fourteen years.[16] Lutherans preached "justification by grace alone," while Pietists focused on the Holy Spirit who converts Scripture text into a living power within someone witnessed by an alteration of a human's lack of morals.[17] Amid furious debates and insults against the spread of Pietism from the Wittenberg University theology faculty,[18] Spencer founded the University of Halle in 1694. Spencer appointed Franke to chair Greek and Oriental languages and he evolved into Spencer's successor.[19]

Under Franke, the University of Halle included an orphanage, boarding schools, homes for widows and beggars, a pharmacy, a publishing house, a Latin school, a preparatory school for upper-class students called Paedagogium, and a Biblical institute.[20] George Frideric Handel (1685–1759) was born and raised a Piest in Halle and attended Halle University from 1702 to 1703 while studying law.[21]

Meanwhile, England saw the first factory built near Derby which used an extraordinary silk machine that unreeled the thread from cocoons in 1702.[22] The French Guinea Company obtained the Spanish Assiento and changed the company's name to the Assiento Company. Their contract stipulated a duty tax paid to Spain's King Philip V upon the delivery of 38,000 African slaves or 48,000 to the Spanish West Indies if the Queen Anne's War (1702-1713) between France and England over who would control North America should end.[23]

King of Denmark and Norway Frederick I asked for two of Franke's brightest students to spread Christianity in India in 1707. Bartholomaes Ziegenbalg and Heinrich Plutschau's letters and reports circulated throughout Germany about their successful mission of[20] Tranquebar. Frederick joined with Pietists to form a missions school to train missionaries to work in Lapland and Greenland. Under the leadership of Franke, Halle University trained a worldwide generation of Pietist pastors and missionaries due to their conversion by the Holy Spirit led pious lives.[25]

Unnoticed by the Church of England who sang psalms from the newly revised collection from 1562 by Nahum Tate and Nicholas Brady written in 1696, Isaac Watts published *Hymns and Spiritual Songs* written for and sung by his 1707 Independent Puritan congregation.[26] Abraham Darby (1678-1717) developed a coke-fired furnace creating marketable iron in 1709. His ever-growing larger coal-based furnaces expanded England's paper and gunpowder mills, distilleries, pottery, glass making, cannon foundries, and sugar refineries.[27] England won Queen Anne's War against the French in 1713 and acquired the slave trade to the Spanish colonies.[28]

Ignoring the dismay of Amsterdam's Dutch reformed church officials, Piest Theodore Jacobus Frelinghuysen's fiery sermons ignited a Rariton Valley, New Jersey revival.[29] Solomon Stoddard enjoyed his sixty years overseeing revivals as a Northhamptom Congressional Church minister in the British colony of Massachusetts. His "harvests" blossomed with higher church attendance as he watched a renewed Christian Spirit flow within his community. Twelve-year-old Benjamin Franklin (1706-1790) abandoned his father's Boston candle-making shop for an apprenticeship at his brother James Franklin's Boston publishing house, which he had set up after returning from London the year before. From December 1719 to August 1720 they printed America's second newspaper, the *Boston Gazette*.[30] Stoddard's grandson Johnathon Edwards (1703–1758) graduated with honors from Yale in 1720 and began serving as a New York Presbyterian minister.[31]

In the East German state of Southern Saxony, Nicolaus Ludwig von Zinzendorf's (1700–1760) grandparents and unwed aunt raised Spencer's[32] godson. His grandmother,[33] Baroness Henrietta Catherine von Gersdorf,[34] read the Bible in Hebrew and Greek. He attended Franke's preparatory school[35] Paedagogium in Halle, at age ten until he turned sixteen. He aspired to become a minister but could not because of his nobility. He graduated from the University of Wittenberg in 1721. In Dresden,[36] while employed as legal counsel at King John Ernest of Saxony's court he received his inheritance and bought the Berthelsdorf Estate,[37] seventy miles away. He appointed Johann Andreas Roth to the estate's pastorship.

Zinzendorf married the sister of Count Heinrich, Erdmuth Dorotheia,[38] and allowed the Unity of Brethren refuge[39] on May 27, 1722, in a partially built farmhouse on a swampy hill often used as a gypsy camp. safely outside the nearest village of Berthelsdorf to avoid problems with the lack of certificates proving orthodoxy. Christian David (1690–1722) led[40] the Bohemian and Moravian remains of the Old Moravian Hussite Church and began building the village Herrnhut, "the Lord watch" on Zinzendorf's Berthelsdorf estate on June 8, 1722.[41]

The Massachusetts Assembly imprisoned James Franklin from June 12 to July 2, for insinuating collusion between local Boston officials and pirates in the Franklin brothers' humor and literary newspaper called the *New England Courant*. James hid from authorities after he printed his final edition of the *Courant,* which repeatably mocked local officials and Puritan ministers by January 1723. The Massachusetts Assembly forbade them from printing any content without prior censorship.[42]

About one hundred fifty miles east of Herrnhut, Johann Sebastian Bach composed religious music from 1723 to 1750 in the large city of Leipzig, in East

Saxony.⁴³ After relocating his family, David advertised his "City of David" in every town he visited. To the disillusion of his guests expecting an actual city, only three houses had been built, and David worked on building number four. On May 12, 1724, Count Zinzendorf laid a stone foundation for a school for the sons of nobles.⁴⁴ Lutheran Pietists joined their community.⁴⁵ David continued to journey between Moravia and Saxony. Loud trombones announced each refugee group's arrival in Herrnhut.⁴⁶ The Harpersdorf Schwenkfelders found refuge from burial with neither song, bells nor procession. Their dead received only prayer being buried at night in a cattle path. They too settled at Herrnhut and Berthelsdorf.⁴⁷ Halle's leadership resented each spurt of Herrnhut's growth as Herrnhut was beyond their control. It would lead to yet another religion. Zinzendorf doubted them.⁴⁸

In 1725, at Lincoln College Oxford, rule-stickler, upper-class, twenty-three-year-old, High Church Anglican deacon John Wesley (1703–1791) Jeremy Talyor's *Rules and Exercises for Holy Living* (1650–1658), which stressed pure intentions and complete dedication to God. Wesley began to write his first version of "A Plain Account of Christian Perfection." The next year, he internalized Thomas A. Kempis' *The Imitation of Christ*, requiring transformation of the heart combined with an altered temperament.[49]

As Herrnhut's population diversified into more Protestant religions, tension rose. Poverty replaced loving each other.[50] Zinzendorf limited emigration to Herrnhut due to persecution and Augsburg Confession-abiding refugees and relocated Schwenkfelders to Berthelsdorf.[51] The Moravian refugees wanted their own church, while Zinzendorf and Rothe, his priest serving at Berthelsdorf, desired to incorporate Herrnhut into the Saxon Lutheran State church.[52]

On Aug. 13, 1727, at Herrnhut, Zinzendorf along with some of the Moravians prayed for their community during Communion service. The Holy Spirit responded by surging through the congregation, strengthening prayer, promoting a disciplined lifestyle, and fostering a passion for mission.[53] Based on monastic precepts, they attended a daily worship service and reared the unmarried in childcare centers separated by sex, learning instrumental and vocal music. They divided their community into choirs based on age, sex, marital status, and religious education. Their return to Apostolic Tradition included the kiss of peace, foot washing, and casting of lots.[54]

In New England, Edwards quit his senior tutoring job at Yale after a "personal religious experience" and began serving as a pastor with his grandfather in Northampton Congregational Church.[55]

John Wesley read William Law's *Serious Call* and *Christian Perfection* persuading him that no one could be half-Christian.[56] The Church of England ordained Wesely in 1728. His younger brother Charles (1707–1788) had formed an Oxford Bible study called the "Holy Club" which John joined and led on returning to Oxford in 1729.[57] He began to study the Bible convincing him to "walk as Jesus walked."[58]

Zinzendorf defended himself against Lutheran attacks, claiming he had started a new sect. On August 12, 1729, he published "Notarius-Instrument" signed by the Herrnhut Brethren. Moravian descendants of the ancient Church of the Brethren, recognized by Luther and Calvin, honored the Augsburg Confession. "We acknowledge no public Church of

God except where the pure Word of God is preached, and where the members live as holy children of God."⁵⁹ Zinzendorf visited Universities and sent delegates to England and Europe to organize societies within the Lutheran Church called Christian Fellowship within the National Church.⁶⁰ Count Leopold of Firman and Archbishop of Salzburg in eastern Bavaria, which currently belonged to Austria, flushed out the Salzburgers from his papal state.⁶¹

Inspired by Law's *Christian Perfection*, under Wesely, students vowed to follow the method spelled out in the Bible of self-denial, fasting and good deeds of visiting prisons, ministering to the needy, communion, praying, and Bible reading. Critics dubbed their pious Holy Club; "Methodists."⁶²

Meanwhile, when his grandfather died, Edwards took over the Northampton Congressional Church. Ealy in 1730, Edwards prayed that he too would lead a revival where the Holy Spirit restored his Christian Community.⁶³ Inspired by the Piest preacher Frelinghuysen's success, North New Jersey Presbyterian preachers William and Gilbert Tennent initiated local revivals.⁶⁴

In Herrnhut on January 7, 1731, Zinzendorf proposed that the Moravians abandon their reconstitution and convert to pure Lutheranism. After a heated debate, two slips of paper were placed in a box. The congregation prayed. The paper vote authorizing the church to become Lutheran was 1 Cor. 9:21 to live outside the law to gain those who live outside the law. Zinzendorf's son Christel picked the pro-Moravian vote: 2 Thessalonians (2 Thes.) 2:15, "So then, brothers, stand firm and hold to the traditions that you were taught by us, either by our spoken word or by our letter."[65]

The first Schwenkfelder exiles from Herrnhut and Berthelsdorf swore allegiance to King George II after arriving in Philadelphia, Pennsylvania on September 24, and celebrated their first Thanksgiving the next day.[66]

In Copenhagen, at the coronation of the king of Denmark Christian VI, Zinzendorf received the Order of Danebrog on June 6, 1731, where he met a dark-skinned man from St. Thomas in the Virgin Islands and Eskimos from Greenland. Although the Tubingen Theological Faculty acknowledged Moravians as "good members of the National

Church," the Saxon Government disagreed. Dresen commissioners investigated Herrnhut from January 19 through the 22, 1732. Their report raised alarm among the German public. Zinzendorf harbored the radical group despised by Protestants and Catholics called the Schwenkfelders at Berthelsdorf.[67]

Moravians specialized in helping the black West Indies slaves and preliterate cultures.[68] Almost thirty thousand Salzburg refugees had marched to Augsburg from Bavarian Catholic persecution. The trustees of the Georgia Colony Charter granted the Society for the Propagation of Christian Knowledge's request for lands and to manage donations but had no funds available.[69] Across the Atlantic, Georgia became an official colony.[70] The Church of England sent Samuel Quincy to serve as the first Anglican priest at the Savannah, Georgia settlement.[71]

According to Franklin's *Autobiography Part Two*, (written in 1784) he paid stewardship funds to the sole Philadelphia Presbyterian Meeting or minister in 1732. The minister's visits convinced Franklin that Presbyterians desired respectable Presbyterians instead of cultivating respectable citizens. Reflecting on Philippians 4:8, "Finally, brothers, whatever is true, whatever is honorable, whatever is just, whatever is pure, whatever is lovely, whatever is commendable, if there is any excellence, if there is anything worthy of praise, think about these things." Franklin mused that other than some form of morality he expected more than reading the Bible, attending church respecting preachers, and partaking in communion. Franklin withdrew from attending Presbyterian services. He attempted to attain "moral Perfection."[72]

After consulting many books, Franklin listed twelve virtues he would conquer one at a time.[73] He planned to rid himself of one virtue each week and kept charts of each virtue per page highlighting his faults in a book that he always carried with him. This project would continue for several years.[74] After a Quaker kindly pointed out that Franklin not only always had to be right but often was "overbearing and rather insolent" Franklin added the thirteenth virtue to strive for with the heading "Humility."[75] His list is found in the Appendix.

Henry, the elector and king of Saxony decreed to evict the Schwenkfelders at Berthelsdorf and that the Moravians could remain at Herrnhut "as long as they behaved quietly" on April 4, 1733.[76]

John Kay invented a flying shuttle that guided threads from one side of a loom to the other repeatedly making weaving material faster than possible in hand-done weaving, revolutionizing the textile industry and increasing the demand for coal.[77] Thanks to 10,000 pounds set aside by the May 1733 House of Commons and another 3,000 pounds from private donations to the Georgia Trustees the Salzburg refugees from Augsburg relocated to England on October 21.[78] In Philadelphia, Franklin published his first edition of *Poor Richard's Almanack* on December 19.[79]

The Salzburg refugees left England on January 19, 1734, headed for Charleston, South Carolina. When they landed in March, the Governor of Georgia General Oglethorpe postponed his return trip to England and helped the Salzburgs settle in Georgia.[80]

Franklin applauded Irish Reverend Samuel Hemphill's sermons bestowing the "Practice of Virtue." The same Hemphill sermons that Franklin applauded outraged the Philadelphia Presbyterian orthodox congregation. The congregation and retired clergy arraigned Hemphill under the charge of Heterodoxy at their Synod.[81]

Edwards' revival began in Northampton, Massachusetts,[82] during his diligently researched exposition on the Scripture readings for that Sunday morning.[83] God had predestined all his congregation as the "elect" predestined to be saved by their repentance.[84] People responded to his sermons "with emotional outbursts." Many people's lives dramatically altered for the better, and they spent time doing devotions. This phenomenon spread as far as Connecticut within two months.[85]

The largest shipful of Schwenkfelder exiles from Herrnhut and Berthelsdorf arrived in Philadelphia, Pennsylvania on September 20, and celebrated their first Thanksgiving two days later.[86]

In 1735,[87] Church of England preacher Daniel Roland ignited the initial Welsh Revival and left Wales their first hymns and the Calvinistic Methodist Church,[88] which grew into the Welsh Presbyterian Church.[89] Howell Harris of Trevecka, Wales, enjoyed Griffith Jones's sermons preached in fields. Jones founded "circulating schools" as he traveled to educate students from the Welsh Bible. From an answered secret prayer that melted his heart with the love of God,

Harris shouted, "Abba Father!" as he knew that Christ saved him, and he was God's child on June 18.[90]

Franklin had written three pamphlets and the April 1735 *Pennsylvania Gazette* published his article favoring Hemphill at the Presbyterian Synod. Many of Hemphill's supporters abandoned him and Franklin when they found out that Hemphill preached his sermon advocating good works had been directly lifted from the British Review on a discourse by Dr. Forster. Franklin wrote in his autobiography, "I stuck by him, however, as I rather approved his giving good sermons composed by others than bad ones of his own manufacture." In September, Franklin quit the Presbyterian church when the Synod ruled against him and his favorite preacher yet continued to donate money to support the ministers.[91]

In Oxford, a tavern boy known for his deceitful foul mouth and foolish jokes, George Whitefield (1714–1770) became a member of the Oxford Holy Club that year.[92] One night according to Whitefield he woke up screaming, "I thirst! I thirst!" After a short time, he explained, "I found and felt in myself that I was delivered from the Burden that so heavily oppressed me! The Spirit of Mourning was taken away from me, and I knew what it was truly to rejoice in God."[93]

The Wesley brothers joined a volunteer mission team for the Society for the Propagation of the Gospel in Foreign Parts (founded in 1701) bound for Georgia to save their souls by living to God's glory by converting the Chickasaw Indians.[94] Newly ordained Charles was the secretary of foreign affairs, while the Church of England sent John to replace Quincy.[95]

Beginning their three-and-a-half-month journey across the Atlantic, their mission party of four boarded a ship named the *Simmonds* at Gravesend dock on October 14, with twenty-six Moravians from Herrnhut led by bishop David Nitschmann.[96] as the first Moravians sent by Zinzendorf to Georgia now required ministers.[97] The *Simmonds* sailed with its sister ship, the *London Merchant*, transporting two hundred Salzburg Moravian refugees. They planned to join the Lutheran Salzburg colony in New Ebenezer, about twenty miles northeast of Savannah. Both pastors in charge of the colony once worked as teachers in the Halle Orphanage under Franke and had been ordained specifically for American mission.[98] On November 25, John Wesely awoke afraid to die as the wind howled and the boat rocked back and forth as the ships sailed through their first Atlantic storm.[99]

In Wales that December, lay preacher Harris's intense door-to-door and "open air" preaching began to inspire many Welsh to confess their sins and ask Christ for forgiveness.[100]

From January 17 until 25, 1736, violent Atlantic storms battered the two ships. Wesley recorded in his journal during the first storm, "The sea broke over us from stern to stern, burst through the windows of the state cabin where three or four of us were, and covered us all over, though a bureau sheltered me from the shock." Wesley felt faithless and did not want to die more than ever. The third storm occurred during the Moravian service. Wesley wrote:

> "In the midst of the psalm wherewith their service began the sea broke over, split the main sail into pieces, covered the ship, and poured in between the decks, as if the great deep had already swallowed us up. A terrible screaming began among the English. The Germans calmly sang on. I asked one of them afterwards, "Was you not afraid?" He

answered, "I thank God, no." I asked, "But were not your women and children afraid?" He replied mildly, "No; our women and children are not afraid to die."[101]

Zinzendorf was banished from Saxony. During his eleven-year exile, he preached Lutheran Pietism everywhere he journeyed.[102] Both London ships reached the Savannah harbor by February 4. Quincy still resided in the rectory, so Wesley lodged with the Moravians and worked at learning German.[103] Wesley asked Bishop August Spangenberg about his conduct during the storms. According to Wesley's journal:

> "My brother, I must first ask you one or two questions. Have you the witness within yourself? Does the Spirit of God bear witness with your spirit, that you are a child of God? I was surprised and knew not what to answer. He observed and asked, "Do you know Jesus Christ?" I paused and said, "I know he is the Saviour of the world." "True," replied he; but do you know he has saved you?" I answered, "I hope he has died to save me." He only added, "Do you know

yourself?" I said, "I do." But I fear they were vain words."[104]

Under Anthony Seifferth's pastorship, the Moravians founded the first American Moravian church on February 28.[105] By March 26, Wesley mastered German enough to read *True Christianity* by Arndt.[106] Edward's report on the Massachusetts revival in *A Narrative of the Surprising Work of the Spirit of God* further inspired Harris and Wesley.[107] By May, Wesley translated many Moravian hymns into English and published America's first hymnal.[108] Charles' failure as the secretary of foreign affairs, his bad health, and gossip against him caused him to return to England in August.[109]

Freshly ordained as an Anglican priest, Methodist Calvinist Whitefield's preaching normally packed churches.[110] His sermons recommended avoiding trying to make oneself fit or "good enough for God" Instead, "depend only upon him for salvation; unless he is your wisdom, righteousness and sanctification, he will never be your redemption. Our salvation is the free gift of God; it is owing to his free love, and the free grace of Jesus Christ, that ever you are saved."[111]

After many conversions, the New England Revival that began at Edward's Congregational Church appeared to have "run its course" and was fading into a nostalgic, "do you remember when" event, that people hoped would someday reoccur.[112] During his mission trip to Georgia in 1737, Whitefield initiated an orphanage patterned after Francke's design in Savannah.[113]

When he returned to England, many Anglican churches banned Whitefield from preaching from their pulpits, accusing him of enthusiasm; he adopted the Welsh open-air method, which drew large crowds and ignited an "Evangelical Revival" across England that fostered numerous riots.[114] The Anglican Church saw emotional conversion-centered worship with prayers deviating from the *Book of Common Prayer*, undercutting the Church of England.[115]

Whitefield answered his critics in his sermon, "Folly and Danger of Not Being Righteous Enough." "When we confine the Spirit of God to this or that particular church; and are not willing to converse with any but those of the same communion; this is to be righteous over-much with a witness: and so it is, to confine our communion within church-walls, and to think that Jesus could not preach in a field as well as on consecrated ground." Jesus spoke at both the sanctified temple and in open-air venues. It remained Whitefield's wish that everyone who heard him preach that their hearts would rejoice in the Church of England's articles, homilies, and liturgies.[116]

The year Lewis Paul developed spinning raw cotton into thread with mechanical rollers in England,[117] Wesley failed as a pastor and then was sued for denying communion to a young woman whom he had courted after she married someone else.[118] On February 1, 1738, Wesley saw the English shore as the *Samuel* sailed into Deal Harbor. He and Whitefield passed each other as Whitefield boarded the *Samuel* and returned to Georgia as he had accepted an offer from the Savannah trustees for a position as a minister.[119]

The Wesley brothers became friends with Peter Bohler, a Moravian. After studying Scripture, Wesley agreed with Bohler that "signs of conversion were dominion over sin and constant peace from a sense of forgiveness."[120] Bohler contested that Wesley lacked the faith necessary to trust in God. He defined faith as "a sure trust and confidence which a man has in God, that through the merits of Christ, his sins are forgiven, and he is reconciled to the favor of God." and that this "faith comes instantaneously."[121] On May 22, Charles Wesely reported a "strange palpitation of the heart" as he understood in his heart that Jesus forgave his sins.

In the afternoon, on May 24, John Wesley attended Evensong at St. Paul's. That evening, he attended a religious society meeting at Aldersgate Street, London. Wesley recounted in his journal that he felt his "heart strangely warmed" as he sensed his trust in Christ, who had set Wesley free for even his sins while listening to Luther's *Preface to the Epistle of Romans*[122] Luther's preface outlines each chapter in Romans, on what Paul wrote about faith:

> "The Holy Spirit inserts "eagerness of unconstrained love into the heart, as Paul says in chapter 5. But the Spirit is given only in, with, and through faith in Jesus Christ, as Paul says in his introduction. So, too, faith comes only through the word of God, the Gospel, that preaches Christ: how he is both Son of God and man, how he died and rose for our sake. Paul says all this

in chapters 3, 4, and 10. That is why faith alone makes someone just and fulfills the law; faith it is that brings the Holy Spirit through the merits of Christ."[123]

Wesley traveled to Germany, introduced himself to Zinzendorf, and visited Herrnhut.[124] He noted in "Journal 69" the powerful sermons preached by an elderly carpenter, Christian David, who founded Herrnhut before preaching to Eskimos in Greenland.[125]

Whitefield preached at Baptist, Congregational, Presbyterian, and Reformed Churches as well as outdoors.[126] His preaching brought a multitude of conversions and visibly repented and joyfully transformed people in the American colonies. Edwards wept while listening to Whitefield's sermon at his New England Congregational Church. Anglicans, Congressionalists, and Presbyterians returned to their pulpits with renewed energy, enjoying the same results as when Whitefield and Edwards preached with the goal of sound doctrine and worship steered by a single conversion that led to devotion and Scripture study.[127]

On New Year's Day 1739, Wesley, Whitefield, their friends, and sixty brethren prayed together at a love feast at Fetters Lane. At 3 a.m., many shouted for joy while others collapsed because "the power of God came mightily" upon them.[128] Wesley watched in horror as Whitefield preached in a muddy field in Bristol in March. Wesley wrote that his conviction that "God wished" all things "to be done in order." It felt sinful to save souls outside church walls.[129] On April 2, Wesley tried preaching outdoors to an audience of about three thousand. From that day on, "All the world" became his parish.[130] Yet, he struggled with the way people responded to his sermons. Some wept. Others crumpled in pain. Then they shouted with great joy that they had been cleansed from Satan. Whitefield invited Wesley to fill in for him in Bristol while he spent time in America.[131] The Wesley brothers published their 1739 *Hymns and Sacred Poems*.[132]

The February 12, 1740, edition of *American Weekly Mercury* blasted Franklin for siding with the anti-Propriety party in his news coverage. The party opposed William Penn's descendants who had moved back to England and the charter that granted them the privilege to select and instruct the colony of Pennsylvania's governor.[133]

Ten million people heard Whitefield preach in the American colonies from 1739 to 1740.[134] His American tour in New England started in the fall.[135] Franklin befriended Whitefield after his outside revival in Philadelphia on November 2 to gain subscriptions allowing him to print Whitefield journals and sermons.[136] Whitefield preached 175 sermons in 45 days,[137] including Northampton, Massachusetts'where he preached several times and finished with a private lecture at Edwards' house.[138]

On Whitefield's return to England, Wesley and Whitefield teamed up. "Therefore repent and return, so that your sins may be wiped away, in order that times of refreshing may come from the presence of the Lord;" (Acts 3:19, NASB) and become a new creature. Conversion always starts with" the Holy Spirit's conviction of your sins. "Nothing but the Holy Spirit can change a person's heart."[139] Wesley became their movement's leader to "awaken and cultivate the masses" for the Church of England.[140] The Wesley brothers created "societies' for new believers in Bristol, charging a penny a week based on a sin-free merit system.[141] John Wesley encouraged the actuality of "Christian Perfection." He defined actual Christian faith as, "No man can be a true Christian without such an inspiration of the Holy Ghost as it fills his heart with peace, joy, and love, which he who perceives it not has it not." Whitefield preached that sin lives even within the hearts of converted Christians since "Jesus taught us to pray..." the Lord's prayer, "Forgive us our trespasses as we forgive others."[142] 1741 London theatergoers witnessed the first performance of Handel's Messiah.[143] while the Anglican church continued their no hymns-only metrical psalms policy.[144] While Wesley and Whitefield saw conversion as a one-time event, Zinzendorf preached Christians need three conversions—first from the world to Christ, next to the church, and finally ministry in the world.[145]

Whitefield helped Roland and Harris in Waterford Southwest Whales organize his church, modeling it after the Moravians. Converts often met in West Yorkshire Moravian Churches in 1743. Converts often met in West Yorkshire Moravian Churches. Whitefield tried to start another revival but quarreled with Zinzendorf and conflict festered due to his belief that Calvin's viewpoint on predestination was completely Scriptural based on Rom. 8:29-33, 9:11-20, 11:7 with Wesley's Arminian stance on free will. Whitefield returned to America in 1744.[146]

The Wesley brothers held the first Conference of Methodists that year at the London Foundry on June 25, defining Christian faith, which resulted in total "assurance" that God loved them from Rom. 8:15, ESV, (the spirit of redemption where we cry, "Abba!"), Ephesians 4:32 (God's forgiveness), 2 Cor. 8:5 (prove your love by giving), Heb. 8:10 (the new covenant), 1 John 4:10 (God's love leading to Jesus' sacrifice for our sins,) and 1 John 4:19 (God loved us first).[147]

A March 2, 1746 letter to Benjamin Franklin from the Reverend Josiah Smith explained after hearing Whitefield preach in Charlestown, South Carolina gentlemen donated two hundred pounds of sterling to encourage him to stay in the American colonies.[148] Another letter from Charleston dated March 11, told of enthused laity donating two to three hundred pounds sterling for Whitefield's orphan house in Georgia.[149] July 31, 1746, Franklin's article printed in *The Pennsylvania Gazette* celebrated Whitefield's triumph over "Armies of invidious Preachers and Pamphleteers; under whose Performances, the Pulpits and Presses, of Great Britain and America, have groaned." After the twentieth time, Whitefield preached twice a day to large congregations at New-Building in Philadelphia, he headed for New York. Franklin quoted Watts' description of Whitefield as "a man raised up by Providence in an uncommon way, to awaken a stupid and ungodly world, to a sense of the important affairs of religion and eternity."[150]

Zinzendorf returned to Herrnhut in 1747 and only visited Britain when working with the Church of England.[151] The Moravian church broke from Lutheranism soon after Zinzendorf died in Herrnhut in 1760.[152] Britain started in 1762 digging the Bridgewater Canal accommodating the increase in goods manufactured in factories in Worsley to Manchester markets and was finished in 1772.[153] Sir Richard Arkwright's new throttle used animal or water power to spin cotton in 1768. By 1774, 30, 000 cotton workers ran Arkwright spindles in Manchester factories. Hungry manufacturing centers filled with filth, poverty, and starvation swallowed English farms and small merchant cities.[154]

John Wesley's evangelical revival sparked another "Great Awakening" (1780–1840) that spread across England to the western United States.[155] By 1771, 26,000 people joined the Methodist movement in England and Wales. By 1791, the number of participating English and Welsh Methodists rose to approximately 57,000. The Wesley brothers published their 1780 hymnal, a *Collection of Hymns for the Use of the People called Methodists*. Together they authored more than 9,000 hymns and poems.[156]

The Moravians of Herrnhut influenced William Carey, the founder of the Baptist Missionary Society, whose goal was to evangelize the world by all Christians despite conflicting denominations.[157] He went to India in 1793 and translated the Bible into thirty-four languages by 1834.[158]

1859 revival leader David Morgan's preaching drove thousands to Christ. The Moriah Calvinistic Methodist Chapel birthed the 1904–1905 Welsh Revival[159] generating revivals in other countries.[160]

---

1. Henry H. Knight III, *John Wesley: Optimist of Grace* (Eugene, OR: Cascade Books, 2018), 15.

2. Woodbridge and James, *Church History Volume Two From Pre-Reformation to the Present Day*, 260.

3. Gonzalez, *Church History An Essential Guide*, 259.

4. Knight III, *John Wesley*, 16; Woodbridge and James, *Church History Volume Two From Pre-Reformation to the Present Day*, 261.

5. Ibid., 260.

6. Clouse, *The Church from Age to Age*, 580; Woodbridge and James, *Church History Volume Two From Pre-Reformation to the Present Day*, 261.

7. Woodbridge and James, *Church History Volume Two From Pre-Reformation to the Present Day*, 398

8. Rusten, "1678 John Bunyan Publishes Pilgrim's Progress,"; "A Tinker's Pilgrimage."

9. "William Penn Timeline" *USHistory.org*, accessed 6/17/2024, https://www.ushistory.org/penn/timeline.htm.

10. Franklin Benjamin, *Franklin Writings The Library of America*, edited by J.A. Leo Lemay (New York, NY: Literary Classics of the United States, Inc.,1987), 1471.

11. McManners, *The Oxford Illustrated History of Christianity*, 694.

12. Clouse, *The Church from Age to Age*, 581.

13. Woodbridge and James, *Church History Volume Two From Pre-Reformation to the Present Day*, 262.

14. Ibid., 323.

15. McManners, *The Oxford Illustrated History of Christianity*, 694.

16. Clouse, *The Church from Age to Age*, 581.

17. Woodbridge and James, *Church History Volume Two From Pre-Reformation to the Present Day*, 263

18. Clouse, *The Church from Age to Age*, 581.

19. Woodbridge and James, *Church History Volume Two From Pre-Reformation to the Present Day*, 262.

20. Clouse, *The Church from Age to Age*, 580; Woodbridge and James, *Church History Volume Two From Pre-Reformation to the Present Day*, 262.

21. Smith and Smith, *Quicknotes Christian History Guidebook*, 361.

22. Lewis, *Great Civilizations*, 56.

23. Davidson, *The African Slave Trade Precolonial History 1450-1850*, 66.

24. Gonzalez, *Church History An Essential Guide*, 262.

25. Knight III, *John Wesley*, 16; Woodbridge and James, *Church History Volume Two From Pre-Reformation to the Present Day*, 262.

26. Smith and Smith, *Quicknotes Christian History Guidebook*, 363–364.

27. Lewis, *Great Civilizations*, 56.

28. Davidson, *The African Slave Trade Precolonial History 1450-1850*, 66.

29. Smith and Smith, *Quicknotes Christian History Guidebook*, 375.

30. Lemay, *Franklin Writings The Library of America*, 1471.

31. Smith and Smith, *Quicknotes Christian History Guidebook*, 378.

32. Woodbridge and James, *Church History Volume Two From Pre-Reformation to the Present Day*, 261.

33. Clouse, *The Church from Age to Age*, 583.

34. Walker, *A History of the Christian Church*, 450.

35. Clouse, *The Church from Age to Age*, 583.

36. Walker, *A History of the Christian Church*, 450.

37. Clouse, *The Church from Age to Age*, 583.

38. Walker, *A History of the Christian Church*, 450.

39. Woodbridge and James, *Church History Volume Two From Pre-Reformation to the Present Day*, 458.

40. Joseph Edmund Hutton, *A History of the Moravian Church*, Second Edition, Book Two. Prepared by John Bechard (London: 1909), 134. Kindle.

41. Woodbridge and James, *Church History Volume Two From Pre-Reformation to the Present Day*, 458.

42. Lemay, *Franklin Writings The Library of America*, 1471–1472.

43. McManners, *The Oxford Illustrated History of Christianity*, 695.

44. Hutton, *A History of the Moravian Church*, 136–138.

45. Walker, *A History of the Christian Church*, 451.

46. Hutton, *A History of the Moravian Church*, 138.

47. "Arrival in Philadelphia," *Schwenkfelders in Pennsylvania* (Society of the Descendants of the Schwenkfeldian Exiles), https://schwenkfelderexilesociety.org/schwenkfelders-in-pennsylvania/.

48. Adelaide L. Fries, "Chapter 1 Antecedent Events. The Province of Georgia. The Salzburgers. Unitas Fratrum. Halle Opposition," *The Moravians in Georgia - 1735-1740* (Winston-Salem NC: Public Domain, 1904), e-Sword.

49. Knight III, *John Wesley*, 1– 4; Kenneth J. Collins, *John Wesley: A Theological Journey* (Nashville, TN: Abingdon Press, 2003), 33–34; Thomas Jackson, ed., "A Plain Account of Christian Perfection, as Believed to be Taught by the Reverend Mr. John Wesley From the Year 1725 to the Year 1777." *The Works of John Wesley*. Vol. 11 (1872), Part 02-03, e-Sword.

50. Hutton, *A History of the Moravian Church*, 141.

51. Ibid., 140, 158.

52. Walker, *A History of the Christian Church*, 451.

53. Woodbridge and James, *Church History Volume Two From Pre-Reformation to the Present Day*, 458.

54. Clouse, *The Church from Age to Age*, 583–4.

55. Smith and Smith, *Quicknotes Christian History Guidebook*, 375.

56. Jackson, *The Works of John Wesley*, Part 04.

57. Woodbridge and James, *Church History Volume Two From Pre-Reformation to the Present Day*, 406.

58. Jackson, *The Works of John Wesley*, Part 05.

59. Hutton, "Edict of Banishment."

60. Hutton, *"The History of Moravian Movement."*

61. Adelaide L. Fries, "Chapter 1 Antecedent Events. The Province of Georgia. The Salzburgers. Unitas Fratrum. Halle Opposition," *The Moravians in Georgia - 1735-1740* (Winston-Salem NC: Public Domain, 1904), e-Sword.

62. Woodbridge and James, *Church History Volume Two From Pre-Reformation to the Present Day*, 406.

63. Smith and Smith, *Quicknotes Christian History Guidebook*, 376.

64. Smith and Smith, *Quicknotes Christian History Guidebook*, 378; Collins, *John Wesley*, 77.

65. Hutton, "Edict of Banishment."

66. "Arrival in Philadelphia."

67. Hutton, "Edict of Banishment."

68. Clouse, *The Church from Age to Age*, 583.

69. Fries, "Chapter 1."

70. Knight III, *John Wesley*, 9.

71. Collins, *John Wesley*, 62.

72. Lemay, *Franklin Writings The Library of America*, 1383, 1394, 1474.

73. Ibid., 1384–1394.

74. Ibid., 1386–1387, 1389.

75. Ibid., 1392–1393.

76. Hutton, *"Edict of Banishment."*

77. Lewis, *Great Civilizations*, 57.

78. Fries, "Chapter 1."

79. Lemay, *Franklin Writings The Library of America*, 1474.

80. Fries, "Chapter 1."

81. Lemay, "The Autobiography Part Three," *Franklin Writings The Library of America*, 1400, 1473.

82. Jessica Parks, ed. *Jonathan Edwards: A Guide to His Life and Writings,* Faithlife Author Guides (Bellingham, WA: Faithlife, 2017). Logos.

83. Gonzalez, *Church History An Essential Guide*, 289.

84. Smith and Smith, *Quicknotes Christian History Guidebook*, 376.

85. Gonzalez, *Church History An Essential Guide*, 288.

86. "Arrival in Philadelphia"; "The Schwenkfelder Story."

87. Woods, "Chapter 3: What is Revival," *Touched by Heaven: When God Sends Revival*.

88. Jessie Penn-Lewis, *The Awakening in Wales* (New Kensington, PA: Whitaker House, 2014). Logos.

89. Fenwick, *Free Church of England*, 17.

90. Woodbridge and James, *Church History Volume Two From Pre-Reformation to the Present Day*, 404–405.

91. Lemay, *Franklin Writings The Library of America*, 1400, 1475.

92. Woodbridge and James, *Church History Volume Two From Pre-Reformation to the Present Day*, 406, 411; Richard Green Edgbaston, *John Wesley-Evangelist* (1905). e-Sword.

93. Woodbridge and James, *Church History Volume Two From Pre-Reformation to the Present Day*, 411.

94. Knight III, *John Wesley*, 5, 9–10; Collins, *John Wesley*, 56; Woodbridge and James, *Church History Volume Two From Pre-Reformation to the Present Day*, 406.

95. Woodbridge and James, *Church History Volume Two From Pre-Reformation to the Present Day*, 404–406; Collins, *John Wesley*, 62.

96. Collins, *John Wesley*, 56–58.

97. Hutton, "Edict of Banishment."

98. Collins, *John Wesley*, 64; Knight III, *John Wesley*, 18.

99. Collins, *John Wesley*, 57.

100. Woodbridge and James, *Church History Volume Two From Pre-Reformation to the Present Day*, 405.

101. Collins, *John Wesley*, 57–58.

102. Clouse, *The Church from Age to Age*, 584.

103. Collins, *John Wesley*, 63.

104. Collins, *John Wesley*, 63; Knight III, *John Wesley*, 19.

105. Edmund De Schweinitz, *The Moravian Manual: Containing an Account of the Moravian Church, or Unitas Fratrum*, (Bethlehem, PA: Moravian Publication Office; A. C. & H. T. Clauder, 1869), 38. Logos.

106. Collins, *John Wesley*, 64.

107. Woodbridge and James, *Church History Volume Two From Pre-Reformation to the Present Day*, 404–405.

108. Collins, *John Wesley*, 70.

109. Ibid., 68.

110. Gonzalez, *Church History An Essential Guide*, 288.

111. George Whitefield, "Folly and Danger of Parting With Christ," *Whitfield, George-Sermons* (Franklin, TN: e-Sword Version 13.0.0, Rick Meyers, 2021).

112. Gonzalez, *Church History An Essential Guide*, 288.

113. Woodbridge and James, *Church History Volume Two From Pre-Reformation to the Present Day*, 404–405.

114. Ibid., 407–408.

115. Hein and Shattuck, *The Episcopalians, Denominations in America*, 26–27.

116. Whitefield, "Folly and Danger of Not being Righteous Enough," *Whitefield, George-Sermons*.

117. Davidson, *The African Slave Trade Precolonial History 1450-1850*, 64.

118. Gonzalez, *Church History An Essential Guide*, 262.

119. Collins, *John Wesley*, 77.

120. Woodbridge and James, *Church History Volume Two From Pre-Reformation to the Present Day*, 407.

121. Knight III, *John Wesley*, 19.

122. Collins, *John Wesley*, 86.

123. Martin Luther, *Preface to Romans by Martin Luther, 1483–1546*, translated by Andrew Thorton (Christian Classics Eternal Library), accessed June 7, 2024, https://www.ccel.org/l/luther/romans/pref_romans.html.

124. Woodbridge and James, *Church History Volume Two From Pre-Reformation to the Present Day*, 459.

125. Hutton, *A History of the Moravian Church*, 131.

126. Hein and Shattuck, *The Episcopalians, Denominations in America*, 27.

127. Gonzalez, *Church History An Essential Guide*, 289.

128. Woodbridge and James, *Church History Volume Two From Pre-Reformation to the Present Day*, 408.

129. Gonzalez, *Church History An Essential Guide*, 264.

130. Collins, *John Wesley*, 103.

131. Gonzalez, *Church History An Essential Guide*, 264.

132. Woodbridge and James, *Church History Volume Two From Pre-Reformation to the Present Day*, 411.

133. Lemay, *Franklin Writings The Library of America*, 1476.

134. Parks, *Jonathan Edwards*.

135. Woodbridge and James, *Church History Volume Two From Pre-Reformation to the Present Day*, 412.

136. Lemay, *Franklin Writings The Library of America*, 1475–1476.

137. Woodbridge and James, *Church History Volume Two From Pre-Reformation to the Present Day*, 412.

138. Parks, *Jonathan Edwards*.

139. Whitefield, "Repentance and Conversion."

140. Gonzalez, *Church History An Essential Guide*, 268.

141. Woodbridge and James, *Church History Volume Two From Pre-Reformation to the Present Day*, 409.

142. Collins, *John Wesley*, 118, 132.

143. McManners, *The Oxford Illustrated History of Christianity*, 695.

144. Smith and Smith, *Quicknotes Christian History Guidebook*, 363.

145. Christian A. Schwarz, *The 3 Colors of Ministry: A trinitarian approach to identifying and developing your spiritual gifts* (St. Charles, IL: ChurchSmart Resources, nd.) 13.

146. Fenwick, *Free Church of England*, 18; Woodbridge and James, *Church History Volume Two From Pre-Reformation to the Present Day*, 414–415; Gonzalez, *Church History An Essential Guide*, 268; Whitefield, "A Letter from George Whitefield."

147. Collins, *John Wesley*, 129–131; Woodbridge and James, *Church History Volume Two From Pre-Reformation to the Present Day*, 409.

148. Lemay, *Franklin Writings The Library of America*, 308-309.

149. Ibid., 309–310.

150. Ibid., 304-305.

151. Clouse, *The Church from Age to Age*, 584.

152. Gonzalez, *Church History An Essential Guide*, 264.

153. Lewis, *Great Civilizations*, 57.

154. Davidson, *The African Slave Trade Precolonial History 1450-1850*, 64.

155. Woods, "Chapter 3: What is Revival," *Touched by Heaven: When God Sends Revival*.

156. Woodbridge and James, *Church History Volume Two From Pre-Reformation to the Present Day*, 411.

157. Booty, "Reformers and Missionaries: The Bible Eighteenth and Early Nineteenth-Century England," 135.

158. Ibid., 137.

159. David Matthews, "The Revivalist," *I Saw the Welsh Revival* (Greenville, SC: Ambassador International, 2018).

160. Woods, "Chapter 3: What is Revival," *Touched by Heaven: When God Sends Revival*.

16

Fueling Revivals

Summary and Aftermath

Noticeably, none of the Christian mystics in English history practiced altered states of conscience, ecstasy, or somehow inducing a trance reproducible with drugs or hypnosis. Instead, they participated in the "mystery of Christ."[1] When one person's spiritual life changes forever, they then can further their relationship with God through faith, prayer, communion, and meditation on Scripture.

This process is called *Christian mysticism,* facilitated by God's grace via the Holy Spirit with one's heart.

Kepler's Trinity and Descartes' proof of God's existence, demonstrate that each seeker's successful techniques and experiences vary and seem to be a personal gift uniquely translated by each sole participant. Kepler and Galileo explained the variance of experience by stating that God expresses himself to humans according to their limitations. This can be found in the Bible. The prophet Isaiah asked in Isa. 40:13-14, "Who has measured the Spirit of the Lord, or what man shows him his counsel? Whom did he consult, and who made him understand? Who taught him the path of justice, and taught him knowledge, and showed him the way of understanding?" In John 13:16, Jesus says, "Truly, truly, I say to you, a servant is not greater than his master, nor is a messenger greater than the one who sent him."

Luther famously pointed out, "salvation happens by faith alone." During conversion as witnessed by Edwards, Wesley, and Whitefield, people often screamed while others burst into tears as the Holy Spirit convicted them of their sins. The quiet resolve afterward marked the moment when a shift toward dropping worldly desires and replacing them with following God's commandments developed within a human.

Wesley preached that this transformation was "Christian Perfection," while Whitefield preached that humans never fully reach "perfection." Both experienced the kindling within their heart that transformed their lives. Wesley knew Scripture and pursued righteousness, but needed faith followed by conversion even though he had already accomplished becoming an ordained Anglican priest before God anointed Wesley's ministry.

At the 1771 Methodist Conference in Bristol, Wesley addressed America's cry for assistance. Francis Asbury (1745–1816) volunteered. Wesley ordained Thomas Coke (1747–1814) as a superintendent in 1784, who promptly ordained Asbury. The 1784 Baltimore Christmas Conference founded the Methodist Church. The Methodists remained a part of the Church of England until 1795. By the 1830s, over 500,000 people belonged to the Methodist Church in the United States.[2]

Despite vast differences in denomination and theology, whenever a large number of people in a specific area's lives change due to the same Holy Spirit while praying and worshiping together, this event becomes a *revival*. When multiple revivals co-occur over a larger land spread, it is labeled an *awakening*.

The Holy Spirit worked through single diverse individuals like the Spirit did with the major and minor Old Testament prophets. Wycliffe's reform in England fully advanced in Bohemia and Moravia.[3] The Bohemians repelled seven crusades preached by the papacy and led by the Imperial Emperor.[4] Luther studied writings from Oxford and Huss before nailing his 95 Theses. The Church of English planted the order of worship into everyone's hands instead of only the clergy.[5] From 1535–1568, five versions, Coverdale, Matthew's, Cranmer, Geneva, and Bishop's Bible, helped formalize the English language.[6] The King James Version, patterned after Shakespearian English, triumphed in prose and verse and shaped English culture as they formed the British Empire.[7] Huss' descendants became Moravians who influenced Wesley's Anglican reforms throughout the British Isles.[8]

As scholars translated the Bible, others strove for extreme wealth by procuring and possessing huge amounts of land by any means and exploiting cheap labor. Ecclesiastics 5:8-10 warned:

> "If you see in a province the oppression of the poor and the violation of justice and righteousness, do not be amazed at the matter, for the high official is watched by a higher, and there are yet higher ones over them. But this is gain for a land in every way: a king committed to cultivated fields. He who loves money will not be satisfied with money, nor he who loves wealth with his income; this also is vanity."

Evil external influences like the devastation of the Thirty Years' War, the tragic slave trade, and the comparable exploitation of European miners and factory workers in the Industrial Revolution led to an outpouring of the Holy Spirit, which had not been recorded since Pentecost. Without the seeds of tolerance throughout Europe and the British Isles, and the decimation of Lutheran-based religious groups, the Moravian Revival could not affect the entire world demonstrating how God continues to work toward human salvation throughout history. Edwards in *The*

Distinguishing Marks of the Spirit of God (1741) and *Thoughts on Revivals of Religion in New England* (1742) described revivals as reoccurring "cyclical works of grace" like "waves breaking on shore" used as a primary tool by God to advance His kingdom.[9] Jesus explained the pursuit of wealth as darkness and the pursuit of turning toward God and loving him with everything one has to offer, recorded in Matt. 6:19-24:

> "Do not lay up for yourselves treasures on earth, where moth and rust destroy and where thieves break in and steal, but lay up for yourselves treasures in heaven, where neither moth nor rust destroys and where thieves do not break in and steal. For where your treasure is, there your heart will be also. The eye is the lamp of the body. So, if your eye is healthy, your whole body will be full of light, but if your eye is bad, your whole body will be full of darkness. If then the light in you is darkness, how great is the darkness! No one can serve two masters, for either he will hate the one and love the other, or he will be devoted to the one and despise the other. You cannot serve God and money."

Revivals and reforms continued during the next century ending in songs of praise against the backdrop of the pursuit of lands and money resulting in apathy, skepticism, and poverty. The British and French allied with warring American Indian nations who fought each other in the French and Indian War (Seven Years War with France) from 1754 to 1763. Britain acquired Canadian New France and parts of India at the war's end by signing the Treaty of Paris.[10] 1768 ushered in more breakthroughs driving the textile industry. James Hargreaves spinning jenny allowed workers to manipulate eight spindles at once. Later models accommodated eighty spindles. 1769 coal mines installed New Comen Atmospheric Engines pumping large amounts of water out of the coal mines. Soon coal miners used James Watts' patented upgrades that quadrupled the water pump's output.[11] The American Revolution (War of Independence) 1775-1783.[12] America declared its independence from Britain in 1776.

Reformed pastors ushered revivals in the Connecticut Valley beginning in the 1780s.[13] A Cornwall December 25, 1781, Christmas morning service evolved into a six-hour prayer meeting. Many returned in the evening after spending Christmas Day with their families. Like all their prayer meetings held until March, Anglicans, Baptists, and Methodists prayed until midnight for England's revival. The many resulting conversions triggered the Second Great Awakening.[14] The Second Great Awakening saw Methodist circuit riders and emotional camp meetings in the western states of Kentucky and Tennessee. Baptist and Methodist membership numerically grew.[15] English newspaper *Gloucester Journal* editor Robert Raikes (1735-1811) wrote about the poor uneducated children factory and mine workers compared to wealthy schooled children. Between 1781 and 1783, he set up Sunday Schools teaching reading, writing, and hygiene.[16]

Many British expected to embrace the new Millennium as the apocalyptic French Revolution in the 1790s. Anne Cutler (1759-1794) and Methodist William Bramwell (1759–1818) led the Yorkshire Revival from 1792 to 1796.[17]

George Stevenson built and opened on September 27, 1825, the first English railroad which ran a ten-mile stretch from Stockton to Darlington.[18] In 1835, American Samuel Morse created the telegraph. By 1836, London boasted of its first railway.[19]

The Royal British Navy ruled the seas. Crowned in 1837, Queen Alexandrina Victoria (1819-1901) witnessed the greatest expanse of the British Empire as the British sang, "Rule, Britannia! Britannia, rule the waves! Britons never shall be slaves." In 1838, the first steam paddle-driven ship, the *Great Western* designed by Isambard Kingdom Brunel to carry 12,000 tons of coal needed for fuel, 6,000 tons of cargo, and 4,000 paying passengers or 10,000 troops sailed from Bristol to New York City in fifteen days.[20]

Victorian romanticism melded with the cold rationalism of the Age of Enlightenment.[21] The High Church stressed the "renewed commitment of the English people to the Anglican Church." Anglo-Catholic Oxford Movement Tractarians published ninety tracts contending that Anglican bishops descended from the Apostolic Church founded by Jesus and pressured churches to incorporate High Church worship procedures.[22] "Broad Church Anglicans" developed into a popular catchphrase for theological liberals throughout the late 1840s.[23] Evangelicals kept the Piest traditions of Wesley and Whitefield and promoted hymn singing in the Anglican Church.[24] Parliament granted permission to build over four hundred railroads from 1844 to 1846.[25] Great Britain controlled twenty-five percent of the world's commerce by 1850.[26]

Great Britain received reports on 1857-1858 New York City Fulton Street prayer meetings led by Jeremiah Lanphier sparking similar noon meetings in Boston, Chicago, and Philadelphia to other United States cities, towns, and villages converting thousands.[27] 1859 Welsh revival leader David Morgan's preaching drove thousands to Christ, founding the Moriah Calvinistic Methodist Chapel in the small hamlet of Lougor in Glamorgan County, which boasted of two Non-conformist churches, a school, and a village hall.[28] Welsh converts danced joyfully during Christmas Evans' prayer meetings.[29] An outpouring of the Holy Spirit broke out in the village of Kells in Ulster Ireland, which spread to Belfast. Three thousand people gathered outside the First Presbyterian Church of Ahoghill where hundreds repented their sins after listening to a lay leader's preaching.[30] Charles Spurgeon preached to London crowds. The hearts of many felt strangely warmed in Wesleyan Methodist Churches throughout Great Britain. William Booth left the Wesleyan

Church to pursue evangelizing London slums as his first call to ministry. Booth would eventually establish the Salvation Army.[31]

During the same year, Darwin published *Origins of Species,* leading people to question the accuracy of Genesis.[32] Broad Church Anglican professors published *Essays and Reviews* in 1860, themed on, "Christianity is a false position" as truth reconciling science with religion. Ecclesiastic courts tried the seven authors. South African missionary J. W. Colenso's 1862 publication *The Pentateuch and the Book of Joshua Critically Examined* denied Moses' authorship of the first five Old Testament books and found no geological evidence of Noah's flood.[33]

England, France, and Italy competed introducing colonies to extend their rule in Africa during the 1870s. Ten years later Germany joined the race. At Victoria's 1887 fiftieth Golden Jubilee and her 1897 sixtieth Diamond Jubilee, commentators compared the British Empire to Rome's.[34] By 1904 the British Empire and her Anglican Church stretched across 11, 000, 000 miles.[35]

1. William Johnston, *The Wounded Stag: Originally published in a cloth edition as Christian Mysticism Today* (New York, NY, Toronto: Haper & Row and Fitzhenry & Whiteside, 1984), 20.

2. Woodbridge and James, *Church History Volume Two From Pre-Reformation to the Present Day*, 410–411.

3. Schweinitz, *The History of the Church Known as the Unitas Fratrum or The Unity of the Brethren*, 18.

4. Harrison and Sullivan, *A Short History of Western Civilization*, 313.

5. Maude, *The History of the Book of Common Prayer*, 74.

6. McCrum, Cran, and MacNeil, *The Story of English*, 110.

7. "How the King James Bible Changed the World," *Baylor Magazine* (Summer 2011), Baylor University, June 21, 2011, accessed June 21, 2023, https://www.baylor.edu/alumni/magazine/0904/news.php?action=story&story=95758.

8. Clouse, *The Church from Age to Age*, 584–88.

9. Kurian, "revival."

10. Lewis, *Great Civilizations*, 54; Woodbridge and James, *Church History Volume Two From Pre-Reformation to the Present Day*, 566.

11. Mitchell Wilson, *American Science and Invention: A Pictorial History* (New York, NY: Simon and Schuster 1954), 51.

12. Lewis, *Great Civilizations*, 54.

13. Woodbridge and James, *Church History Volume Two From Pre-Reformation to the Present Day*, 573.

14. Rusten, "1781 Cornwall's Christmas Revival Focuses on Prayer."

15. Woodbridge and James, *Church History Volume Two From Pre-Reformation to the Present Day*, 573.

16. Ibid., 604.

17. Ibid., 573.

18. Lewis, *Great Civilizations*, 58.

19. Woodbridge and James, *Church History Volume Two From Pre-Reformation to the Present Day*, 529.

20. Woodbridge and James, *Church History Volume Two From Pre-Reformation to the Present Day*, 563, 566-567; Douglas Lobley, *Ships Through the Ages* (London: Octopus Books Ltd., 1972), 97, 118.

21. Wallace Henley, "We Need Lightning Now," *Call Down Lightning: What the Welsh Revival of 1904 Reveals About the End Times* (Nashville, TN: Thomas Nelson, 2019). Logos.

22. Woodbridge and James, *Church History Volume Two From Pre-Reformation to the Present Day*, 579.

23. Ibid., 578, 608.

24. Ibid., 580.

25. Lewis, *GreatCivilizations*, 58.

26. Woodbridge and James, *Church History Volume Two From Pre-Reformation to the Present Day*, 563.

27. Ibid., 595.

28. David Matthews, "The Revivalist," *I Saw the Welsh Revival* (Greenville, SC: Ambassador International, 2018). Logos.

29. Stanley Howard Frodsham, *Smith Wigglesworth: Apostle of Faith* (Springfield, MO: Gospel Publishing House, 2010), 9. Logos.

30. Woodbridge and James, *Church History Volume Two From Pre-Reformation to the Present Day,* 595.

31. Frodsham, *Smith Wigglesworth: Apostle of Faith,* 9.

32. Woodbridge and James, *Church History Volume Two From Pre-Reformation to the Present Day,* 611

33. Ibid., 610, 612.

34. Ibid., 566-567.

35. Mark D. Chapman, *Anglicanism A Very Short Introduction* (Oxford NY: Oxford University Press, 2006), 8.

17

The 1904-1906 Welsh Revival

As secularism rose, Anglicans and Non-Conformists stopped attending church. Social work for the poor declined. Agnosticism became the social norm among students and the upper class during the 1880s.[1] In 1893, coal miner John Evan Roberts (1878–1951) started praying daily that God would use him in a great revival.[2] Tithe Wars from 1886 to 1890 erupted between farmers refusing to pay one-tenth of their income to the Church of England despite no church affiliation and soldiers backing the tax collectors.[3] Although Evan Roberts had no skill as a preacher, in 1901, he attended a New Castle Grammar School evangelical campaign aimed at the non-church-attending masses by the Calvinistic Methodist Forward Movement led by Reverend Seth Joshuah. No conversions resulted.

The movement attended a service on the coast of Cardigan Bay. Joshuah prayed that God "Bend us." Roberts repeated him and fell off his chair, looking semi-conscious, lying flat on the church floor and sweating. Roberts arose as a changed man. Studying at school became impossible. He prayed and sighed and cried for a "great spiritual awakening."[4]

In December 1902, seventy-three-year-old St. David's Reverend Dean Howell saw himself on the "brink of eternity with earthbound thing fading from his gaze the light of heaven shining upon him." He foretold the Welsh about a great spiritual awakening as in Isa. 64:1–2, "Oh that you would rend the heavens and come down, that the mountains might quake at your presence—as when fire kindles brushwood and the fire causes water to boil— to make your name known to your adversaries, and that the nations might tremble at your presence!"

Three disgruntled ministers formed a prayer circle in May 1903 to pray for each other and their churches. Two ladies in Monmouthshire also prayed for a revival between 1903–1904.[5] William L. Courtney published letters in an article "Do We Believe?" *The Telegraph* newspaper in 1904 concluded that "advances in science applied to history and biology, turned people into skeptics.[6]

The Holy Spirit commanded Roberts to return to Lougor and tell his story to the congregation at his home church, the Moriah Calvinistic Methodist Chapel.[7] In January 1904, in New Quay, Cardigan, Wales,[8] Evan Roberts started prayer meetings where people prayed or read Scripture[9] at his church, which ignited a revival that quickly spread across Glamoganshire.

Spontaneously, the Holy Spirit swooped upon and mingled with crowds. People confessed their sins, prayed, testified, and sang as God's Spirit directed.[10] Thousands endlessly sang hymns praising God in their churches, homes, and in the coal mines.[11] Individuals reported the day and the hour that, according to Welsh historian R.Tudur Jones, "suddenly as flood gates opened," "suddenly the fire came down," or "suddenly the baptism happened."[12]

Workers brought their entire earnings home to their families. Alcohol and gambling establishments, along with theaters, closed due to a lack of customers. Fans and players lost interest in playing and watching football(soccer).[13] Athletes, performers, and repentant agnostics volunteered to serve in various ministries. Profane blastomeres transformed into eloquent arbitrators of God. As singers' hearts changed toward God, they sang old gospel hymns.[14]

Politics shut down. Members of Parliament attended revival meetings. Courthouses remained empty since judges lacked cases to try. The illegitimate birthrate declined by 44%. The mules in the mines needed retraining as no one cussed while ordering them about. Church denominations worshiped together.[15] Booksellers had trouble keeping up with the new demand for Bibles.[16] *The South Wales Dailey News* reported,

> "Infidels were converted, drunkards healed, thieves and gamblers saved, and many thousands reclaimed to respectability and

honored citizenship. Confessions of awful sins were heard on every side, and everywhere. Old debts were remembered and paid. Theatres and public houses were in distress for lack of patronage. Several police courts had clean sheets and were idle. In five weeks, 20,000 conversions were recorded."[17]

Between 1904 and 1905, 150,000 joined Welsh Churches, and 70,000 converted to following Christ within the first two months.[18] Worldwide, church leaders of multiple religions visited to witness the revival, generating revivals in other countries.[19] As people prayed for the outpouring of the Holy Spirit in Europe, Denmark, Norway, Germany, and Sweden reported revivals.[20] Revivals spread to Africa, Asia, and North and South America.[21] On January 20, 1905, the *Denver Post* headline proclaimed, "Entire City Pauses for Prayer Even at the High Tide of Business." Ministers in Atlantic City boasted only fifty adults remained unconverted to Christianity from their population of fifty thousand. Two hundred forty department stores signed agreements to close from 11 a.m. to 2 p.m. every day, allowing their customers and employees time to attend prayer meetings.[22]

The Western Mail, the Cardiff, Wales news reported that Roberts advised:

> "You desire an outpouring of the Holy Spirit in your city? You do well. But remember, four conditions must be observed. They are essential."

> "First, is there any sin in your past with which you have not honestly dealt—not confessed to God? On your knees at once. Your past must be put away and cleansed."[23]

> "Second, is there anything in your life that is doubtful—anything you cannot decide whether it is good or evil? Way with it.[24] There must not be a trace of a cloud between you and God.[25] Have you forgiven everybody—EVERYBODY?[26] If not, don't expect forgiveness for your sins.[26] Better

offend ten thousand friends than grieve the Spirit of God[28]—or quench Him."[29]

"Third, do what the Holy Spirit prompts without hesitation or fear. Obedience—prompt, implicit, unquestioning obedience, at whatever cost."[30]

"Fourth, a public confession of Christ as personal Savior.[31] Profession and confession are vastly different! Multitudes are guilty of long and loud profession. Confession of Christ as Lord is of recent date. We forget that there is a Trinity in the Godhead, and that the three Persons are on absolute equality.[31] We praise the Father and we praise the Son. Can anyone produce a satisfactory reason why we should not, and do not, praise the Holy Spirit? When we speak of Him as a 'thing,' or 'something,' are we not greatly in error, since the Scriptures claim for Him absolute equality with the other sacred Persons in the Holy Trinity? Is He not ignored entirely in hundreds of the churches? Hear the word of the Lord: 'Quench not the Spirit.' That is the one way to revival. When the fire burns, it purifies. And when purified, you are fit to be used in the work of God."33

News articles quoted from Matthews, "That They All May Be One." See Endnotes for supporting Scripture.

---

1. Chapman, *Anglicanism A Very Short Introduction*, 615.

2. Ibid., 597.

3. Woodbridge and James, *Church History Volume Two From Pre-Reformation to the Present Day*, 597.

4. David Matthews, "The Revivalist."

5. Jessie Penn-Lewis, "The Prophet of the Revival in Wales," *The Awakening in Wales* (New Kensington, PA: Whitaker House, 2014). Logos.

6. Woodbridge and James, *Church History Volume Two From Pre-Reformation to the Present Day*, 615.

7. David Matthews, "The Revivalist."

8. Rusten, "1904 Welch Revival Spreads Around the World."

9. Ralf Andrus, "1904 Welsh Revival," (Sermons by Logos, 2008), accessed June 25, 2024.

10. Kurian, "Roberts, Evan John."

11. Matthews, "Reminiscences of the Great Revival."

12. Henley, "We Need Lightning Now."

13. Andrus, "1904 Welsh Revival."

14. Henley, "We Need Lightning Now."

15. Andrus, "1904 WelshRevival."

16. Henley, "We Need Lightning Now."

17. Matthews, "That They All May Be One."

18. Henley, "We Need Lightning Now."

19. Woods, "Chapter 3: What is Revival," *Touched by Heaven: When God Sends Revival*; Matthews, "Reminiscences of the Great Revival."

20. Woodbridge and James, *Church History Volume Two From Pre-Reformation to the Present Day*, 598.

21. Rusten, "1904 Welch Revival Spreads Around the World."

22. Andrus, "1904 Welsh Revival."

23. 2 Chronicles 7:14; Prov. 28:13; Psa. 32; James 5:16; 1 John 1:9.

24. Deu. 30:15-16— Choose between good and evil; Heb. 5:14 —Train; Psa. 143— prayer for God's aid in discernment.

25. Lamentations 3:44.

26. Matt. 5:22–24; Ephesians 4:31–32.

27. Mark 11:25; Matt. 6:14–15, 18:15–35; Luke 17:3–4.

28. Isa. 63:9–10; Eph. 4: 30.

29. 1 Thes. 1:11, 5:19–21; Matt. 12:31–32, 23.

30. Psa. 119; Eze. 36:23–29; Rom. 8:4–6; 2 Thes. 2:10–16; Luke 6:46–49; Acts 16:6–15.

31. Matt. 10:32–33; Rom. 1:1–7; Heb. 13:12–15.

32. Matt. 28:18–19; John 14:15–17.

33. 1 Peter 1:23-25, Malachi 3:2-3.

18

Conclusion

Invite the Holy Spirit to Church

Revival historian Lewis Drummond wrote:

"God is in control of His church and will give His people what they need when they need it." God's wisdom far supersedes ours, and we must place the timing of these awakenings in the divine economy of things." Revivals do not come by caprice or just because the church does certain things in a formal, structured fashion, [though] the people of God do have a part, [but] the sovereignty of God is central."[1]

Although 1990s critics of fourteenth-century mysticism found fault with "an exclusive interest in religion," the Offices of Morning and Evening Prayer intended to support and preserve the inner life of love and prayer.[2] Thornton quotes K. E. Kirk, who recommends a positively charged response to God's grace. Holy Communion and Confession sacraments straightforwardly offer mercy, love, and Christ's resurrection. Like the Hussites who left the Catholic Church so they could receive Communion at every service, Kirk sees the Eucharist as the heart of Christian life, supported by the Office and private devotion: "prayer." Connecting with God is not "fasting, mortification, bare boards, and hair shirts, but getting up on cold mornings to go to Mass, rising earlier to recite the Office."[3] A revival is an extraordinary event performed by the Holy Spirit when Christ's bride, the universal apostolic church, reaches a point of teetering on death.

Whether a Christian worships as an Anglican, Baptist, Catholic, Lutheran, non-denominational,

Pentecostal, or one of the many Reformed Churches based on Calvinism, prayer is the conduit that connects all people to God via the Holy Spirit.[4] 1 Cor. 12:4–6 shows the triune nature of God, "Now there are varieties of gifts, but the same Spirit; and there are varieties of service, but the same Lord; and there are varieties of activities, but it is the same God who empowers them all in everyone."[5]

The prayer techniques developed by Christian mystics are as diverse as the unique personalities of people who spent their time experiencing God. Each revival started with one faithful person. John Wesley's story shows one can grow up in a Christian environment, work hard to be a good Christian, become ordained, and have zero faith. Without faith in God, one lacks the power to transform the world into a more joyful place. When the converted Welsh spoke at special events in America, they had no power because they lacked the background in learning and studying Scripture.

Conversion is the moment a person gains an unshakeable confidence in God. Start with prayer or start by reading or listening to Scripture. Once a person develops faith God may choose to lend the power of the Holy Spirit. If one person tries and decides on which of the many ways Christian mystics used to enrich their conversation and understanding of the supreme ruler and creator of multiple universes explored in *Inviting The Holy Spirit to Church*, then that one person will experience the "peace that passes understanding." That "peace" is what Jesus hoped his disciples would exhibit while they braved a storm on the Sea of Galilee, but He was disappointed in His traumatized disciples in Luke 8:22–25, Mark 4: 35–40, Matt. 8:23–27. The faithful Moravians had the faith required to remain calm while the fury of the Atlantic ravaged the ship as they worshiped.

God, in His own time, responds to prayers for revival. Backed with the power of God, that person might begin another non-denominational church, transforming lives within a community. Like the original disciples in Luke 24:49, And behold, "I am sending the promise of my Father upon you. But stay in the city until you are clothed with power from on high." A person must wait for the Holy Spirit before expecting anything else to occur.[6] As the Lutherans pointed out when arguing with the Pietists, God does the work through grace.

In John 3:8, Jesus explained to the pharisee Nicodemus, "The wind blows where it wishes, and you hear its sound, but you do not know where it comes from or where it goes. So it is with everyone who is born of the Spirit." Remember, one faithful person's prayer for revival in the eighteenth century led to the first Great Awakening in the case of Edwards in the British American Colonies. Another faithful person Evan Roberts' prayers led to a country following God and spreading worldwide, affecting an estimated five million people at the beginning of the twentieth century.[7]

A revival does not last forever yet reoccurs. God's revivals continued into the twentieth century. For example, a year after the Welsh Revival in Benton Harbor, Michigan, the Flying Rollers of the House of David Mary McDermitt damned San Francisco, promising "earthquake, fire, and pestilence within a month."

A week later,[8] the *Los Angeles Times* ran an article on April 18, 1906, titled "Weird Bable of Tongues," featuring a new religious movement that showed the outburst of the Holy Spirit by speaking in tongues at the city's Azura Street Mission. The newspaper ran headlines about the San Francisco earthquake on the same day. Los Angeles Frank Bartleman distributed 125,000 copies of a tract titled *Earthquake!* from San Diego to San Francisco, calling people to repentance. Azura Street Mission transformed from a fire-damaged sanctuary on Easter to a vibrant church hosting 1,500 each Sunday by August.[9] This was the first of many revivals that led to the Pentecostal Church.

News of the Welsh Revival sparked a Khasi Hills revival in India in 1906. In a nearby Lushai, India, Mizo Christians prayed for a revival in their mostly pagan village. As they sang "God be with you as we Meet Again" honoring the departure of three friends, they felt the outpouring of the Holy Spirit. Others joined them as they sang praises and prayed for the rest of the night. Several Lushains traveled to witness to neighboring villages, but the Holy Spirit had already transformed surrounding villages. These Christians were persecuted.[10]

The Great 1907 Korean Revival ignited in Pyongyang and spread.[11] Canadian Presbyterian missionary Jonathon Goforth (1859–1936)) served in China as a missionary. When he traveled to Korea, he witnessed thousands weeping as they confessed their sins, repented, and turned toward God. They reconciled with their enemies, continually prayed, eagerly listened to Scripture readings, and sensed the power of the Holy Spirit at their gatherings. His testimony to the Chinese on returning to China started to Manchurian Revival.[12]

Daniel Deforest London is a priest serving at Christ Episcopal Church in Eureka, CA.[13] In his introduction to *The Cloud of Unknowing Distilled*, London quotes Jesuit theologian Karl Rahner, who warned, "The Christian of the future will either be a mystic or will not exist at all." If a church fails to discover its 'mystical roots," the church probably will be forced to close its doors for the final time. Most people crave a "direct encounter with God's love.[14] This church reform must use "creative compassion" to switch from a "me" society into a "we" society[15] with your heart, mind, body, and soul" (Luke 10:27, Mark 12:29–31, Matt. 22:37–39). The more one feeds the Holy Spirit's link between oneself and God, the stronger the tie. Both the Moravian, Welsh, and Pentecostal revivals show when a group of people pray, meditate, and follow God together, God changes the world for the better. People's prayers, meditations, and conformity to God's Will will shape the current century.

---

1. Henley, "We Need Lightning Now."

2. Thornton, *English Spirituality*, 183.

3. Ibid., 73.

4. "Veni, Creator Spiritus," accessed June 23, 2023, https://www.preces-latinae.org/thesaurus/Hymni/VeniCreator.html.

5. Schwarz, *The 3 Colors of Ministry*, 15.

6. Ibid., 19.

7. Rusten, "Welsh Revival Spreads Around the World."

8. Gordon Thomas and Max Morgan Witts, *The San Francisco Earthquake* (New York: Stein and Day/Publishers/, 1971), 218.

9. Cecil M., Jr. Robeck, "Series Foreword." *How Pentecost Came to Los Angeles: The Story behind the Azusa Street Revival*, edited by Cecil M. Robeck Jr. and Darrin Rodgers, 6. Azusa Street Book Series. (Springfield, MO: Gospel Publishing House, 2017), 10. Logos.

10. Rusten, "1906 Revival Overflows Among the Mizo People."

11. Anthony C. Thiselton, *Systematic Theology* (Grand Rapids, MI; Cambridge, U.K.: William B. Eerdmans Publishing Company, 2015). 291. Logos.

12. Woodbridge and James, *Church History Volume Two From Pre-Reformation to the Present Day,* 598–599.

13. "Daniel Deforest London," Daniel Deforest London, accessed June 9, 2023, https://deforestlondon.wordpress.com/.

14. London, *The Cloud of Unknowing Distilled,* Kindle location, 99–100.

15. Fox, "Spirituality for Protestants–Religion Online."

Appendix

Benjamin Franklin's Catalogue of Virtues

1. Temperance: Eat not to dullness; drink not to elevation.

2. Silence: Speak not but what may benefit others or yourself; avoid trifling conversation.

3. Order: Let all your things have their places; let each part of your business have its time.

4. Resolution: Resolve to perform what you ought; perform without fail what you resolve.

5. Frugality: Make no expense but to do good to

others or yourself; *i. e.*, waste nothing.

6. Industry: Lose no time; be always employ'd in something useful; cut off all unnecessary actions.

7. Sincerity: Use no hurtful deceit; think innocently and justly; and, if you speak, speak accordingly.

8. Justice: Wrong none by doing injuries, or omitting the benefits that are your duty.

9. Moderation: Avoid extreams; forbear resenting injuries so much as you think they deserve.

10. Cleanliness: Tolerate no uncleanliness in body, cloaths, or habitation.

11. Tranquillity: Be not disturbed at trifles, or at accidents common or unavoidable.

12. Chastity: Rarely use venery but for Health or Offspring; Never to Dulness, Weakness, or the Injury of your own or another's Peace or Reputation.

13. Humility: Imitate Jesus and Socrates.[1]

ABBREVIATIONS

- 1 Cor.................1 Corinthians
- 1 Thes..............1 Thessalonians
- 2 Cor............... 2 Corinthians
- 2 Pet.................2 Peter
- 2 Thes..............2 Thessalonians
- Deu...................Deuteronomy
- Eph...................Ephesians
- Gal...................Galatians
- Gen...................Genesis
- Heb...................Hebrews
- Isa....................Isaiah
- Matt.................Matthew

- Num...................Numbers

- Prov..................Proverbs

- Rev...................Revelation

- Rom..................Romans

---

1. Lemay, "The Autobiography Part Two," *Franklin Writings The Library of America*, 1384-1385.

BIBLIOGRAPHY

Addis, William E., and Thomas Arnold. *A Catholic Dictionary*. New York: The Catholic Publication Society Co., 1887.

Allmand, Christopher. *Henry V*. Berkeley and Los Angeles, CA: The University of California Press, 1992.

Annaidh, Seamas Mac, *Irish History*. Bath BA1 1HE: Parragon Publishing, 1999.

Aries, Philippe and Georges Duby, eds. *A History of Private Life Revelations of the Medieval World*. Translated by Arthur Goldhammer, Cambridge, MA, London, England: The Belknap Press of Harvard University Press, 1988.

Aubigne, J. H. Merle d'. *The Reformation in England Volume One*. Translated by H. White. Edinburgh, England: Carlise, PA: The Banner of Truth Trust, 1977.

- *The Reformation in England Volume Two*. Translated by H. White, London, England: Carlise, PA: The Banner of Truth Trust, 1972.

Avis, Paul. *The Anglican Understanding of the Church: An Introduction*. Second edition. London: SPCK, 2013.
- "Great Britain." *The SPCK Handbook of Anglican Theologians*. Edited by Alister E. McGrath. London: SPCK, 1998. Logos.

Bailey, George. *Germans The Biography of an Obsession*. Toronto, New York: The Free Press, Maxwell Macmillan Canada and Maxwell Macmillan International, 1991.

Banowshky, William S. "The Holy Spirit Fifth Annual Fort Worth Christian College Lectureship March 22- 26, 1964." *The Gift of the Holy Spirit*. Fort Worth, TX: Fort Worth Christian College, 1964.

Barry, John D., et al., "Pelagianism." *The Lexham Bible Dictionary*. Bellingham, WA: Lexham Press, 2016. Logos.

Bede. *A History of the English Church and People*. Translated by Leo Sherley Price. Baltimore, MD: Penguin Books, 1955.

Blunt, John Henry. *A Key to the Knowledge of Church History*. London, Oxford, and Cambridge: Rivingtons Waterloo Place, 1877. e-Sword.

Booty, John. "Reformers and Missionaries: The Bible in Eighteenth and Early Nineteenth-Century England." *Anglicanism and the Bible*. 117–142. The Anglican Studies Series. Denver, CO: Morehouse Pub Co, 1984.

Booty, John E., and Owen C Thomas. *The Spirit of Anglicanism Hooker, Maurice, Temple*. Edited by William J. Wolf. Wilton, CT Morehouse-Barlow Co. Inc., 1979.

Borsch, Frederick H. "All Things Necessary to Salvation," *Anglicanism and the Bible*. 203–227. The Anglican Studies Series. Denver, CO: Morehouse Pub Co, 1984.

Bray, Gerald. *Anglicanism: A Reformed Catholic Tradition*. Bellingham, WA: Lexham Press, 2021. Logos.

Bromiley, G. W., D. M. Beegle, and W. M. Smith. "English Versions." *The International Standard Bible Encyclopedia*, Revised. Edited by Geoffrey W. Bromiley. Wm. B. Eerdmans, 1979–1988.

Bulgakov, Sergius. *The Comforter*. Translated by Boris Jakim. Grand Rapids, MI; Cambridge, U.K.: William B. Eerdmans Publishing Company. 2004. Logos.

Cantor Norman F. *The Civilization of the Middle Ages A Completely Revised and Expanded Edition of Medieval History*. New York, NY: HarperCollins Publishers, 1993.

Chapman, Mark D., *Anglican Theology*. London; New Delhi; New York; Sydney:Bloomsbury, 2012. Logos.

- *Anglicanism A Very Short Introduction*. Oxford NY: Oxford University Press, 2006.

Clark, Mary T. "Introduction: The Spirituality of St. Augustine." *Augustine of Hippo: Selected Writings*. Edited by John Farina, Translated by Mary T. Clark. The Classics of Western Spirituality. Mahwah, NJ: Paulist Press, 1984. Logos.

Clouse, Robert G. et. al. *The Church from Age to Age A History from Galilee to Global Christianity*. Edited by Edward A. Saint Louis, MO: Concordia Publishing House, 2011.

Cole, Graham A. *He Who Gives Life*. Wheaton, IL: Crossway, 2007.

Collins, Kenneth J. *John Wesley: A Theological Journey*. Nashville, TN: Abingdon Press, 2003.

Costain, Thomas B., *The Three Edwards The Pageant of England*. Garden City, NY: Doubleday & Company, Inc., 1958.

Cross F. L. and Elizabeth A Livingstone, eds. *The Oxford Dictionary of the Christian Church*. Oxford; New York: Oxford University Press, 2005.

Davidson, Basil. *The African Slave Trade Precolonial History 1450¬1850*. Boston, MA; Toronto: Atlantic Monthly Press Book Little Brown and Company, 1961.

Dent, J. M *The Anglo-Saxon Chronicle*. Edited and Translated by M. J. Swanton. University of Exeter. Routledge, NY: Routledge, 1996.

Dersin, Denise, ed. *What Life Was Like In The Realm of Elizabeth England AD 1533–1603*. 5th Printing. Alexandria, VA: Time-Life Books, 1998.

Desplenter, Pieters, and Melion. "Introduction: Exploring the Decalogue in Late Medieval and Early Modern Culture." *The Ten Commandments in Medieval and Early Modern Culture*. Intersections, Volume 52, The Ten Commandments in Medieval and Early Modern Culture. Leiden Boston: Brill, 2017, 1-12.

Desplenter, Youri, Jürgen Pieters, and Walter S. Melion, eds. *The Ten Commandments in Medieval and Early Modern Culture.* Intersections, Volume 52. Leiden Boston: Brill, 2017.

De Schweinitz, Edmund. *The Moravian Manual: Containing an Account of the Moravian Church, or Unitas Fratrum.* Bethlehem, PA: Moravian Publication Office; A. C. & H. T. Clauder, 1869. Logos.

Dever, William G., *Did God Have a Wife? Archaeology and Folk Religion in Ancient Israel.* Grand Rapids, MI; Cambridge, U.K: William B. Eerdmans Publishing Company, 2008. Logos.

DeVries. Kelly. *Infantry Warefare in the Early Fourteenth Century Discipline, Tactics, and Technology.* Woodbridge, Suffolk UK, Rochester, NY USA: The Boydell Press, 1996.

Dinkova-Bruun, Greti. "The Ten Commandments in the Thirteenth-Century Pastoral Manual Qui Bene Presunt." *The Ten Commandments in Medieval and Early Modern Culture.* Edited by Desplenter, Pieters, and Melion. Intersections, Volume 52, Leiden Boston: Brill: The Ten

Commandments in Medieval and Early Modern Culture, 2017, 113-132.

Durant Will & Ariel, *The Story of Civilization: 7 The Age of Reason Begins*. New York, NY: MJF Books, 1961.

Earle, Mary C., ed. *Celtic Christian Spirituality: Essential Writings-Annotated and Explained*. SkyLight Illuminations Series. Woodstock, VT: Skylight Paths Publishing, 2011.

"England," *Darkness of the Dark Ages*. London: G. Morrish, nd. e-Sword.

Edgbaston, Richard Green. *John Wesley-Evangelist* 1905. e-Sword.

Evans, G. R., and J. Robert Wright. *The Anglican Tradition: A Handbook of Sources*. London: SPCK, 1991. Logos.

Feldmeth, Nathan P. Pocket Dictionary of Church History: Over 300 Terms Clearly and Concisely Defined. The IVP Pocket Reference Series. Downers Grove, IL: IVP Academic, 2008. Logos.

Fenwick, John. The Free Church of England: *Introduction to an Anglican Tradition*. London; New York: T&T Clark, 2004. Logos.

Ferguson, Everett. *Church History Volume One: From Christ to the Pre-Reformation, The Rise and Growth of the Church in Its Cultural, Intellectual, and Political Context*. Grand Rapids, MI: Zondervan Academic, 2013.

Finney, Charles G. *Holy Spirit Revivals*. New Kensington, PA: Whitaker House, 2016. Logos.

Flisher, Jr., Allan C., et al., "York and the Northern Counties." *This England*. Edited by Melville Bell Grosvenor and Franc Shor. Washington, D. C.: National Geographic Society, 1966.

Foxe John, Foxe's Book of Martyrs. London, England: John Day, 1563. e-Sword.

Franklin Benjamin. *Franklin Writings The Library of America*. Edited by J.A. Leo Lemay. New York, NY: Literary Classics of the United States, Inc., 1987.

Fremantle, Anne, and Bryan Holme. *Europe A Journey with Pictures*. Scranton, PA: The Studio Publications, Inc., 1954.

Fries, Adelaide L. *The Moravians in Georgia - 1735-1740*. Winston-Salem NC: Public Domain, 1904, e-Sword.

Frodsham, Stanley Howard. *Smith Wigglesworth: Apostle of Faith*. Springfield, MO: Gospel Publishing House, 2010.

Galli, Mark, and Ted Olsen. "Martyrs: Thomas Cranmer, Reform and Reversals." *131 Christians Everyone Should Know*. Nashville, TN: Broadman & Holman Publishers. 2000. Logos.

Geoffrey, Thomas. *The Holy Spirit*. Grand Rapids. MI: Reformation Heritage Books. 2011. Logos.

Gies, Frances and Joseph Gies. *Cathedral, Forge, and Waterwheel Technology and Invention in the Middle Ages*. New York, NY: HarperCollins Publishers, 1994.

Gilmore, Alec "Rolle, Richard," *A Concise Dictionary of Bible Origins and Interpretation*. London; New York: T&T Clark, 2006. Logos.

Gonzalez, Justo L. *The Story of Christianity Volume II The Reformation to the Present Day*. New York, NY: HarperCollins, 2010.

Groeschel, Craig. *The Christian Atheist*. Grand Rapids, MI, Zondervan, 2010.

Greer, Rowan A., *Anglican Approaches to Scripture From the Reformation to the Present*. New York, NY: The Crossroad Publishing Company, 2006.

Grieb, Katherine A., "Anglican Interpretations of Scripture: Can Scriptural Reasoning Provide a Way Forward?" *Canterbury Studies in Anglicanism.* Edited by Martyn Percy and Ian Markham, 29–42. A Point of Balance The Weight and Measurement of Anglicanism. New York, NY; Harrisburg, PA; Denver, CO: Morehouse Publishing, 2012.

Guilbert, Charles Mortimer. *The Book of Common Prayer and Administration of the Sacraments and Other Rites and Ceremonies of the Church According to the Use of the Episcopal Church.* New York: The Church Hymnal Corporation and The Seabury Press, 1977.

Gurst, John D. *Saga of a Sceptred Isle.* Printed, 15"x10", 1966, inside "This England." National Geographic Society cover. 1966.

Hale. *The Civilization of Europe in the Renaissance.* American, Atheneum Macmillan Publishing Company, 1994.

Hanson, Brian L. *The Essential Lexham Dictionary of Church History.* Edited by Michael A. G. Haykin. Bellingham, WA: Lexham Press, 2022.

Harrison, John B., and Richard E. Sullivan. *A Short History of Western Civilization*. New York: Alfred A. Knopf, Inc., 1962.

Haugaard, William P. "The Bible in the Anglican Reformation." *Anglicanism and the Bible* (The Anglican Studies Series). Wilton, CT: Morehouse Pub Co, 1984. PDF.

Heath, Duncan, and Judy Boreham. *Introducing Romanticism*. London: Icon Books Ltd, 2012.

Hein, David, and Gardiner H. Shattuck Jr., *The Episcopalians, Denominations in America*. Number 11. Westport, CT; London: Praeger Publishers, 2004.

Henley, Wallace. Call Down Lightning: *What the Welsh Revival of 1904 Reveals About the End Times*. Nashville, TN: Thomas Nelson, 2019. Logos.

Hodge, Charles. *Systematic Theology. Vol. 1*. Oak Harbor, WA: Logos Research Systems, Inc., 1997. Logos.

Holder, Ward R., *Crisis and Renewal The Era of the Reformations* (Westminster History of Christian Thought). Louisville, KY: Westminster John Knox Press, 2009. Kindle.

Holmes, S. R. "Lateran Councils," *New Dictionary of Theology: Historical and Systematic*. Edited by Martin Davie et al., London; Downers Grove, IL: InterVarsity Press, 2016. Logos.

Hornbeck II, Patrick, et al., *Wycliffite Spirituality*. Translated by J. Patrick Hornbeck II et al., The Classics of Western Spirituality. New York; Mahwah, NJ: Paulist Press, 2013. Logos.

Horton, C. J., "The Holy Spirit Fifth Annual Fort Worth Christian College Lectureship March 22–26, 1964." *The Holy Spirit in Christian Growth*. Fort Worth, TX: Fort Worth Christian College, 1964. e-Sword.

Hutton J. E., M.A., *The History of The Moravian Movement*. Second edition, 1909. e-Sword.

- *A History of the Moravian Church*. Second Edition, Book Two. Prepared by John Bechard. London: 1909. Kindle.

Irvin, Dale T, and Scott W. Sunquist. *History of the World Christian Movement: Modern Christianity from 1454–1800*. Maryknoll, NY: Orbis Books, 1970. www.maryknollsociety.org.

Jackson, Thomas ed. "A Plain Account of Christian Perfection, as Believed to be Taught by the Reverend Mr. John Wesley From the Year 1725, to the Year 1777." *The Works of John Wesley*. Vol. 11. 1872. e-Sword.

Jefferson, Kurt W. *Celtic Politics: Politics in Scotland, Ireland, and Wales*. Lanham, MA; Boulder; New York; Toronto; Plymouth, UK: University Press America, Inc., 2011.

Johnson, Paul. *A History of the American People*. New York, NY: HarperCollins Publishing, 1997.

Johnston, William. *The Wounded Stag: Originally published in a cloth edition as Christian Mysticism Today*. New York, NY, Toronto: Haper & Row and Fitzhenry & Whiteside, 1984.

Jones, Christopher M., "Song of Songs, Book Of, Critical Issues." Edited by John D. Barry et al., *The Lexham Bible Dictionary*. Bellingham, WA: Lexham Press, 2016.

Jones, E. A. ed, *Hermits and Anchorites in England 1200–1550*. Manchester Medieval Sources Series, Manchester, Manchester University Press, 2019. Kindle.

Keener, Craig S., Gift & Giver *The Holy Spirit for Today*. Grand Rapids, MI: Baker Academic, 2001. Logos.

Kempe, Margery. *The Book of Margery Kempe*. Edited and translated by B. A. Windeatt, London, England: Penguin Classics, 2005. Kindle.

Kempis, Thomas à, *The Imitation of Christ Translated from Latin to Modern English*. Translated by Aloysius Croft and Harold Bolton. Oak Harbor, WA: Logos Research Systems, 1996. Logos,

Kilcrease, Jack "Purgatory," *Lexham Survey of Theology*. Edited by Mark Ward et al. Bellingham, WA: Lexham Press, 2018. Logos.

Knight III, Henry H. *John Wesley: Optimist of Grace*. Eugene, OR: Cascade Books, 2018.

Kuh, Michael, et al., "The Age of Chivalry," *Questing Life of the Scholar*. Edited by Merle Serverly and Fredrick G. Vosburgh. Man Library, Washington, D. C.: National Geographic Society, 1969.

Kurian, George Thomas. *Nelson's New Christian Dictionary: The Authoritative Resource on the Christian World*. Nashville, TN: Thomas Nelson Publishers, 2001.

Lawson, James Gilchrist. *Deeper Experiences of Famous Christians First published in 1911.* White Tree Publishing, 2018. Kindle.

Lewis, Brenda Ralph ed. *Great Civilizations.* Bath, BA HE, UK: Parragon Publishing, 2003.

Lights and Shadows of the Reformation. London, Great Briton: G. Morrish, 1915. e-Sword.

Lin, Timothy. *How the Holy Spirit Works in Beleivers' Lives Today.* Carmel, IN: Biblical Studies Ministries International, Inc., 2002.

Lobley, Douglas. *Ships Through the Ages.* London: Octopus Books Ltd., 1972.

London Daniel DeForest. *The Cloud of Unknowing Distilled.* Hannacroix, NY: Apocryphile Press, 2021. Kindle.

Lützow, Francis. *The Hussite Wars.* London; New York: J. M. Dent & Sons; E. P. Dutton & Co., 1914. Logos.

M'Clintock D.D., John, and James Strong. "Bradwardine, Thomas," *Cyclopedia of Biblical, Theological and Ecclesiastical Literature.* New York: Harper Brothers, Publishers, 1895.

MacGregor, Geddes. *The Bible in the Making*. Philadelphia; New York: J. B. Lippincott Company, 1959.

Manser, Martin, and Mike Beaumont. *Handbook of Bible Prayers*. Manser and Beaumont, 2020.

Matthews, David. *I Saw the Welsh Revival*. Greenville, SC: Ambassador International, 2018. Logos.

Mattingly, Garett. *The Armada*. USA: The Riverside Press Cambridge, Houghton Mifflin Company Boston, 1959.

Maude, J. H., *The History of the Book of Common Prayer*. Edited by Leighton Pullan, Second edition. London: Rivingtons: Oxford Church Text Books, 1900. Logos.

McCrum, Robert, William Cran, and Robert MacNeil. *The Story of English*. New York, NY: Elisabeth Sifton Books, Viking, Viking Penguin Inc., 1986.

McGinn, Bernard, ed., *Celtic Spirituality*. Translated by Oliver Davies. The Classics of Western Spirituality, New York: Mahwah, NJ: Paulist Press, 1999. Logos.

McManners, John ed., *The Oxford Illustrated History of Christianity*. Oxford, New York: Oxford University Press, 1991.

Meiklejohn, J. W., et al., *New Bible Dictionary*. Leicester, England; Downers Grove, IL: InterVarsity Press, 1996. Logos.

Meyer, Michael C., and William H. Breezley ed. *The Oxford History of Mexico*. New York, NY: Oxford University Press, 2000.

Miller, Robert P. ed., *Chaucer Sources and Backgrounds*. New York: Oxford University Press, 1977.

Morris, Colin. "Christian Civilization." *The Oxford Illustrated History of Christianity*. Edited by John McManners. Oxford, New York: Oxford University Press, 1991.

Morison, Samuel Eliot. *The European Discovery of America: The Southern Voyages A. D. 1492-1616*. Oxford, NY: Oxford University Press, 1974.

Oden, Thomas C. ed., "Song of Solomon 1:1-4 The Bride and the Lover." *Ancient Christian Commentary on Scripture*. Downers Grove, IL InterVarsity Press, 2010. e-Sword.

O'Loughlin, Thomas, "Hagiography," *Celtic Spirituality*. Edited by Bernard McGinn, translated by Oliver Davies. The Classics of Western Spirituality, New York; Mahwah, NJ: Paulist Press, 1999. Logos.

Pacwa, Mitch. *The Holy Spirit A Bible Study Guide for Catholics*. Huntington, IN: Our Sunday Visitor, 2016. Kindle.

Parks, Jessica. "The Decline of the Papacy in the Middle Ages." *In Church History Themes*. Edited by Zachariah Carter. Bellingham, WA: Faithlife, 2022. Logos.

- ed. *Jonathan Edwards: A Guide to His Life and Writings*. Faithlife Author Guides. Bellingham, WA: Faithlife, 2017.

Penn-Lewis, Jessie. *The Awakening in Wales*. New Kensington, PA: Whitaker House, 2014.

Penn, William. *A Brief Account of the Rise and Progress of the People Called Quakers*. Transcribed by David Price. London: Harris & Crofield, 1834, e-Sword.

Peters, Greg "Asceticism," Glen G. Scorgie ed. *Dictionary of Christian Spirituality*. Grand Rapids, MI: Zondervan, 2011. Logos.

Prosper Grech, *An Outline of New Testament Spirituality*. Grand Rapids, MI; Cambridge, UK: William B. Eerdmans Publishing Company, 2011.

Robeck, Cecil M., Jr. "Series Foreword." *How Pentecost Came to Los Angeles: The Story behind the Azusa Street Revival.* Edited by Cecil M. Robeck Jr. and Darrin Rodgers, 6. Azusa Street Book Series. Springfield, MO: Gospel Publishing House, 2017. Logos.

Roberts, Evan, Arthur Goodrich, G. Campbell Morgan, W. T. Stead, Evan Hopkins, E.W. Moore. *The Story of the Welsh Revival by Eyewitnesses*, published in 1905. JawboneDigital, 2015. http://www.JawboneDigital.com. Kindle.

Rusten, Sharon with E. Michael. *The Complete Book of When & Where in the Bible and throughout History.* Wheaton, IL: Michael E Rusten, 2005. Logos.

Sanders, Frank Knight, and Charles Foster Kent. "1. Introduction to Canticles, 4. Recognition of a Literal Sense." *Volume 1: The Messages of the Earlier Prophets Arranged in the Order of Time Analyzed, and Freely Rendered in Paraphrase.*

Third edition. New York: Charles Scribner's Sons, 1899. e-Sword.

Schaff, Philip. *The Creeds of Christendom, with a History and Critical Notes: The History of Creeds.* Vol. 1. New York: Harper & Brothers, Publishers, 1878. Logos.

- *The Creeds of Christendom, with a History and Critical Notes: The History of Creeds.* Vol. 7. New York: Harper & Brothers, Publishers, 1878, Logos.

- *The Creeds of Christendom, with a History and Critical Notes: The History of Creeds.* Vol. 8. New York: Harper & Brothers, Publishers, 1878, Logos.

Schama, Simon. *A History of Britain At the Edge of the World? 3500 B.C.–1603 A.D..* New York, NY: Hyperion, 2000.

Schwarz, Christian A. *The 3 Colors of Ministry: A trinitarian approach to identifying and developing your spiritual gifts.* St. Charles, IL: ChurchSmart Resources, nd.

Schweinitz, Edmund De. *The History of the Church Known as the Unitas Fratrum or The Unity of the Brethren*. Bethlehem, PA: Moravian Publication Office, 1885. Logos.

Sharon with Rusten and E. Michael. *The Complete Book of When & Where in the Bible and throughout History*. Wheaton, IL: Michael E Rusten, 2005.

Singer, Isidore, ed. "Akiba Ben Joseph." *The Jewish Encyclopedia: A Descriptive Record of the History, Religion, Literature, and Customs of the Jewish People from the Earliest Times to the Present Day, 12 Volumes*. New York; London: Funk & Wagnalls, 1901–1906. Logos.

Smith, Carol and Roddy Smith. *Quicknotes Christian History Guidebook*. Uhrichsville, OH: Barbour Publishing, Inc., 2001.

Smith, Lesley. "The Ten Commandments in the Medieval Schools: Conformity or Diversity." "Introduction: Exploring the Decalogue in Late Medieval and Early Modern Culture." *The Ten Commandments in Medieval and Early Modern Culture*. Edited by Desplenter, Pieters, and Melion. Intersections, Volume 52, The Ten

Commandments in Medieval and Early Modern Culture. Leiden Boston: Brill, 2017. 13–29.

"Song of Solomon." *Biblical Dead Sea Scrolls: Bible Reference Index.* Bellingham, WA: Lexham Press, 2011. Logos.

St. Augustine, *Saint Augustine Confessions.* "Introduction." Translated by R. S. Pine-Coffin. New York: Barnes & Noble Books, 1992.

Stead, William T. *The Welsh Revival A Narrative of Facts* and Morgan, G. Campbell. *Revival: its Power and Source, Book Two: The Story of the Welsh Revival As told by Eyewitnesses Together With a Sketch of Evan Roberts and His Message to The World.* Trumpet Press 2022. Kindle.

Strayer, Joseph R. and Dana C. Munro, *The Middle Ages 395-1500.* Fourth edition. New York: Appleton-Century-Crofts, Inc. 1959.

Suplee, Curt. *Milestones of Science.* Washington D. C.: National Geographic, 2000.

Thiselton, Anthony C. *Systematic Theology.* Grand Rapids, MI; Cambridge, U.K.: William B. Eerdmans Publishing Company, 2015. Logos.

Thomas, Gordon and Max Morgan Witts, *The San Francisco Earthquake*. New York: Stein and Day/Publishers/, 1971.

Thompson, Jeremy. *Lists from Church History. Faithlife Biblical and Theological Lists*. Bellingham, WA: Faithlife, 2022. Logos.

Thornton, Martin. *English Spirituality: An Outline of Ascetical Theology According to the English Pastoral Tradition*. Eugene, OR: Wipf & Stock Publishers, 2012. Logos.

Time-Life Books. *What Life Was Like in the Age of Chivalry Medieval Europe AD 800–1500*. Time-Life Education, 1997.

Torrell, Jean-Pierre. *Christ and Spirituality in St. Thomas Aquinas*. Edited by Matthew Levering and Thomas Joseph White. Translated by Bernhard Blankenhorn. Vol. 2. Thomistic Ressourcement Series, Washington, D.C.: The Catholic University of America Press, 2011. Logos.

Tuchman, Barbara W. *Bible and Sword: England and Palestine from the Bronze Age to Balfour*. New York: Ballantine Books. 1984.

Underhill, Evelyn. *The Mystics of the Church*. New York: George H. Doran Company, 1925. Logos.
- **Mysticism: A Study in the Nature and Development of Man's Spiritual Consciousness*. Dutton and Company. 1912. Logos.

Ussher, James. *The Annals of the World*. Revised and updated by Larry and Marion Pierce. Green Forest AR: Master Books, 2003.

Volz, Carl A. *The Medieval Church: From the Dawn of the Middle Ages to the Eve of the Reformation*. Nashville, TN: Abingdon Press. 1997.

Walker, Williston, *A History of the Christian Church*. Third Edition. New York, NY: Charles Scribner's Sons, 1970.

Whitefield, George. "Folly and Danger of not Being Righteous Enough," *Whitfield, George-Sermons*. Franklin, TN: e-Sword Version 13.0.0, Rick Meyers, 2021.

Wilson, Mitchell. *American Science and Invention: A Pictorial History*. New York, NY: Simon and Schuster 1954.

Woodbridge, John D. and Frank A. James III. *Church History Volume Two From Pre-Reformation to the Present Day*. Grand Rapids, MI: Zondervan, 2013.

Woods, Robin. *Touched by Heaven: When God Sends Revival*. Greenville, SC: Ambassador International, 2017. Logos.

Wright, Louis B. "The Thames Mirrors Britain's Glory." *This England*. Edited by Merle Serverly, Seymour L. Fishbein, and Edwards Park. World in Color Library, Washington, D. C.: National Geographic Society, 1966.

Youngblood, Ronald F. et al., "Bible Versions and Translations." *Nelson's New Illustrated Bible Dictionary*. Nashville, TN: Thomas Nelson, Inc., 1995.

Principal Resources from the Web

https://www.academia.edu/

https://www.africanhistoryextra.com

http://akensidepress.com/thornton/about/index.html.

https://anglicanfocus.org.au/2021

https://archives.history.

https://avalon.law.yale.edu/17th_century/westphal.asp.

https://banneroftruth.org/

https://www.baylor.edu/

https://berkeleydivinity.yale.edu/news/frederick-h-borsch

https://www.bl.uk/people/anselm-of-canterbury.

https://bibleinterp.arizona.edu/sites/bibleinterp.arizona.edu/files/docs/Smith1.pdf.

https://bibleinterp.arizona.edu/sites/bibleinterp.arizona.edu/files/docs/Smith1.pdf.

https://books.google.com/

https://www.britannica.com/
https://byzantinebronzes.ancients.info/
https://www.catholictextbookproject.com/
https://www.ccel.org/
http://web.cn.edu/kwheeler/
https://collections.bristolmuseums.org.uk
http://courses.washington.edu/

https://d.lib.rochester.edu/
https://deforestlondon.wordpress.com/
https://digitalcommons.luthersem.edu/
https://doi.org/10.17570/stj.2020.v6n1.a.
https://ebookcentral-proquest-com.ezproxy.regent.edu/
https://www.emperorcharlesv.com/
https://www.encyclopedia.com/
https://www.english-heritage.org.uk/
https://www.englishmonarchs.co.uk/
https://www.episcopalchurch.org/
https://www.geni.com/
https://ghdi.ghi-dc.org/
https://www.globalsecurity.org/
https://www.gresham.ac.uk/
https://www.heeve.com/modern-history/

https://www.historyextra.com/
http://www.historyfish.net/
https://www.historyhit.com/
https://www.historynaked.com/
https://www.historyofinformation.com/
https://www.historyofparliamentonline.org/
https://www.historytoday.com/
https://www.historic-uk.com/
http://www.holyromanempireassociation.com/
https://www.historytoday.com/
https://ia600204.us.archive.org/
https://www.jewishvirtuallibrary.org/
https://lux.lawrence.edu/
https://libguides.fau.edu/
https://www.luminarium.org/
https://msa.maryland.gov/
https://www.military-history.org/
https://museeprotestant.org/en/
https://muse.jhu.edu/
https://www.mzv.cz/teheran/en/
https://www.nationaltrust.org.uk/
https: //nasa.gov.
https://northumberlandkt.com/
https://oll.libertyfund.org/

https://origins.osu.edu/
https://pillars.taylor.edu/
https://plato.stanford.edu/
https://www.preces-latinae.org/
https://pure.royalholloway.ac.uk/
https://www.religion-online.org/
https://rhqrmp.org/
https://www.ria.ie/
https://www.royal.uk/
https://sermons.logos.com/sermons/
https://www.stdavidscathedral.org.uk/discover/history/
https://textandcanon.org/
https://www.thecollector.com/
http://theconversation.com/
https://www.ushistory.org/
https://www.warhistoryonline.com/
https://www.wired.com/
https://www.worldhistory.org/
https://www.wondriumdaily.com/
https://www.uh.edu/

Battles, Councils, People, Places Index

A

- *A Discourse of the Religion Anciently Professed by the Irish and the British*, 240

- *A History of the English Church and People*, 30

- Abelard, 54, 58

- Act of Supremacy, 201

- *Adages*, 191

- Adam, (Gen. 1-5), 102, 126, 128

- Aelred of Rievaulx, v, 54–57, 75

- Alaric and the Goths, 31

- American Revolution, 313

- *Analogy of Religion*, 15
- *Ancrene Wisse*, 74–75
- Anselm, 8, 11, 40–43, 140–141, 147, 162, 234
- Aquinas, Thomas 80, 187
- archbishop(s), vii, 67, 165, 167, 225, 245
  - Archbishop of Armagh,
    - James Ussher, 240, 246
  - Archbishop of Canterbury, 39–40, 85, 125, 126, 162, 225, 227
    - Anselm, See Anselm
    - Arundel, Thomas, See Arundel
    - Courtenay, William, 125, 129
    - Cranmer, See Cranmer, Thomas in Denomination and Founder Index
    - Lanfranc, 39
    - Laud, William, 241, 243, 244

- Parker, Matthew, 222
- Reginald, 67–68
- Sudbury, Simon, 128
- Warham, William, 192, 193, 199
  - Archbishop of Genoa,
    - Jacobus de Voragine, 60
  - Archbishop of Mainz, Cologne, Trier, 166
  - Archbishop of Prague, 140
    - Zbynek, 171
  - Archbishop of Salzburg, Bavaria, 275
  - Archbishop of York, 40, 152
    - Thurstan, 54
- archdeaconries, 79
- Arndt, Johann, 265, 285
- Arthur of Brittany, 66–67

- Arundel, Thomas
  - Abbot, 150
  - Canterbury Archbishop, 143, 144
  - Chancellor, 146, 148–150
- Asbury, Francis, 309
- *Assertion of the Seven Sacraments*, 196
- Augsburg Confession, 230, 273, 274

B

- Bacon, Francis, 238
- Bacon, Roger, 80, 82, 192
- Bakongo, 189
- Ball, John, 126, 128
- Balliol, John, King of Scotland, 92–93
- Balliol College, 98, 119

- Barclay, Robert, 265

- Baron's War, 84

- Baroness Henrietta Catherine von Gersdorf, 270

- Bartleman, Frank, 336

- battle, 189

  - Battle of Bovines, 69

  - Battle of Crecy, 101, 105

  - Battle of Hastings, 39

  - Battle of Marignano, 193

  - Battle of Mohacs, 199

  - Battle of Novara, 193

  - Battle of Poitier, 108

  - Battle of White Mountain, 237

- Bavaria, 96, 166, 234, 237, 238, 275

- Bede, 29, 30, 33–34
- Belgic Confession, 235
- Bernard of Clairvaux, v, 36, 45, 56, 97, 140
  - mysticism, 55, 147
- Blessed Sacrament or Rosary Societies, 186
- Blount, William, 191
- Bohler, Peter, 287
- Bonaventure of Bagnoregio, 80, 82–83, 140
- *Book of Invasions*, 28
- *Book of Margery Kempe*, 152
- *Book of Nature*, 38
- Booth, William, 317
- Bradwardine, Thomas, 98–99, 100, 102–103, 141
- Brahe, Tycho, 221, 223-224, 227-228

- Bramwell, William, 314

- Brethren of Common Life, 141, 183–184, 188

- *Breviary*, 77

- Bridget of Sweden, St., 141, 143, 148

- Bridgewater Canal, 294

- Bristol, 127, 151, 183, 248-249, 290, 291, 309, 315

- British and the Foreign Bible Society, 14

- British Colonies, 248, 317

    - American, 266, 289, 291, 293, 335

- British Empire, 310, 314-317

- Brunel, Isambard Kingdom, 315

- Brutus (Noah's son), 28

- Bull(s), 82, 125, 172, 184, 195, 196

    - Gold Bull, 165

- Golden Bull, 166
- Bullinger, Henry, 200
- Bunyan, John, 247
- Burnell, Hugh, 144

C

- Calvet, George, Baron of Baltimore, 240
- Cambridge, 15, 67, 191, 192, 194, 228, 240
  - Chancellor, 77, 191
  - Platonists, 242
  - Trinity College, 246
- Canterbury, 8, 39-40, 42, 128, 148, 172
  - Latin and Old English documents, 39
  - Shrine of Archbishop Beckett, 60
  - Warden of Canterbury Hall, 119

- *Canterbury Tales*, 60, 131
- cardinal, 70, 126, 172, 178, 195
- Carey, William, 294
- Catherine of Sweden, St., 141
- *Charter of Love*, 44
- *Château d'Amour*, 79
- Chaucer, 60, 131
- *Chronicle of the Augustine Canon*, 130
- Cluny, 43
- Coke, Thomas, 309
- Colenso, J. W., 317
- Colet, John, 191, 192
- College of St. George, 104–105
- Cologne, 166, 186, 192, 196, 198, 204
  - College/University, 81, 83, 184, 187

- Columbus, Cristopher, 189
- Copernicus, Nicolaus, 203, 224, 227, 233, 239, 247
- Cortes, Hernan, 199
- Council of Constance, 172–174, 177
- Council of Orange, 32
- Council of Whitby, 11, 33
- Council of Venice, 95
- Council of Zurich, 198
- Cromwell, Oliver, 243, 245-246, 247
- Cromwell, Thomas, 202
- Courtney, William L., 323
- *Cur Deus Homo?*, 41, 42
- Cutler, Anne, 314

D

- Darby, Abraham, 269
- Darwin, Charles, 317
- *De Antiquitate Britannicae Ecclesiae*, 222-223
- De Haerectico Comburendo. statute, 144
- *De Processione Spiritus Sancti*, 43
- *Defensor Pacis*, 95
- Descartes, Rene, 247-248, 308
- Diet, 190, 206
    - Diet in Prague, Bohemian, 221, 230
    - Diet at Worms, 190
    - General, 190, 230
    - Protestant Estates, 235
- Digges, Thomas, 222

- Dionysius, 35, 242

- Dominican(s), 66, 76, 80, 83, 186

- *Domus Conversorum*, 79

- Drummond, Lewis, 331-332

- Durham Cathedral, 102

E

- Early Cathedral schools, study, 38, 58

- Edinburgh Castle, 93, 96

- Edwards, Johnathon, 270, 274, 275, 280, 289, 291, 308, 312, 335

- Elizabethan Settlement, 4

- Episcopius, Simon, 230

- *Epistle on Mixed Life*, 148

- *Exposition on the Canticle of Canticles*, 32

- Evans, Christmas, 316

F

- First Council of Lyon, 81

- Fisher, John, 191, 201

- Fountains Abbey, 44,

- *Four Books of Sentences*, 58–59, 69, 81, 83

- Fourth Lateran Council, 70

  - of 1201, 66–67

  - of 1214, 68

  - of 1215, 69

  - of 1220, 77

- *Foxe's Book of Martyrs*, 120

- Fox, Richard, 191

- Francis of Assisi, 68, 77, 121

- Franciscan(s), 66, 76–77, 80, 99, 151
- Franke, August Herman, 266, 267, 268, 270, 282
- Franklin, Benjamin, 269, 271, 277-278, 279, 281, 290-291, 293-294, 340-341
- Franklin, James, 270, 271
- Franklin, Josiah, 266
- Frederick di Lavagna 81
- Frederick of Hohenstaufen, 68
- Fredrick of Austria, 95
- Fredrick the Wise of Saxony, 195
- Frelinghuysen, Theodore Jacobus, 269
- French and Indian War (Seven Year War with France), 313
- French Revolution, 314
- Frisian Nethread peasant revolt, 197

- Frisian peasant revolt, 193

G

- Galileo, 231-232, 233, 241, 242, 247, 308
- Geoffrey of Monmouth, 29
- Georgia, 277, 279, 282, 286, 287, 293
- Glastonbury, 29
- Goforth, Jonathon, 336
- Great Schism, 126–127, 172–173
- Grosseteste, Robert, 36, 70, 79–82, 141, 192
- Guillaume de Nogaret, 94
- Gutenberg, Johann, 179, 185

H

- Habsburg(s), 193, 195, 197, 199, 230, 233,

234-235, 238, 245
- Hamburg, Germany, 199
- Hampole, Yorkshire, 97–98
- Handel, Frideric, 267
- Harding, Steven, 44
- Hargreaves, James, 313
- *Harmonies of the World*, 237
- Hemphill, Samuel, 279, 281
- Henrietta-Marie de Bourbon, 240
- Henry de Beauchamp, 153
- Henry of Lancaster (Prince Henery), 143, 144–145, 149
- Henry the Navigator, 183, 184
- Herrnhut, 271–272, 273, 274, 276-277, 278, 280, 282, 289, 294, 295
- Hinton, Simon, 83–84

- *Historia Britonum*, 29
- Holy Roman Emperor, 165–167, 245
  - Charles the Bald, 35
  - Charles V, (Charles I king of Spain), 194, 195, 200, 201
- Ferdinand II, Holy Roman Emperor, 234, 235, 237, 238
- Ferdinand III, Holy Roman Emperor, 243
- Fredrick II, Holy Roman Emperor, 166
- Fredrick III, Holy Roman Emperor, 190
- Henry VII, 166
- Louis the Bavarian, 95–96
- Matthias, 233
- Maximilian I, 190, 194
- Maximilian II, 223
- Rudolf II, 223, 228, 233

- Sigismund, 173, 174
- Holy Roman Empire, 166, 169, 195, 197, 221, 230, 237, 240
- Hooker, Richard, 224, 225, 227
- House of Orange, 222, 236
- Howell, Dean, 322
- Hugh de Lusignan, 66, 67
- Hugh of St. Victor, 55
- Hundred Years War, 98, 126

I

- Ignatius of Loyola, 202
- *In Praise of Folly*, 191
- Inquisition(s), 69, 149, 187, 203, 205, 206, 222, 233, 242
- Ireland, 44, 68, 248

- Armagh, 246
- Kells, Ulster Ireland, 316
- Mount Sandel near Coleraine, Ireland, 29

- Isabella of Angouleme, 66
- Isabella of Gloucester, 66

J

- J. H. Newman, 14
- Jamestown, 4, 229, 232
- Jerome of Prague, 169, 176
- Jesuit(s), 202, 203, 206, 222, 230, 234, 238, 337
- John "the Scot" Ericgena, 35–36
- John of Gaunt, 122, 124, 125, 127–128, 129
- John of Jandun, 95

- John of Reading, 99
- Jones Griffith, 280
- Joshuah, Seth, 322
- Joyce, George, 193–194

K

- Kay, John, 278
- Keating, Thomas, 145
- Keble, John, Tractarian leader, 15
- Kepler, Johannes, 226-228, 229, 231, 233, 237, 238, 247, 308
- Kempe, Margery 142, 147–148, 150, 152, 163
- Khan, Genghis, 103
- Khasi Hills. 336
- King(s), 11, 40, 75, 76, 79, 107, 139, 166, 189, 190, 193, 221, 228, 239, 240, 311

BATTLES, COUNCILS, PEOPLE, PLACES INDEX

- Affono, Dom of the Congo, 188, 193, 195
- Arthur, 30, 99–100
- Balliol, John, of Scotland, see Balliol, John
- Cazimir of Poland, king of Bohemia, 186
- Charles I, 4, 240, 241, 242, 244, 245
- Charles I, of Spain, (Charles V Holy Roman Emperor), 194-195, 196, 199, 200, 201, 206, 224
- Charles II, 228, 241, 247, 266
- Charles IV, of Bohemia, 140, 166
- Christian IV, Prince, Duke of Holstein, of Denmark and Norway, 239
- Christian VI, King of Denmark, 276
- David I of Scottland, 40, 54–55
- David Bruce of Scottland, 95, 96, 101
- Earl Harold Godwinson, 38-39

- (King continued)
  - Edward of Woodstock (king of Wales),
    - Black Knight, 100, 105
    - Black Prince, 101, 108, 120, 124
  - Edward I, 85, 92–94
  - Edward II, 95
  - Edward III, 99–101, 103–105, 107, 108, 119–121, 122, 124, 125
  - Edward VI, 202, 205, 207
  - Edward the Confessor, 38, 104, 143
  - Ferdinand II of Bohemia, (Ferdinand von Habsburg), 218, 220, 233, 234, 235
  - Ferdinand of Castile (Fredrick II of Aragon) and Queen Isabella, 187-188, 194
  - Francis I of France, 195, 201
  - Frederick I of Denmark and Norway, 268

- Fredrick II of Denmark, 221, 224
- Fredrick V, Elector Palatine, king of Bohemia, 233, 236, 237
- George II, 276
- Harold Godwinson, 38, 39
- Henry Elector and King of Saxony, 278
- Henry I, 43, 101
- Henry II, 59, 69, 163
- Henry III, 77, 78–79, 84, 104
- Henry IV, 143, 144–145
- Henry V, 127, 149–150, 152–153, 172
- Henry VI (infant king of England and France), 153
- Henry VII of Germany, 165
- Henry VIII, 12, 15, 17, 153, 162, 195, 200, 201, 204

- (Kings continued)
  - James I, 4, 222, 229, 236, 238, 239
  - James II, 266
  - John, vi, 65–70, 77, 78, 119–120, 162
  - John III of Portugal, 205
  - John Ernest of Saxony, 270
  - John the Good of France, 108
  - Ladislaus, of Naples, 172
  - Manuel of Portugal, 195
  - Malcom III of Scotland, Canmore, 40
  - Matthias of Bohemia, 233
  - Maximilian I of Germany, 190
  - Maximilian II of Bohemia, 211, 223
  - of the Romans, 166, 173
  - Nizinga of the Congo, (Jooao I), 188

- Otto of Germany, 69
- Philip II of France, 59, 66–67, 68–70
- Philip II of Spain, 206
- Philip IV of France, 93–94
- Philip V of Spain, 268
- Philip VI of France, 96, 99, 107
- Premysl Otakor I, first king of Bohemia, 165
- Richard the Lionhearted, 66
- Richard II, 126, 127, 128–129, 138–139, 140, 141, 143, 145, 150, 151
- Robert the Bruce, 94
- Sigismund, of Bohemia, King of the Romans, 173
- Soyo, Mwene of Soya, Congo 189
- Wenceslaus of Bohemia, 170
- William and Mary, 248

- William the Bastard, 38
  - William the Conqueror, 39, 40, 42–43, 101, 162
- Wladislas of Bohemia, 149
- Knighton, Henry, 130–131
- Korean Revival, 336

L

- Lanphier, Jeremiah, 316
- Langland, William, 126
- Latimer, William, 192
- Lauf, William, 240
- *Laws*, 224
- Leicester, 142, 155,
- Lincoln, 79, 81–82, 150

BATTLES, COUNCILS, PEOPLE, PLACES INDEX   399

- - Banbury, 142

  - Lincolnshire, 56

- Lombard, Peter, 58–59, 69, 83, 162

- London, 59, 79, 93, 94, 125, 150, 151, 153, 185, 224-226, 232, 246, 270, 284, 288, 292, 315, 316-317

  - bishop, 125, 126, 197, 225, 227

  - Company, 229, 236, 246, 293

  - Tower, 128, 142, 243

- Lord Mountjoy, 191, 193

- Lord Percy, 125

- Luthia, India, 336

M

- *Magna Carta*, 69, 77

- Manchurian Revival, 337

- *Man of Laws Tale*, 131
- Maryland, 241
- Marsilius of Padua, 95
- Maurice of Nassau, 227, 229, 236
- *Maximus the Confessor*, 35, 36
- McDermitt, Mary, 335
- *Meditations on the Passion*, 97, 148
- Melanchthon, Philip, 197, 204
- Meninger, William, 145
- Merton, 84, 98, 108
- Milton, John, 247, 248
- *Mind's Journey to God*, 82
- *Monologion*, 41
- More, Thomas, 191-192, 199, 201
- Morning and/or Evening Prayer, 12

- Morning, Noonday, Evening Office, 8, 147, 332

- Morse, Samuel, 315

- Moses, (Gen. Exo., Leviticus, Numbers, and Deu.) 5, 199, 317

- Mount Tavor, 178

N

- New England, 238, 271, 274, 286, 289, 291, 312

- New York, 270, 294, 315, 316

- Newton, Isaac, 247-248

- Nicene Creed, 1

- Noah (Gen. 6:11-9:19), v, 28, 317

- Normandy, 8, 11, 38, 66, 69, 162
  - Bec, 40

- Rouen, 67

- Northampton Congressional Church, Massachusetts, 274, 275, 280, 291

- Notre Dame, 58

O

- *Of the Laws of Ecclesiastical Polity*, 225

- Oglethorpe, General, 279

- Old English, vi, vii, 39

- Oldenbarnevelt, Johan van, 232, 236-237

- *On Friendship*, 57

- *On the Church*, 172, 174

- *Order of the Church*, 16

- Oxford, 15, 59, 67, 69–70, 79-80, 97, 121, 125, 146, 153, 163, 229, 310

  - All Soul's College, 241

- anchorites, 85
- Balliol College, 119
- chancellor, 70, 148
- Dominican, 83
- Franciscan, 80
- Holy Club, 274, 275, 281
- Lincoln Colledge, 272
- Merton, 84, 98, 108
- movement, 14, 315
- professor 83, 120–122, 173, 191
- student(s), 67, 97, 107–108, 141–142, 144, 170, 281
- theology, 15, 98, 102, 120, 141

P

- Palace of the Popes at Avignon, 95, 96, 103, 105, 127
- Palatine, 166, 197, 207, 234, 237, 238
- Parchmyner, William, 150
- Paris, 43, 79, 80, 81, 104, 163, 185, 313
    - Notre Dame, 58
    - schools, 54, 55
        - University, 55, 59, 76, 78–79, 82, 95
            - St. Genevieve's Mount, 55
- Parliament, 120, 124, 131, 142, 143–144, 149, 190, 226, 240, 242–244, 245, 316, 324
    - beginnings, 79, 80, 82, 84
    - statutes, 107, 144, 201, 226, 242, 267
        - Statute of Laborers, 107, 127

- Statute of Praemunire, 107
- Statute of Provisors, 106
- Paul, Lewis, 287
- Paul (the apostle), 3, 38, 124, 288-289
- Peace of Augsburg, 206, 207
- Peasant Revolt of 1381, 127–129
- Pennington, Basil, 145
- Pennsylvania, 266, 276, 280-281, 291, 293
- *Piers Plowman*, 126
- Pilgrim's Progress. 266
- *Plague Song*, 190
- Plato/ Platonist 57, 84, 242
- *Poor Richard's Almanack*, 279
- Pope(s), vi, 11–12, 16, 34, 40, 43, 106–107, 120, 126, 139, 162, 166, 172, 173-174, 187, 191, 203

- Alexander V, 171
- Alexander VI, 192
- Benedict XI, 94
- Benedict XII, 96
- Boniface VIII, 94, 172
- Clement V, 94–95
- Clement VI, 99, 100
- Clement VII, 126, 199, 200
- Eugene IV, 179
- Gregory IX, 79
- Gregory XI, 125, 126
- Gregory XII, 173
- Innocent III, vi, 67–68, 69, 70, 131
- Innocent IV, 81-82
- John XXII, 95–96

- John XXIII, 171–173
  - Julius II, 192
  - Leo X, 195, 196
  - Martin V, Roman, 178, 179, 184
  - Paschal II, 43
  - Paul III, 202-203
  - Paul IV, 205
  - Urban II, 43
  - Urban V, 119
  - Urban VI, 126, 141
  - Zosimus, 32
- *Power of the Papacy*, 127
- Prague, 169–172, 177–180, 221-222, 223-224, 227, 230, 235, 270
  - University, 140, 141, 169–171, 233

- Procopius the Great, Taborite general, 179
- *Proslogion*, 42

Q

- Queen
  - Anne's War, 268, 269
  - Boleyn, Anne, 200
  - Elizabeth, 3, 228
  - Jane Seymore, 202
  - Mary Tudor, (Bloody Mary), 205, 206
  - Phillipa, 120
  - Victoria, Alexander, 315, 317
- *Qui bene present*, 78
- Quincy, Samuel, 277

R

- *respublica Christiana*, 11
- Richard de Beauchamp, 152–153
- Richard of Caister, 151
- Richard of St. Victor, 36
- Richard of Wetheringsett, 78
- Rievaulx, 44, 54, 56–57
- Rhineland, 166, 179, 185
- Rhine River, 95, 174, 234
- Robert of Artois, 99
- Robert of Newminister, 44
- Roberts, Evan John, 321-323, 326-327, 335
- Rochester, 39
- Robin Hood, 126

- Roland, Daniel, 280, 292
- Rolle, Richard, 97–98, 148
- Roman Empire, 85
  - Romans, 11, 33
  - Rome, 77
  - sack of, 31, 199
- *Rules and Exercises for Holy Living*, 272

S

- Scholastic, 16, 58
- Scotland, 4, 54–55, 56, 92–93, 95, 96, 100, 221, 222, 246, 248
  - oral tradition, 76
  - Bannockburn, Scotland, 95
  - Berwick, Scotland, 93

- ○ Scone, Scotland, 93, 95
- Seymour, Jane, 202
- Shakespeare, William, v, 229, 232-233
- Simon de Montfort, 84
- Sir John of Oldcastle, 142, 144–145, 148–150, 152
- Sir Richard Arkwright, 294
- Sir William Marshal, 77
- Slavonian Monastery of Emmaus, 140
- Southfields, William, 150
- *Spiritual Friendship*, 57
- St. Paul's, Canterbury, 33
- St. Paul's Cathedral, London, 99, 143, 150, 199, 224, 226, 246, 288
- St. Paul's Lady Chapel, London, 125
- St. Peter Monastery, 33

- St. Peter, Northampton, 142
- St. Victor, 36, 54–55, 97, 151
- Stevenson, George, 314
- Stoddard, Solomon, 269
- Stone of Destiny, 93
- *Summa ad instructionem*, 83
- *Summa Theologiae*, 84
- *Summa, or Mirror of Churchmen*, 78
- Swinderby, William, 142

T

- Taylor, Jeremy, 241, 244, 246
- Tennent, William, and Gilbert, 275
- *The Adventures of Simplicissimus*, 248
- *The Cloud of Unknowing*, 145, 337

- *The Fire of Love*, 148
- *The Forme of Perfect Living*, 97
- *The Imitation of Christ*, 183, 273
- *The Labyrinth*, 194
- The Second Statute of Praemunire, 139
- *The Scale of Perfection*, 146, 148
- The Stations of the Cross, 77
- *The Tempest*, 232
- Thirty-Nine Articles, 15, 17, 222
- Thirty Years War, 239, 243, 245, 248
- Thomas a Kempis, 183, 273
- Thornton, Martin, 6–8, 10, 17, 18, 33, 40, 139–140, 151, 186, 332
- Tithe Wars, 321
- towns and gowns, 59, 107

- Tractarian(s), 14–15, 315
- Travers, Walter 224–225
- Treaty of Amiens, 93
- Treaty of Bretigny, 108
- TULIP, 236
- Tunstall, Cuthbert, bishop of London, 192, 197, 199
- Tyler, Wat, 128-129

U

- Ussher, James, 240, 246

V

- Vaughan, Richard, 244
- Victorine(s), 55, 140

- Virginia Company, 3

- Wallace, William, 93, 94
- Wales, 30, 76, 144, 280, 283, 295, 326
    - Black Knight, King Edward, King of, 100
    - Church of, 4
    - Earl of Pembroke, 77
    - Golden Grove, 244
    - New Quay, Cardigan, 323
    - Prince of, 143–144
    - Waterford, 292
- Walter Hilton of Thurgarton, 97, 146–148
- Warde, Thomas, 145
- Watts, Isaac, 269, 294

- Watts, James, 313
- West India(n), 193, 231, 238, 240, 248
- Westminster, 93, 215, 229, 243
    - Abby, 93, 94, 145, 149, 247
    - anchorites, 153
    - Confession, 246
    - Hall, 143
- William of Champeaux, 54
- William of Malmesbury, historian, 29
- William of Occam, 98
- William of St. Thierry, 36, 80
- Worchester, 39
- Worms, Germany, 190–192, 198
- Wtenbgaert, John, 231

Y

- York, 40, 44, 54, 82, 149, 151, 152, 172
- Yorkshire, 44-45, 54, 97, 292
  - Beverley, 151
  - Cawood, 151

Z

- Zbinco von Hasenburg, Johann, 171
- Zelivsky, Jan, 178
- Zizka, John, Taborite general, 179
- Zurich, Switzerland, 196, 200, 201
  - Consensus, 205
  - Council of, 198
- Zwingli, Ulrich, 15, 17, 193, 195-196, 200, 204

Denomination and Founders Index

A

- Angle-Saxon Church, 38–39, 162

  - Aidan, Columba, David, Dewi Sant, Ninan, 30

  - Patrick, 30, 40

- Anglo-Catholic Church, 16, 315

- Anglican(s), 7, 11, 310, 321, 332

  - Broad Church, 315, 317

  - Church, vi–viii, 8, 10–11, 13–14, 17, 65, 163, 240, 289, 292, 314, 315-316, 317

  - clergy/laity, 3, 4, 6, 13–14, 17, 277, 285, 286, 309

- elitism (High Anglican), 241, 242, 272
- Evangelical, 310, 315-316
- spirituality, 7, 12–13, 15–16
- theology, 15–16, 225
- tradition, 16
- apostolic church, 15, 19, 44, 315, 332
  - Apostolic Tradition, 274
    - Joseph of Arimathea, v, 29
    - Philip, the apostle, 29

B

- Baptist, 289, 295, 314, 332
- Brethren of Common Life, 141, 183, 184, 188
- Bohemia(n), 140, 165, 199, 221, 223, 230, 233, 234, 271

- Bible/hymns, 172
- Catholic, 238, 245
- Crown of, 166
- Confession, 223, 230
- Church/clergy, 140, 170
- Diet, 221
- nationalism, 171, 177
- noble(s), 149, 166, 170, 194, 235, 237
- Protestants, 230
  - Bohemian Brethern (Unitas Fratrum), 223
  - Calixtines, 178
  - Taborites, 178-179
  - Unity of the Bohemian Brothers, 179
  - Unity of Brethren, 172, 271

- Utraquists, 177–178, 179, 206, 226, 227

  ○ Rebellion, 169–174, 177-179, 310

C

- Calvin, John, 17, 103, 201, 205, 206, 228, 236, 243, 274, 293

  ○ Calvinism, 207, 236, 333

  ○ Calvinist(s)/Calvanistic, 221, 223, 233, 234, 236-237, 241

    - Calvinist Methodist, 280, 285, 322

      ○ Harris, Howell, 280-281, 283, 285, 292

      ○ Morgan, David (Moriah Calvinistic Methodist Chapel), 295, 316

      ○ Rolands, Daniel, 280, 292

      ○ Whitefield, Gorge, 281, 285-287, 292, 289-290, 291-294, 308-309, 316

- Ecclesiastical Ordinances, 203
- Five Points of Calvinism, 236
- Synod, 231, 236–237
  - of Dort, 236
- Catholic(s), 9, 33, 40, 163, 172, 186-187, 188, 199, 224, 230, 233, 235, 238, 240, 241, 242, 246, 266-267, 277
- Church/Roman Catholic Church, 30, 77, 95, 162-163, 171, 178, 188, 223, 226, 227, 229, 241, 332
  - Catholicism, 30, 188-189, 206, 238, 241, 267
  - Congregation of Index, 233
  - countries, 3, 199, 202, 234-235, 237, 239, 277
  - Early Church Fathers, 16, 34, 57
    - Augustine, 30-32, 40, 97, 100, 102–103, 194, 233

- Cannon, 130, 146
- *City of God*, 31–32
- *Confessions*, 30
- Victorian, 140
- Pelagius controversy, 31-32
- Clement I, Bishop of Rome, 16
- Clement of Alexandria, 80
- Gregory the Great, 55
- Jerome of Stridon (St.), 188, 191, 192, 194
- Origen, 20, 80

- *Roman Catholic Lexicon*, 13
- Reformation, 186
- publications, 13, 40, 226

- Celtic, 30, 223, 241
  - Celts, vii, 30, 35, 55, 163
    - churches, 32–33
    - legends, 29–30
    - spirituality, v, 163
- Church of England, 4, 6–8, 11–17, 29, 74, 162, 200-201, 207, 222, 223, 224, 225, 229, 243, 245, 247, 269, 274, 277, 280, 282, 286-287, 291, 294, 309, 331
  - Cranmer, Thomas, 12, 194, 200, 202, 206, 207, 310
    - *Book of Common Prayer*, 8, 12–13, 17, 204
    - *Book of Homilies*, 204
    - Forty-two Articles of Faith, 205
- Congressional, 269, 274, 275, 286, 289

E

- Episcopal, v, 1-2, 6, 7, 8, 14, 167, 246, 337

H

- Huss, John, 10, 103, 149, 169–172, 174, 177, 178, 185, 195, 310
  - Hussites, 178–180, 186, 226, 271, 332
    - Four Articles of Prague, 179

J

- Jewish, 20–21, 55, 57, 83, 85
  - Jews, 36, 69, 79, 81, 83, 85, 104, 183, 246

L

- Lollard(s), vi, 97, 121–122, 127-128, 129–131, 142–144, 146, 149–153, 200

  - Preacher/clergy, 122, 125, 126, 128, 149

  - Wycliffe, John, vi, 10, 95, 103, 119–131, 142, 143, 148–149, 151, 163, 170–172, 173, 185, 200, 310

    - *Dialogue between a Wise Man and a Fool*, 123

    - *Form of Confession*, 123

    - *Of Wedded Men and Wives*, 123

    - *On Civil Lordship*, 122

    - *Seven Works of Mercy*, 123

    - *The Five Questions of Love*, 124

    - *The Lantern of Light, On Love*, 124

DENOMINATION AND FOUNDER INDEX   427

- Luther, Martin, v, 15, 17, 103, 194–195, 196-197, 204, 273, 307, 309

  - *Preface to the Epistle of Romans,* 287

  - "Short Confession on the Holy Sacramt," 204

  - Lutheran(s), v, 197, 200, 206, 207, 221, 223, 226, 265, 267, 273, 274-275, 276, 311, 332, 334

    - Lutheranism, 197, 200, 201, 206, 226, 276, 294

    - Moravia, 166, 199, 221, 272

      - Moravian(s), 11, 140, 161, 179, 271, 273, 274, 276-277, 282, 283-285, 287, 292, 294, 295, 310, 334, 337

        - Revival, v, 10, 273-274, 311

          - David, Christian, 271, 272, 289

- Zinzendorf, Nicolaus Ludwig von, 270-271, 272, 273, 274-275, 276-277, 282, 284, 289, 292, 294

- Pietism, v, 265, 267, 284

    - Piet(ist), 267, 268, 272, 334

        - Spencer, Philip Jakob, 265, 266, 267, 270

            - *Pia Desideria*, 265

- Salzburg(ers), 275, 277, 279, 282

M

- Methodist, 6, 275, 309, 314

    - Baltimore Christmas Conference, 309

    - Methodist Conference in Bristol, 293, 295, 309

        - Wesley Charles, 274, 282, 288, 290, 291, 295

- Wesley, John, 272, 274, 282, 283-285, 288-289, 290, 291, 292, 293, 295, 308, 309, 310, 316, 333
  - Wesleyan Methodist, 317
- Mitzo Christians, 336
- Muslim(s), 13, 37, 58, 77, 184, 187, 188

N

- Non-Conformist, 316, 321
- Non-denominational, 332, 334

P

- Pentecostal, 6, 333, 336, 337
  - Azura Street Mission, 335-336
- Protestant(s), 2, 9, 205-206, 234
  - Bohemian, 230, 234-235, 238

- Dutch, 234
- English, 33, 205, 220
- German, 195, 198, 239, 265, 273, 277
- Reformation, vi, 37
- theology, 15–16
  - Protestantism, 203, 205
- Presbyterian, 224-225, 241, 289, 316
  - Canadian, 336
  - New Jersey, 275
  - New York, 270
  - Philadelphia 277-278, 279
    - Synod, 279, 281
  - Scotland, 222, 246
  - Welsh, 280

- Puritan(s), 16, 103, 224, 228, 229, 240-242, 243, 247, 266, 269, 271

  - Puritanism, 225

Q

- Quaker, 246, 265-266, 278

  - Fox, George, 243, 244, 246, 266

  - Penn Jr., William, 266, 290

R

- Reformed, 204, 236, 269, 289, 313, 333

- Remonstrant Brotherhood, 242

  - Arminian, 234, 236, 293

    - Arminianism, 232, 236, 241

    - Arminius, Jacob, 228, 231, 232

- Gomarus, Franciscus, 228
- Grotius, Hugo, 234, 236-237
- Five Points of Arminianism, 232, 236
- *Remonstrance*, 232
- Remonstrant(s), 234, 236, 240
- Remonstrant party, 231, 236
- Netherlands Synod, 231, 237–237
  - of Dort, 236

S

- Saxon Catholic Christianity, 163
- Schwenkfeld, Casper von, 197-198, 199, 204
- Schwenkfelders, 272, 273, 276-277, 278, 280

SCRIPTURAL INDEX

I

- 1 Corinthians (1 Cor.) 6:19 (bodies and lives, God's creation), 32

- 1 Cor. 9:21 (outside the law to win over), 276

- 1 Cor. 12:4-6 (Trinity of God), 333

- 1 John 1:9 (confess sin), 327

- 1 John 4:10, (God's love leading to Jesus' sacrifice for our sins), 293

- 1 John 4:19 (God loved us first), 293

- 1 Peter 1:23-25 (the Word purifies like fire), 328

- 1 Thessalonians (1 Thes.) 1:11, 5:19-21 (quenching the Spirit), 327

2

- 2 Chronicles 7:14 (confess), 325
- 2 Corinthians (2 Cor.) 4:6 (Christ's light), 243
- 2 Cor. 5:10 (Jesus judges), 41
- 2 Cor. 8:5 (Prove your love by giving), 293
- 2 Cor. 2 11:14–15a (Satan's disguise), 3
- 2 Cor. 13:5 (Determine if you choose God as Jesus lives within), 244
- 2 Cor. 13:14 (Holy Spirit, personal), 14
- 2 Peter 1:21 (God's prophecy from the Holy Spirit), 2
- 2 Thessalonians (2 Thes.) 2:15 (stand firm), 276
- 2 Thes. 2:10-16 (obeying the Spirit), 327

A

- Acts 2:4, 4:31, 13:9–10 (speaks the Word of God when full), 5

- Act 3:19, (Repent), 291

- Acts 4:32-33 (unity of the church) 243

- Acts 5:32 (the key of obedience), 18

- Acts 10:42, 17:31 (Jesus judges), 41

- Acts 16:6-15 (obeying the Spirit), 326

- Acts 17:34 (Dionysius the Areopagite), 242

C

- Colossians 1:16 (God created all), ix

D

- Deuteronomy (Deu.) 5:6–21 (Ten

Commandments), 55, 69, 78, 83, 123, 162

- Deu. 30:15-16 (Choose between good and evil), 326

E

- Ecclesiastics 5:8-10 (pursuing riches), 311
- Ephesians (Eph.) 4:31 (forgive everyone), 326
- Eph. 4:32 (God's forgiveness), 293
- Eph. 4:30 (greive the Spirit), 327
- Exodus 20 (Ten Commandments), 123
- Ezekiel 36:23-29 (obeying the Spirit), 327

G

- Galatians (Gal.) 5:14 (fulfilling the law by loving your neighbor), 124
- Genesis (Gen.) 1:1-19 (creation), v

- Gen. 9:19 (Noah's sons), viii

H

- Hebrews (Heb.) 4:13 (God is everywhere), 32
- Heb. 5:14 (Train to discern between good and evil.) 326
- Heb. 8:10, (the new covenant), 293
- Heb. 11:6 (impossible without faith), viii
- Heb. 11:1-40 (faith conquers), 244
- Heb. 12:1 (cloud of witnesses), 32
- Heb. 12:1-3 (lay aside sin), 244
- Heb. 12:2 (Jesus on the Cross leads to glory), 244
- Heb. 13:8 (Jesus stays the same), 13, 163
- Heb. 13:12-15 (proclaiming God), 327-328

I

- Isaiah (Isa.) 11:2–3 (gifts of the Holy Spirit), 58

- Isa. 40:13, 48:16, 63:10–11 (divinity of the Holy Spirit), 14

- Isa. 40:13-14 (God's superiority), 308

- Isa. 55:6-8 (seek the Lord), viii

- Isa. 63:9-10 (greive the Spirit), 327

- Isa. 64:1-2 (spiritual awakening), 322

J

- James 1:6, 2:14–26 (ask in faith and obey), 18

- James 2:8 (Golden Rule) 124

- James 5:16 (confess), 326

- John 1:3 (non-existence without Christ), 36

- John 1:12, (gift of the right to God's Children), 244

- John 3:8 (the Spirit of God), 335

- John 5:22, 27, 9:39 (Jesus judges), 41

- John 6:1-15, 22-59 (feeding 5,000), 197-198

- John 13:16 (God's superiority), 308

- John 14:16–17, 16:13–15 (Holy Spirit, personal), 14, 327

- John 14:22-24 (indwelling of Jesus), 198

L

- Lamentations 3:44 (cloud blocking God), 326

- Luke 1:15–16, 41–42, 67 (speaks the Word of God when full), 5

- Luke 6:46-49 (obeying the Spirit), 327

- Luke 8:22-25 (Calming the Storm), 92, 334

- Luke 10:27 (Golden Rule), 124, 337
- Luke 11:13 (prayer conduit for Holy Spirit), 18
- Luke 17:3-4 (forgiven as you forgive), 326
- Luke 23:50–56 (tomb), 29
- Luke 24:49 (wait on God), 334

M

- Malachi 3:2-3 (God will purify like fire), 328
- Mark 4:35–41 (calming the storm), 92, 334
- Mark 8:34 (take up the cross), 41
- Mark 11:25 (forgiven as you forgive), 326
- Mark 12:29–31 (Golden Rule), 124, 337
- Mark 15:42–47 (tomb), 29
- Matthew (Matt.) 5–8 (Blessed the pure of heart), 81

- Matt. 5:14 (Christ's light within), 243
- Matt. 5:22-24 (forgive everyone), 326
- Matt. 6:9–13 (Lord's Prayer/Our Fathers), 75, 78, 123, 147, 207, 292
- Matt. 6:14-15, 18:15-35 (forgiven as you forgive), 326
- Matt, 6:19-24 (Pursue God instead of wealth), 312
- Matt. 8:23–27 (calming the storm), 92, 334
- Matt. 10:32-33 (proclaiming God), 326
- Matt. 12:31-32, 23 (quenching the Spirit), 328
- Matt. 16:27, 25:31–46 (Jesus judges), 41
- Matt. 22:37–39 (Golden Rule), 124, 337
- Matt. 27:57–61 (tomb), 29
- Matt. 28:19 (divinity of the Holy Spirit), 14, 327-328

N

- Numbers (Num.) 11:27–29 (Holy Spirit at Moses' camp), 5

P

- Philippians 4:8 (meditate on goodness), 277-278
- Proverbs (Prov.) 15:3 (God is everywhere), 32
- Prov. 28:13 (confess), 326
- Psalm 32 (confess), 326
- Psalm 33, 34 (tasting the Lord's sweetness), 102
- Psalm 90:12 (bodies and lives, God's creation until death), 32
- Psalm 104:24-25 (God created all), ix

- Psalm 119 (obeying the Spirit), 327
- Psalm 143 (prayer for God's aid in discerning good and evil), 326
- Psalms, 38, 74, 77, 97, 147, 269, 283, 292

R

- Revelation 1:4–4:22 (seven letters), 6
- Romans (Rom.) (Luther overview), 288-289
- Rom. 1:1-7 (proclaiming God), 327
- Rom. 2:16 (Jesus judges), 41
- Rom. 8 (indwelling of Jesus over fleshly desires), 198
- Rom. 8:4-6 (obeying the Spirit), 327
- Rom. 8:9–11 (dependence on Holy Spirit), 18
- Rom. 8:15, (the spirit of redemption where we cry, "Abba!"), 293

- Rom. 8:26–27 (Holy Spirit, personal), 14

- Rom. 8:29-33, 9:11-20, 11:7 (predestined elect), 293

- Rom. 13:10 (fulfilling the Law, of loving your neighbor), 124

S

- Song of Solomon (Song of Songs), 20–21

Topic and Related People Index

A

- abbess, 34, 141

- abbot(s), 34–35, 40, 44, 56, 185

- Age of Enlightenment, 16, 247, 315

- allegory, 58, 266

- anchoress, 39, 74–76, 139, 148, 154

  - days, (typical), 76

    - Amy Palmer, anchoress, 142

    - Emma Rawghton, anchoress, 152–153

    - Julian of Norwich, anchoress, 97, 121, 139–140, 150

- anchorite(s), 8–9, 12, 39, 74–75, 85, 97, 129, 148, 149, 153

- Aristotelian philosophy/physics, 80, 81, 203, 231, 248

    - Aristotle, 57, 58, 84, 223, 238

- ascetical theology, 40-41

- awakening(s), 66, 310, 322, 331

    - Great Awakening, 335

        - Second Great Awakening, 295, 314

B

- barons, 40, 69, 70, 75, 77, 79, 84, 177

    - Baron of Baltimore, 241

    - Baroness, 270

- belief(s), 13, 42, 43, 98, 146, 204, 245, 293

    - church heretical, 127, 153

TOPIC INDEX 447

- believe(d) (s), x, 14, 17, 36, 123, 141, 145-146, 151, 171, 266, 323

- believer(s), 7, 232, 244, 291

- Bible(s), 4, 5, 13-15, 18, 38, 58, 122, 146, 169, 178, 184, 192, 198, 202, 204, 233, 265, 266, 270, 274, 275, 278, 295, 308, 311, 324

  - Bishop's, 310

  - Bohemian, 172

  - French, 205

  - German, 192, 197

  - Geneva, 220, 222, 310

    - Whittingham, William, 206, 200 (English NT)

  - Great Bible First Edition (Cromwell's), 17, 202, 221, 310

    - Coverdale, Miles, 17, 194, 199, 201

- (Bibles continued)
  - Cloverdale's Great Bible second edition, (Cranmer's), 202, 310
- Tyndale, William 17, 194, 197, 198-201, 229
  - English New Testament, 197, 199, 200
  - Englis Old Testament, 199, 200
- Gutenberg Bible, 185
- Erasmus, 188, 191, 192-193, 194, 195, 196
  - Greek New Testament, 194, 195, 196
- Hebrew Bible/Old Testament, 12, 20, 38, 41, 56, 187, 200, 221, 270, 310, 317
- Italian, 192
- King James Bible/Version, v, 229, 232-233, 310
- Lollard Bible, 129-130

- Luther, 194,-195, 196, 200, 204-205, 274, 308, 310
  - New Testament, 196-197, 288
  - Old Testament, 200
    - Complete, 204
- LXX, 58
- Matthew's, 310
- New Testament, 12, 41, 125, 194, 195, 196, 198-199, 200, 206
- Origen Parallel Bible, 20
- Poor Man's Bible, 185
- Slavonian, 140
- Welsh 280
- Wycliffe Middle English Bible, 125, 129-131
- Vulgate (Latin), vi, 58, 130, 188, 189, 191, 192, 194

- Black Death (Plague), 96, 104-107, 121, 127-128, 248

- book(s), vii, 10, 28, 30, 33, 58, 78, 80, 85-86, 97, 123, 125, 148, 152, 170, 185, 225-226, 227, 247, 278, 317

    - banned/outlawed, 196, 199-200, 203, 206, 222, 233-234

    - censorship, 187, 189, 192, 271

    - Latin, 43, 130, 148, 183, 185, 192, 194, 246

    - hand copied/printed, vi-vii, 34, 85

    - heretical, 149, 173

C

- climate/weather, 11, 37, 92, 95

    - hotter temperatures, 246

    - hundred-year cold spell, 221

- Little Ice Age, 94
  - Medieval warm period, 37, 92
- Communion (bread/wine/Lord's Supper), 6, 58, 69, 75, 127, 141, 169, 171, 173, 178, 179, 197, 204, 222, 230, 273, 275, 278, 286, 287, 307, 332
- confession(s), 9, 68, 127, 325, 327, 332
  - confess(ed)(ing), 106, 123, 141, 149, 283, 323, 326, 336
- contemplate Christ/creation, v, 147
  - contemplate Scripture, 12–13, 57
- contemplation, 34, 39, 44, 55, 152, 163, 183
- contemplative,
  - meditation, 139, 146
  - life, 97, 148
  - prayer, 9

- science, 81

D

- Dark Ages, 85

F

- faith, viii, x, 7–8, 15–19, 31, 69, 78, 82, 84, 141, 146, 228, 244, 246, 287-289, 307, 308, 309
  - Catholic, 30, 96, 196, 199, 234, 238
  - mystical union with God, 82, 84
  - Protestant, 16, 131, 205, 232, 234, 244, 266, 292, 293, 334
  - through meditation of prayer, 41–42
- faithful, 96, 163, 333, 334, 335
  - living, 13

- service, 122, 162

- faithfulness, 8, 98, 141

- faithless/decline in, 31, 126, 283, 287, 333

G

- God's

  - compassion/grace/mercy/forgiveness, 18, 30, 33, 36, 102, 293, 308, 332

  - creation/breath, 32, 83, 102, 198, 227

  - image/child, 31, 35, 240, 281

  - law/commandments, 42, 123, 203, 309

  - love, 42, 97, 102, 146–147, 249, 293, 337

  - life, nature, 34, 42

  - mystery, 84

  - presence/Spirit, 76, 98, 308, 323

- rewards/promise/glory, 56, 224, 282
- will/pleasure/wisdom, 2, 13, 19, 38, 102, 164, 198, 228, 331, 338
- wrath, 9, 100
- Word, 3, 4, 14, 21, 51, 225
- work/revivals, 11, 12, 16, 335

- grace, 17–18, 30–32, 36, 41, 97, 139, 145–147, 224, 228, 312
  - above merit/works (gift), 32, 100, 102, 267, 285, 334
  - accessed through, 102, 147, 332
  - fall from, 232
  - inner, 55
  - irresistible, 232, 236
  - mystical, 81, 308

H

- hermits, vii, 8–9, 12, 35, 37, 39, 76, 96, 148

- Holy Grail, 29, 105

- Holy Spirit, v–vii, 1–20, 33, 35–36, 43, 58, 65, 69, 78, 80–81, 147, 164, 186, 198, 227, 232, 244-245, 267, 273, 275, 288-289, 291, 308, 310-311, 316, 323, 325-328, 332-338

- hymn(s), 6, 41, 77, 147, 172, 198, 269, 285, 292, 295, 316, 323, 324

  - Luther's 198

  - Moravian, 285

  - Unity of Brethren, 172

  - Welsh, 280

  - Wesleyan,

    - *Hymns and Sacred Poems*, 290

- *Collection of Hymns for the Use of the People called Methodists*, 295
  - Hymn Sings (Methodist), 6

I

- inventions,
  - American, 315
  - Chinese, 19–20, 37, 81, 86, 101, 145
  - English, 313, 314-315
  - eyeglasses, 82, 85
  - Gregorian calendar, 226, 246
  - gun-barrows, 86
  - gunpowder, 80
  - Korean, 145, 179
  - paper, 19–20, 37, 85, 187, 249, 269, 276

- parchment, 20, 85

- printing press, vii, 37, 145, 179, 187, 192, 196, 226
  - Gutenberg, 185
  - London, 225-226
  - Venice, 192
  - woodblock, 37, 179, 185

- telescope, 230, 231

J

- justification, 7, 41, 267

K

- knight(s), 38, 82, 104–105, 107, 122, 124, 126, 131, 138, 150, 153, 167, 186, 230
  - of the Blue Garter, 100, 104

    - Poor Knight, 104-105
    - Templar, 45, 77, 94–95

L

- Labor(ers)/working class, 59, 66, 107, 127, 144, 311
    - domestic, 34
    - manual, 44, 76, 130
    - of the Holy Spirit, 33
    - peasants, 39, 101, 128-129, 163, 183, 187, 193, 197, 221
    - serf(s), 59, 127, 129, 183
    - slaves/slavery, 4, 13, 69, 103, 182-183, 184-185, 188, 193, 196, 205, 236, 240, 248-249, 268, 269, 277, 311, 315
- Law(s), 30, 107, 165, 184, 221, 227, 231, 238, 267

- canon, 196
- divine/God's, 33, 42, 203, 234, 289
- international, 234
- Jewish/Old Testament, 20, 38, 41
- moral/ceremonial, 83
- New Testament, 124
- lord(s), 5, 34, 55, 166, 216, 230
  - lordship, 66, 123, 199
    - overlord, 122
- Lord, (God/Spirit of/Christ), ix-x, 1-2, 5, 58, 102, 122, 139, 225, 271, 291, 308, 327-328, 333

M

- meditation, 2, 9, 55, 76, 97, 102, 139, 141, 147, 337

- Contemplative, 146
- five-step process, 151
- of Christ's Passion, 147, 148
- of prayer, 41
- on Christ, 151
- Scripture, 307
- meditating on symbols, 186-187
- three-point, 102, 139
* miracle(s), 10, 45, 143, 235
* monasteries, 57, 85, 162
  - Benedict, 8-9, 43
    * Benedictine Abby/monasteries, 44, 188
  - Cistercian(s), 43-45
    * monasteries, 34, 66, 141, 145
    * monastery, 28, 35, 44, 54, 56

- nunnery, 97
- Reform, 44–45
- Monastery of Emmaus, 140
- monastery life, 76
- monastic, 39, 55, 56, 59, 273
- monk(s), 8–9, 12, 34–35, 42, 57, 74, 76, 85, 102, 183, 185
  - anonymous, 145–146
  - Augustine, 194
  - Benedict, 8, 17, 33, 43
    - Benedictine monk's practice, 75, 140
  - Carthusian, 201
  - Cistercian, 43–45, 54, 57
  - Church of Christ, 67
  - Irish, 76

- Syrian, 35
- mystic, 55, 80, 97, 139, 146, 184, 241
  - mystics, vi, vii, 141, 163, 242, 305, 333, 334, 337
  - mystical, 80–81, 82, 152, 186, 242, 244, 337
  - mysticism, v–vii, 21, 55, 81, 147, 152, 308, 332

N

- nationalism, vi, 42, 125, 162, 177
- nobles, 66, 76, 93, 107, 125, 170, 172, 188, 221, 272
- nun(s), 34, 35, 85, 97, 98, 154, 183, 185

P

- penance, 41, 58, 60, 69, 108, 179

- prayer, 7–9, 18–19, 76, 102, 139, 179, 272, 273, 333

    - Centering, 145

    - contemplative, 9, 34

    - Jewish (Judaic), 8, 85

    - liturgical prayers, 17, 74, 242

        - liturgical songbook, 77

    - services/meetings, 12, 77, 313-314, 316, 323, 326

- prayers, 3, 102, 127, 143, 147, 163, 177, 244, 286, 307, 325, 334-335, 337

    - life of, 35, 332

    - services (times), 8, 207, 313-314

- short, private, 98, 147, 280
- to the Virgin Mary, 74
- the soul, 42
- written/penned, 76, 186
  - by Church Fathers, 74
- prayer structure, 41–42, 146–148, 333
  - *Breviary*, 77
  - Celtic, 32
  - *Book of Common Prayer*, 8, 12–13, 17, 205, 225, 286
  - for each other, 57, 130, 332
  - Lord's Prayer, 75, 78, 123, 147, 207, 292
  - Passion of Christ, 41
  - Office of Prayer, 147, 332
  - murmured confessions, 68

- mystical/communion with God, 141, 151–152, 332-335

- Scripture/Psalms (Bible passages), 13, 32, 38, 74, 77, 97, 102, 147, 269, 283, 292

- string of pearls/Rosary, 68, 186-187

- Threefold Rule, 8

- priest(s), 34, 74, 106, 107, 126, 127, 128, 129, 130, 142, 151, 152, 163, 185, 187, 273

  - Anglican, 3, 6, 277, 285, 309

  - Brethren of the Common Life, 183

  - Catholic, 226

  - Church of England, 224

  - Episcopal, 337

  - Hexham, 54

  - Lollard, 124, 126

  - parish, 69, 106

- Prague, 169
- Swiss, 193
- Yorkshire, 44

• piety, 14, 19, 60, 141, 146, 162, 184, 191, 198, 265

• pilgrimage(s), 60, 127, 142–143, 148, 150, 194

• purgatory, 80, 106

R

• reading, 57, 76, 146, 171, 197, 314
  - forbade (prohibited/unauthorized), 146, 191, 196, 204
  - Scripture (Bible), 8, 97, 102, 130, 163, 183, 197, 204, 275, 278, 280, 333, 337

• readings, 16, 98, 202

• recluse(s), 2–3, 29, 35

- revival(s), vi–vii, 4, 9–11, 19, 66, 103, 163, 313, 324-325, 328, 331-335

  - English, 286, 295, 314

    - Yorkshire, 314

  - Great 1907 Korean Revival, 337

  - Manchurian Revival, 337

  - Moravian, 311, 337

  - New England, 269, 275, 280, 285, 286, 291, 312, 313, 335

  - Pentecostal, 336, 337

  - Welsh, 280, 295, 316, 321-328, 335, 337

S

- salvation, 16, 124, 204, 285, 312

  - by conforming to God's will, 38

  - by grace/God's will, 32, 100, 285, 308

- by the Trinty, 84, 139
- by works/good deeds, 32, 100
- mystery, 44, 84
- Arminianism, 224, 228, 232

- Satan/ the devil, 3, 8, 41, 92, 177, 290
- Scripture, 2, 8, 12–17, 57, 82, 130, 145, 148, 163, 172, 195, 197-198, 280, 289, 307, 309, 323, 327, 337
  - extending God's power, 12, 102
  - interpretation, 55, 81, 84, 98, 121, 215, 228, 233, 267, 287
  - knowledge of, 19, 147, 225
  - study, vii, 7, 33–34, 80, 183, 333
- sin(s), 3, 121, 130, 140, 172, 228, 244, 292
  - absolvement, 143, 293

- atonement/cleansing/remission, 8, 18, 31, 80, 234, 266, 291, 316

- confessing, 106, 123, 124, 141, 283, 323, 325, 326, 337

- conviction of, 266, 291, 308

- forgiveness of, 172, 283, 287-288

- original, 31, 36

- seven deadly, 55, 58

- spiritual, 122, 126, 181, 216, 269, 322

  - church, 122-123, 230

  - direction/guidance/supervision, 3, 7, 18, 75, 97, 148, 183

  - expression/practices, 7, 9, 16-17, 32, 41, 98, 143

  - path/life, 33, 66, 148, 307

- spiritualism, 2, 9

- spirituality, 2–3, 7, 9, 44, 122-123, 161
  - Anglican, 12, 163
  - Celtic, v, 163
  - Christian, 17, 161
  - English, 7, 17, 33, 122
  - individual/Reformation, 9, 16, 122

T

- theology, 56–57, 79–84, 120, 141, 231, 233, 267, 310
  - ascetical, 40–42
  - Anglican, 14-16, 225
  - European Protestant, 15, 165
  - Jesuit(s), 202-203, 337
  - Oxford, 98, 120, 141

- Trinity, 2, 8, 19, 36, 43, 83, 102, 125, 139, 171, 226, 308, 327-328

- vision(s), 139–140, 141, 142, 143, 147, 150, 152, 192

NOTES

www.ingramcontent.com/pod-product-compliance
Lightning Source LLC
Chambersburg PA
CBHW021913180426
43198CB00035B/439